Python Feature Engineering Cookbook

Over 70 recipes for creating, engineering, and transforming
features to build machine learning models

Soledad Galli

BIRMINGHAM - MUMBAI

Python Feature Engineering Cookbook

Copyright © 2020 Packt Publishing

Commissioning Editor: Pravin Dhandre
Acquisition Editor: Devika Battike
Content Development Editor: Nathanya Dias
Senior Editor: Ayaan Hoda
Technical Editor: Manikandan Kurup
Copy Editor: Safis Editing
Project Coordinator: Aishwarya Mohan
Proofreader: Safis Editing
Indexer: Manju Arasan
Production Designer: Aparna Bhagat

First published: January 2020

Production reference: 1210120

Published by Packt Publishing Ltd.
Livery Place
35 Livery Street
Birmingham
B3 2PB, UK.

ISBN 978-1-78980-631-1

www.packt.com

Subscribe to our online digital library for full access to over 7,000 books and videos, as well as industry leading tools to help you plan your personal development and advance your career. For more information, please visit our website.

Why subscribe?

- Spend less time learning and more time coding with practical eBooks and Videos from over 4,000 industry professionals

- Improve your learning with Skill Plans built especially for you

- Get a free eBook or video every month

- Fully searchable for easy access to vital information

- Copy and paste, print, and bookmark content

Did you know that Packt offers eBook versions of every book published, with PDF and ePub files available? You can upgrade to the eBook version at www.packt.com and as a print book customer, you are entitled to a discount on the eBook copy. Get in touch with us at customercare@packtpub.com for more details.

At www.packt.com, you can also read a collection of free technical articles, sign up for a range of free newsletters, and receive exclusive discounts and offers on Packt books and eBooks.

Contributors

About the author

Soledad Galli is a lead data scientist with more than 10 years of experience in world-class academic institutions and renowned businesses. She has researched, developed, and put into production machine learning models for insurance claims, credit risk assessment, and fraud prevention. Soledad received a Data Science Leaders' award in 2018 and was named one of LinkedIn's voices in data science and analytics in 2019. She is passionate about enabling people to step into and excel in data science, which is why she mentors data scientists and speaks at data science meetings regularly. She also teaches online courses on machine learning in a prestigious Massive Open Online Course platform, which have reached more than 10,000 students worldwide.

About the reviewer

Greg Walters has been involved with computers and computer programming since 1972. He is well versed in Visual Basic, Visual Basic .NET, Python, and SQL, and is an accomplished user of MySQL, SQLite, Microsoft SQL Server, Oracle, C++, Delphi, Modula-2, Pascal, C, 80x86 Assembler, COBOL, and Fortran. He is a programming trainer and has trained numerous people on many pieces of computer software, including MySQL, Open Database Connectivity, Quattro Pro, Corel Draw!, Paradox, Microsoft Word, Excel, DOS, Windows 3.11, Windows for Workgroups, Windows 95, Windows NT, Windows 2000, Windows XP, and Linux. He is semi-retired and has written over 100 articles for the *Full Circle* magazine. He is open to working as a freelancer on various projects.

Packt is searching for authors like you

If you're interested in becoming an author for Packt, please visit authors.packtpub.com and apply today. We have worked with thousands of developers and tech professionals, just like you, to help them share their insight with the global tech community. You can make a general application, apply for a specific hot topic that we are recruiting an author for, or submit your own idea.

Table of Contents

Preface

Python Feature Engineering Cookbook covers well-demonstrated recipes focused on solutions that will assist machine learning teams in identifying and extracting features to develop highly optimized and enriched machine learning models. This book includes recipes to extract and transform features from structured datasets, time series, transactions data and text. It includes recipes concerned with automating the feature engineering process, along with the widest arsenal of tools for categorical variable encoding, missing data imputation and variable discretization. Further, it provides different strategies of feature transformation, such as Box-Cox transform and other mathematical operations and includes the use of decision trees to combine existing features into new ones. Each of these recipes is demonstrated in practical terms with the help of NumPy, SciPy, pandas, scikit-learn, Featuretools and Feature-engine in Python.

Throughout this book, you will be practicing feature generation, feature extraction and transformation, leveraging the power of scikit-learn's feature engineering arsenal, Featuretools and Feature-engine using Python and its powerful libraries.

Who this book is for

This book is intended for machine learning professionals, AI engineers, and data scientists who want to optimize and enrich their machine learning models with the best features. Prior knowledge of machine learning and Python coding is expected.

What this book covers

Chapter 1, *Foreseeing Variable Problems in Building ML Models*, covers how to identify the different problems that variables may present and that challenge machine learning algorithm performance. We'll learn how to identify missing data in variables, quantify the cardinality of the variable, and much more besides.

Chapter 2, *Imputing Missing Data*, explains how to engineer variables that show missing information for some observations. In a typical dataset, variables will display values for certain observations, while values will be missing for other observations. We'll introduce various techniques to fill those missing values with some additional values, and the code to execute the techniques.

Chapter 3, *Encoding Categorical Variables*, introduces various classical and widely used techniques to transform categorical variables into numerical variables and also demonstrates a technique for reducing the dimension of highly cardinal variables as well as how to tackle infrequent values. This chapter also includes more complex techniques for encoding categorical variables, as described and used in the 2009 KDD competition.

Chapter 4, *Transforming Numerical Variables*, uses various recipes to transform numerical variables, typically non-Gaussian, into variables that follow a more Gaussian-like distribution by applying multiple mathematical functions.

Chapter 5, *Performing Variable Discretization*, covers how to create bins and distribute the values of the variables across them. The aim of this technique is to improve the spread of values across a range. It also includes well established and frequently used techniques like equal width and equal frequency discretization and more complex processes like discretization with decision trees and many more.

Chapter 6, *Working with Outliers*, teaches a few mainstream techniques to remove outliers from the variables in the dataset. We'll also learn how to cap outliers at a given arbitrary minimum/maximum value.

Chapter 7, *Deriving Features from Dates and Time Variables*, describes how to create features from dates and time variables. Date variables can't be used as such to build machine learning models for multiple reasons. We'll learn how to combine information from multiple time variables, like calculating time elapsed between variables and also, importantly, working with variables in different time zones.

Chapter 8, *Performing Feature Scaling*, covers the methods that we can use to put the variables within the same scale. We'll also learn how to standardize variables, how to scale to minimum and maximum value, how to do mean normalization or scale to vector norm, among other techniques.

Chapter 9, *Applying Mathematical Computations to Features*, explains how to create new variables from existing ones by utilizing different mathematical computations. We'll learn how to create new features through the addition/difference/multiplication/division of existing variables and more. We will also learn how to expand the feature space with polynomial expansion and how to combine features using decision trees.

Chapter 10, *Creating Features with Transactional and Time Series Data*, covers how to create static features from transactional information, so that we obtain a static view of a customer, or client, at any point in time. We'll learn how to combine features using math operations, across transactions, in specific time windows and capture time between transactions. We'll also discuss how to determine time between special events. We'll briefly dive into signal processing and learn how to determine and quantify local maxima and local minima.

Chapter 11, *Extracting Features from Text Variables*, explains how to derive features from text variables. We'll learn to create new features through the addition of existing variables. We will learn how to capture the complexity of the text by capturing the number of characters, words, sentences, the vocabulary and the lexical variety. We will also learn how to create Bag of Words and how to implement TF-IDF with and without n-grams

To get the most out of this book

Python Feature Engineering Cookbook will help machine learning practitioners improve their data preprocessing and manipulation skills, empowering them to modify existing variables or create new features from existing data. You will learn how to implement many feature engineering techniques with multiple open source tools, streamlining and simplifying code while adhering to coding best practices. Thus, to make the most of this book, you are expected to have an understanding of machine learning and machine learning algorithms, some previous experience with data processing, and a degree of familiarity with datasets. In addition, working knowledge of Python and some familiarity with Python numerical computing libraries such as NumPy, pandas, Matplotlib, and scikit-learn will be beneficial. You are required to be experienced in the use of Python through Jupyter Notebooks, in iterative Python through a Python console or Command Prompt, or have experience using a dedicated Python IDE, such as PyCharm or Spyder.

Download the example code files

You can download the example code files for this book from your account at www.packt.com. If you purchased this book elsewhere, you can visit www.packtpub.com/support and register to have the files emailed directly to you.

You can download the code files by following these steps:

1. Log in or register at www.packt.com.
2. Select the **Support** tab.
3. Click on **Code Downloads**.
4. Enter the name of the book in the **Search** box and follow the onscreen instructions.

Once the file is downloaded, please make sure that you unzip or extract the folder using the latest version of:

- WinRAR/7-Zip for Windows
- Zipeg/iZip/UnRarX for Mac
- 7-Zip/PeaZip for Linux

The code bundle for the book is also hosted on GitHub at `https://github.com/PacktPublishing/Python-Feature-Engineering-Cookbook`. In case there's an update to the code, it will be updated on the existing GitHub repository.

We also have other code bundles from our rich catalog of books and videos available at `https://github.com/PacktPublishing/`. Check them out!

Download the color images

We also provide a PDF file that has color images of the screenshots/diagrams used in this book. You can download it here: `https://static.packt-cdn.com/downloads/9781789806311_ColorImages.pdf`.

Conventions used

There are a number of text conventions used throughout this book.

`CodeInText`: Indicates code words in text, database table names, folder names, filenames, file extensions, pathnames, dummy URLs, user input, and Twitter handles. Here is an example: "The `nunique()` method ignores missing values by default."

A block of code is set as follows:

```
import pandas as pd
from sklearn.datasets import load_boston
from sklearn.model_selection import train_test_split
from sklearn.preprocessing import PolynomialFeatures
```

When we wish to draw your attention to a particular part of a code block, the relevant lines or items are set in bold:

```
X_train['A7'] = np.where(X_train['A7'].isin(frequent_cat), X_train['A7'],
'Rare')
X_test['A7'] = np.where(X_test['A7'].isin(frequent_cat), X_test['A7'],
'Rare')
```

Any command-line input or output is written as follows:

```
$ pip install feature-engine
```

Bold: Indicates a new term, an important word, or words that you see on screen. For example, words in menus or dialog boxes appear in the text like this. Here is an example: "Click the **Download** button."

Warnings or important notes appear like this.

Tips and tricks appear like this.

Sections

In this book, you will find several headings that appear frequently (*Getting ready*, *How to do it...*, *How it works...*, *There's more...*, and *See also*).

To give clear instructions on how to complete a recipe, use these sections as follows:

Getting ready

This section tells you what to expect in the recipe and describes how to set up any software or any preliminary settings required for the recipe.

How to do it...

This section contains the steps required to follow the recipe.

How it works...

This section usually consists of a detailed explanation of what happened in the previous section.

There's more...

This section consists of additional information about the recipe in order to make you more knowledgeable about the recipe.

See also

This section provides helpful links to other useful information for the recipe.

Get in touch

Feedback from our readers is always welcome.

General feedback: If you have questions about any aspect of this book, mention the book title in the subject of your message and email us at customercare@packtpub.com.

Errata: Although we have taken every care to ensure the accuracy of our content, mistakes do happen. If you have found a mistake in this book, we would be grateful if you would report this to us. Please visit www.packtpub.com/support/errata, selecting your book, clicking on the Errata Submission Form link, and entering the details.

Piracy: If you come across any illegal copies of our works in any form on the internet, we would be grateful if you would provide us with the location address or website name. Please contact us at copyright@packt.com with a link to the material.

If you are interested in becoming an author: If there is a topic that you have expertise in, and you are interested in either writing or contributing to a book, please visit authors.packtpub.com.

Reviews

Please leave a review. Once you have read and used this book, why not leave a review on the site that you purchased it from? Potential readers can then see and use your unbiased opinion to make purchase decisions, we at Packt can understand what you think about our products, and our authors can see your feedback on their book. Thank you!

For more information about Packt, please visit packt.com.

1
Foreseeing Variable Problems When Building ML Models

A variable is a characteristic, number, or quantity that can be measured or counted. Most variables in a dataset are either numerical or categorical. Numerical variables take numbers as values and can be discrete or continuous, whereas for categorical variables, the values are selected from a group of categories, also called labels.

Variables in their original, raw format are not suitable to train machine learning algorithms. In fact, we need to consider many aspects of a variable to build powerful machine learning models. These aspects include variable type, missing data, cardinality and category frequency, variable distribution and its relationship with the target, outliers, and feature magnitude.

Why do we need to consider all these aspects? For multiple reasons. First, scikit-learn, the open source Python library for machine learning, does not support missing values or strings (the categories) as inputs for machine learning algorithms, so we need to convert those values into numbers. Second, the number of missing values or the distributions of the strings in categorical variables (known as cardinality and frequency) may affect model performance or inform the technique we should implement to replace them by numbers. Third, some machine learning algorithms make assumptions about the distributions of the variables and their relationship with the target. Finally, variable distribution, outliers, and feature magnitude may also affect machine learning model performance. Therefore, it is important to understand, identify, and quantify all these aspects of a variable to be able to choose the appropriate feature engineering technique. In this chapter, we will learn how to identify and quantify these variable characteristics.

This chapter will cover the following recipes:

- Identifying numerical and categorical variables
- Quantifying missing data
- Determining cardinality in categorical variables

- Pinpointing rare categories in categorical variables
- Identifying a linear relationship
- Identifying a normal distribution
- Distinguishing variable distribution
- Highlighting outliers
- Comparing feature magnitude

Technical requirements

Throughout this book, we will use many open source Python libraries for numerical computing. I recommend installing the free Anaconda Python distribution (`https://www.anaconda.com/distribution/`), which contains most of these packages. To install the Anaconda distribution, follow these steps:

1. Visit the Anaconda website: `https://www.anaconda.com/distribution/`.
2. Click the **Download** button.
3. Download the latest Python 3 distribution that's appropriate for your operating system.
4. Double-click the downloaded installer and follow the instructions that are provided.

 The recipes in this book were written in Python 3.7. However, they should work in Python 3.5 and above. Check that you are using similar or higher versions of the numerical libraries we'll be using, that is, NumPy, pandas, scikit-learn, and others. The versions of these libraries are indicated in the `requirement.txt` file in the accompanying GitHub repository (`https://github.com/PacktPublishing/Python-Feature-Engineering-Cookbook`).

In this chapter, we will use pandas, NumPy, Matplotlib, seaborn, SciPy, and scikit-learn. pandas provides high-performance analysis tools. NumPy provides support for large, multi-dimensional arrays and matrices and contains a large collection of mathematical functions to operate over these arrays and over pandas dataframes. Matplotlib and seaborn are the standard libraries for plotting and visualization. SciPy is the standard library for statistics and scientific computing, while scikit-learn is the standard library for machine learning.

To run the recipes in this chapter, I used Jupyter Notebooks since they are great for visualization and data analysis and make it easy to examine the output of each line of code. I recommend that you follow along with Jupyter Notebooks as well, although you can execute the recipes in other interfaces.

The recipe commands can be run using a `.py` script from a command prompt (such as the Anaconda Prompt or the Mac Terminal) using an IDE such as Spyder or PyCharm or from Jupyter Notebooks, as in the accompanying GitHub repository (`https://github.com/PacktPublishing/Python-Feature-Engineering-Cookbook`).

In this chapter, we will use two public datasets: the KDD-CUP-98 dataset and the Car Evaluation dataset. Both of these are available at the UCI Machine Learning Repository.

Dua, D. and Graff, C. (2019). *UCI Machine Learning Repository* (`http://archive.ics.uci.edu/ml`). Irvine, CA: University of California, School of Information and Computer Science.

To download the KDD-CUP-98 dataset, follow these steps:

1. Visit the following website: `https://archive.ics.uci.edu/ml/machine-learning-databases/kddcup98-mld/epsilon_mirror/`.
2. Click the `cup98lrn.zip` link to begin the download:

← → C 🔒 https://archive.ics.uci.edu/ml/machine-learning-databases/kddcup98-mld/epsilon_mirror/

Index of /ml/machine-learning-databases/kddcup98-mld/epsilon_mirror

- Parent Directory
- cup98dic.txt
- cup98doc.txt
- cup98lrn.txt.Z
- cup98lrn.zip ⬅
- cup98que.txt
- cup98val.txt.Z
- cup98val.zip
- instruct.txt
- readme
- testing.txt
- valtargt.readme
- valtargt.txt

Apache/2.4.6 (CentOS) OpenSSL/1.0.2k-fips SVN/1.7.14 Phusion_Passenger/4.0.53 mod_perl/2.0.10 Perl/v5.16.3 Server at archive.ics.uci.edu Port 443

---

3. Unzip the file and save `cup98LRN.txt` in the same folder where you'll run the commands of the recipes.

To download the Car Evaluation dataset, follow these steps:

1. Go to the UCI website: `https://archive.ics.uci.edu/ml/machine-learning-databases/car/`.

2. Download the `car.data` file:

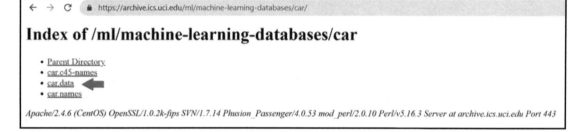

3. Save the file in the same folder where you'll run the commands of the recipes.

We will also use the Titanic dataset that's available at `http://www.openML.org`. To download and prepare the Titanic dataset, open a Jupyter Notebook and run the following commands:

```python
import numpy as np
import pandas as pd

def get_first_cabin(row):
    try:
        return row.split()[0]
    except:
        return np.nan

url = "https://www.openml.org/data/get_csv/16826755/phpMYEkMl"
data = pd.read_csv(url)
data = data.replace('?', np.nan)
data['cabin'] = data['cabin'].apply(get_first_cabin)
data.to_csv('titanic.csv', index=False)
```

The preceding code block will download a copy of the data from `http://www.openML.org` and store it as a `titanic.csv` file in the same directory from where you execute the commands.

There is a Jupyter Notebook with instructions on how to download and prepare the titanic dataset in the accompanying GitHub repository: `https://github.com/PacktPublishing/Python-Feature-Engineering-Cookbook/blob/master/Chapter01/DataPrep_Titanic.ipynb`.

Identifying numerical and categorical variables

Numerical variables can be discrete or continuous. Discrete variables are those where the pool of possible values is finite and are generally whole numbers, such as 1, 2, and 3. Examples of discrete variables include the number of children, number of pets, or the number of bank accounts. Continuous variables are those whose values may take any number within a range. Examples of continuous variables include the price of a product, income, house price, or interest rate. Categorical variables are values that are selected from a group of categories, also called labels. Examples of categorical variables include gender, which takes values of male and female, or country of birth, which takes values of Argentina, Germany, and so on.

In this recipe, we will learn how to identify continuous, discrete, and categorical variables by inspecting their values and the data type that they are stored and loaded with in pandas.

Getting ready

Discrete variables are usually of the `int` type, continuous variables are usually of the `float` type, and categorical variables are usually of the `object` type when they're stored in pandas. However, discrete variables can also be cast as floats, while numerical variables can be cast as objects. Therefore, to correctly identify variable types, we need to look at the data type and inspect their values as well. Make sure you have the correct library versions installed and that you've downloaded a copy of the Titanic dataset, as described in the *Technical requirements* section.

How to do it...

First, let's import the necessary Python libraries:

1. Load the libraries that are required for this recipe:

```
import pandas as pd
import matplotlib.pyplot as plt
```

2. Load the Titanic dataset and inspect the variable types:

```
data = pd.read_csv('titanic.csv')
data.dtypes
```

The variable types are as follows:

```
pclass            int64
survived          int64
name              object
sex               object
age               float64
sibsp             int64
parch             int64
ticket            object
fare              float64
cabin             object
embarked          object
boat              object
body              float64
home.dest         object
dtype: object
```

 In many datasets, integer variables are cast as `float`. So, after inspecting the data type of the variable, even if you get `float` as output, go ahead and check the unique values to make sure that those variables are discrete and not continuous.

3. Inspect the distinct values of the `sibsp` discrete variable:

```
data['sibsp'].unique()
```

The possible values that `sibsp` can take can be seen in the following code:

```
array([0, 1, 2, 3, 4, 5, 8], dtype=int64)
```

4. Now, let's inspect the first 20 distinct values of the continuous variable fare:

```
data['fare'].unique()[0:20]
```

The following code block identifies the unique values of fare and displays the first 20:

```
array([211.3375, 151.55  ,   26.55 ,   77.9583,   0.    ,   51.4792,
        49.5042, 227.525 ,   69.3  ,   78.85 ,  30.    ,   25.925 ,
       247.5208,  76.2917,   75.2417,  52.5542, 221.7792,  26.    ,
        91.0792, 135.6333])
```

Go ahead and inspect the values of the embarked and cabin variables by using the command we used in *step 3* and *step 4*.

> The embarked variable contains strings as values, which means it's categorical, whereas cabin contains a mix of letters and numbers, which means it can be classified as a mixed type of variable.

How it works...

In this recipe, we identified the variable data types of a publicly available dataset by inspecting the data type in which the variables are cast and the distinct values they take. First, we used pandas read_csv() to load the data from a CSV file into a dataframe. Next, we used pandas dtypes to display the data types in which the variables are cast, which can be float for continuous variables, int for integers, and object for strings. We observed that the continuous variable fare was cast as float, the discrete variable sibsp was cast as int, and the categorical variable embarked was cast as an object. Finally, we identified the distinct values of a variable with the unique() method from pandas. We used unique() together with a range, [0:20], to output the first 20 unique values for fare, since this variable shows a lot of distinct values.

There's more...

To understand whether a variable is continuous or discrete, we can also make a histogram:

1. Let's make a histogram for the sibsp variable by dividing the variable value range into 20 intervals:

```
data['sibsp'].hist(bins=20)
```

The output of the preceding code is as follows:

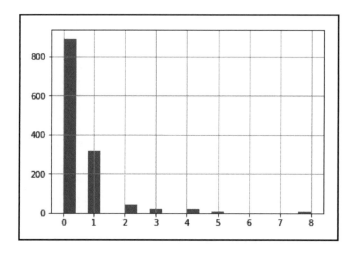

Note how the histogram of a discrete variable has a broken, discrete shape.

2. Now, let's make a histogram of the `fare` variable by sorting the values into 50 contiguous intervals:

```
data['fare'].hist(bins=50)
```

The output of the preceding code is as follows:

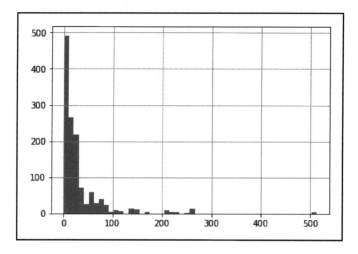

The histogram of continuous variables shows values throughout the variable value range.

See also

For more details on pandas and variable types, check out `https://pandas.pydata.org/pandas-docs/stable/getting_started/basics.html#basics-dtypes`.

For details on other variables in the Titanic dataset, check the accompanying Jupyter Notebook in this book's GitHub repository (`https://github.com/PacktPublishing/Python-Feature-Engineering-Cookbook`).

Quantifying missing data

Missing data refers to the absence of a value for observations and is a common occurrence in most datasets. Scikit-learn, the open source Python library for machine learning, does not support missing values as input for machine learning models, so we need to convert these values into numbers. To select the missing data imputation technique, it is important to know about the amount of missing information in our variables. In this recipe, we will learn how to identify and quantify missing data using pandas and how to make plots with the percentages of missing data per variable.

Getting ready

In this recipe, we will use the KDD-CUP-98 dataset from the UCI Machine Learning Repository. To download this dataset, follow the instructions in the *Technical requirements* section of this chapter.

How to do it...

First, let's import the necessary Python libraries:

1. Import the required Python libraries:

```
import pandas as pd
import matplotlib.pyplot as plt
```

2. Let's load a few variables from the dataset into a pandas dataframe and inspect the first five rows:

```
cols = ['AGE', 'NUMCHLD', 'INCOME', 'WEALTH1', 'MBCRAFT',
'MBGARDEN', 'MBBOOKS', 'MBCOLECT', 'MAGFAML','MAGFEM', 'MAGMALE']
```

```
data = pd.read_csv('cup98LRN.txt', usecols=cols)
data.head()
```

After loading the dataset, this is how the output of `head()` looks like when we run it from a Jupyter Notebook:

	AGE	NUMCHLD	INCOME	WEALTH1	MBCRAFT	MBGARDEN	MBBOOKS	MBCOLECT	MAGFAML	MAGFEM	MAGMALE
0	60.0	NaN	NaN	NaN	NaN	NaN	NaN	NaN	NaN	NaN	NaN
1	46.0	1.0	6.0	9.0	0.0	0.0	3.0	1.0	1.0	1.0	0.0
2	NaN	NaN	3.0	1.0	0.0	0.0	1.0	0.0	0.0	0.0	0.0
3	70.0	NaN	1.0	4.0	0.0	0.0	0.0	0.0	0.0	0.0	0.0
4	78.0	1.0	3.0	2.0	1.0	0.0	9.0	0.0	4.0	1.0	0.0

3. Let's calculate the number of missing values in each variable:

```
data.isnull().sum()
```

The number of missing values per variable can be seen in the following output:

```
AGE          23665
NUMCHLD      83026
INCOME       21286
WEALTH1      44732
MBCRAFT      52854
MBGARDEN     52854
MBBOOKS      52854
MBCOLECT     52914
MAGFAML      52854
MAGFEM       52854
MAGMALE      52854
dtype: int64
```

4. Let's quantify the percentage of missing values in each variable:

```
data.isnull().mean()
```

The percentages of missing values per variable can be seen in the following output, expressed as decimals:

```
AGE          0.248030
NUMCHLD      0.870184
INCOME       0.223096
WEALTH1      0.468830
MBCRAFT      0.553955
MBGARDEN     0.553955
```

```
MBBOOKS     0.553955
MBCOLECT    0.554584
MAGFAML     0.553955
MAGFEM      0.553955
MAGMALE 0.553955
dtype: float64
```

5. Finally, let's make a bar plot with the percentage of missing values per variable:

```
data.isnull().mean().plot.bar(figsize=(12,6))
plt.ylabel('Percentage of missing values')
plt.xlabel('Variables')
plt.title('Quantifying missing data')
```

The bar plot that's returned by the preceding code block displays the percentage of missing data per variable:

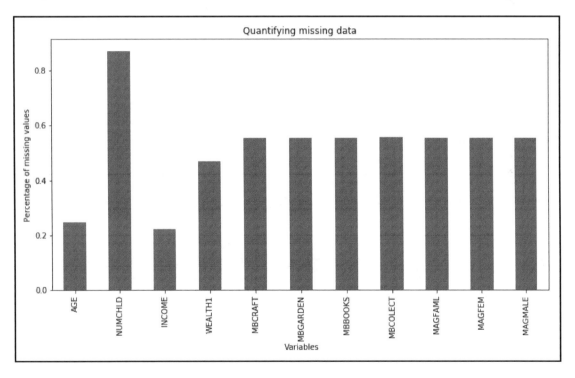

We can change the figure size using the figsize argument within pandas plot.bar() and we can add *x* and *y* labels and a title with the plt.xlabel(), plt.ylabel(), and plt.title() methods from Matplotlib to enhance the aesthetics of the plot.

How it works...

In this recipe, we quantified and displayed the amount and percentage of missing data of a publicly available dataset.

To load data from the `txt` file into a dataframe, we used the pandas `read_csv()` method. To load only certain columns from the original data, we created a list with the column names and passed this list to the `usecols` argument of `read_csv()`. Then, we used the `head()` method to display the top five rows of the dataframe, along with the variable names and some of their values.

To identify missing observations, we used pandas `isnull()`. This created a boolean vector per variable, with each vector indicating whether the value was missing (`True`) or not (`False`) for each row of the dataset. Then, we used the pandas `sum()` and `mean()` methods to operate over these boolean vectors and calculate the total number or the percentage of missing values, respectively. The `sum()` method sums the `True` values of the boolean vectors to find the total number of missing values, whereas the `mean()` method takes the average of these values and returns the percentage of missing data, expressed as decimals.

To display the percentages of the missing values in a bar plot, we used pandas `isnull()` and `mean()`, followed by `plot.bar()`, and modified the plot by adding axis legends and a title with the `xlabel()`, `ylabel()`, and `title()` Matplotlib methods.

Determining cardinality in categorical variables

The number of unique categories in a variable is called cardinality. For example, the cardinality of the `Gender` variable, which takes values of `female` and `male`, is 2, whereas the cardinality of the `Civil status` variable, which takes values of `married`, `divorced`, `singled`, and `widowed`, is 4. In this recipe, we will learn how to quantify and create plots of the cardinality of categorical variables using pandas and Matplotlib.

Getting ready

In this recipe, we will use the KDD-CUP-98 dataset from the UCI Machine Learning Repository. To download this dataset, follow the instructions in the *Technical requirements* section of this chapter.

How to do it...

Let's begin by importing the necessary Python libraries:

1. Import the required Python libraries:

```
import pandas as pd
import numpy as np
import matplotlib.pyplot as plt
```

2. Let's load a few categorical variables from the dataset:

```
cols = ['GENDER', 'RFA_2', 'MDMAUD_A', 'RFA_2', 'DOMAIN', 'RFA_15']
data = pd.read_csv('cup98LRN.txt', usecols=cols)
```

3. Let's replace the empty strings with NaN values and inspect the first five rows of the data:

```
data = data.replace(' ', np.nan)
data.head()
```

After loading the data, this is what the output of `head()` looks like when we run it from a Jupyter Notebook:

	DOMAIN	GENDER	RFA_2	RFA_15	MDMAUD_A
0	T2	F	L4E	S4E	X
1	S1	M	L2G	NaN	X
2	R2	M	L4E	S4F	X
3	R2	F	L4E	S4E	X
4	S2	F	L2F	NaN	X

4. Now, let's determine the number of unique categories in each variable:

```
data.nunique()
```

The output of the preceding code shows the number of distinct categories per variable, that is, the cardinality:

```
DOMAIN      16
GENDER       6
RFA_2       14
RFA_15      33
MDMAUD_A     5
dtype: int64
```

The `nunique()` method ignores missing values by default. If we want to consider missing values as an additional category, we should set the `dropna` argument to `False`: `data.nunique(dropna=False)`.

5. Now, let's print out the unique categories of the GENDER variable:

```
data['GENDER'].unique()
```

We can see the distinct values of GENDER in the following output:

```
array(['F', 'M', nan, 'C', 'U', 'J', 'A'], dtype=object)
```

pandas `nunique()` can be used in the entire dataframe. pandas `unique()`, on the other hand, works only on a pandas Series. Thus, we need to specify the column name that we want to return the unique values for.

6. Let's make a plot with the cardinality of each variable:

```
data.nunique().plot.bar(figsize=(12,6))
plt.ylabel('Number of unique categories')
plt.xlabel('Variables')
plt.title('Cardinality')
```

The following is the output of the preceding code block:

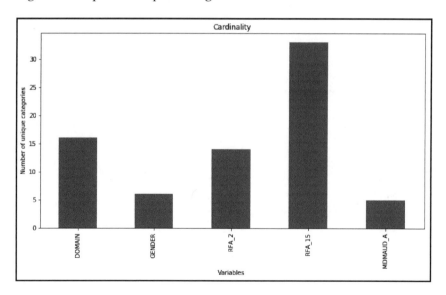

We can change the figure size with the `figsize` argument and also add *x* and *y* labels and a title with `plt.xlabel()`, `plt.ylabel()`, and `plt.title()` to enhance the aesthetics of the plot.

How it works...

In this recipe, we quantified and plotted the cardinality of the categorical variables of a publicly available dataset.

To load the categorical columns from the dataset, we captured the variable names in a list. Next, we used pandas `read_csv()` to load the data from a `txt` file onto a dataframe and passed the list with variable names to the `usecols` argument.

Many variables from the KDD-CUP-98 dataset contained empty strings which are, in essence, missing values. Thus, we replaced the empty strings with the NumPy representation of missing values, `np.nan`, by utilizing the pandas `replace()` method. With the `head()` method, we displayed the top five rows of the dataframe.

To quantify cardinality, we used the `nunique()` method from pandas, which finds and then counts the number of distinct values per variable. Next, we used the `unique()` method to output the distinct categories in the GENDER variable.

To plot the variable cardinality, we used pandas `nunique()`, followed by pandas `plot.bar()`, to make a bar plot with the variable cardinality, and added axis labels and a figure title by utilizing the Matplotlib `xlabel()`, `ylabel()`, and `title()` methods.

There's more...

The `nunique()` method determines the number of unique values for categorical and numerical variables. In this recipe, we only used `nunique()` on categorical variables to explore the concept of cardinality. However, we could also use `nunique()` to evaluate numerical variables.

We can also evaluate the cardinality of a subset of the variables in a dataset by slicing the dataframe:

```
data[['RFA_2', 'MDMAUD_A', 'RFA_2']].nunique()
```

The following is the output of the preceding code:

```
RFA_2        14
MDMAUD_A      5
RFA_2        14
dtype: int64
```

In the preceding output, we can see the number of distinct values each of these variables can take.

Pinpointing rare categories in categorical variables

Different labels appear in a variable with different frequencies. Some categories of a variable appear a lot, that is, they are very common among the observations, whereas other categories appear only in a few observations. In fact, categorical variables often contain a few dominant labels that account for the majority of the observations and a large number of labels that appear only seldom. Categories that appear in a tiny proportion of the observations are rare. Typically, we consider a label to be rare when it appears in less than 5% or 1% of the population. In this recipe, we will learn how to identify infrequent labels in a categorical variable.

Getting ready

To follow along with this recipe, download the Car Evaluation dataset from the UCI Machine Learning Repository by following the instructions in the *Technical requirements* section of this chapter.

How to do it...

Let's begin by importing the necessary libraries and getting the data ready:

1. Import the required Python libraries:

    ```python
    import pandas as pd
    import matplotlib.pyplot as plt
    ```

2. Let's load the Car Evaluation dataset, add the column names, and display the first five rows:

```
data = pd.read_csv('car.data', header=None)
data.columns = ['buying', 'maint', 'doors', 'persons', 'lug_boot',
'safety', 'class']
data.head()
```

We get the following output when the code is executed from a Jupyter Notebook:

	buying	maint	doors	persons	lug_boot	safety	class
0	vhigh	vhigh	2	2	small	low	unacc
1	vhigh	vhigh	2	2	small	med	unacc
2	vhigh	vhigh	2	2	small	high	unacc
3	vhigh	vhigh	2	2	med	low	unacc
4	vhigh	vhigh	2	2	med	med	unacc

By default, pandas `read_csv()` uses the first row of the data as the column names. If the column names are not part of the raw data, we need to specifically tell pandas not to assign the column names by adding the `header = None` argument.

3. Let's display the unique categories of the variable class:

```
data['class'].unique()
```

We can see the unique values of `class` in the following output:

```
array(['unacc', 'acc', 'vgood', 'good'], dtype=object)
```

4. Let's calculate the number of cars per category of the `class` variable and then divide them by the total number of cars in the dataset to obtain the percentage of cars per category. Then, we'll print the result:

```
label_freq = data['class'].value_counts() / len(data)
print(label_freq)
```

The output of the preceding code block is a pandas Series, with the percentage of cars per category expressed as decimals:

```
unacc     0.700231
acc       0.222222
good      0.039931
vgood     0.037616
Name: class, dtype: float64
```

5. Let's make a bar plot showing the frequency of each category and highlight the 5% mark with a red line:

```
fig = label_freq.sort_values(ascending=False).plot.bar()
fig.axhline(y=0.05, color='red')
fig.set_ylabel('percentage of cars within each category')
fig.set_xlabel('Variable: class')
fig.set_title('Identifying Rare Categories')
plt.show()
```

The following is the output of the preceding block code:

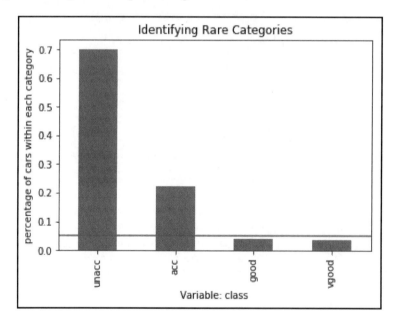

The good and vgood categories are present in less than 5% of cars, as indicated by the red line in the preceding plot.

How it works...

In this recipe, we quantified and plotted the percentage of observations per category, that is, the category frequency in a categorical variable of a publicly available dataset.

To load the data, we used pandas `read_csv()` and set the `header` argument to `None`, since the column names were not part of the raw data. Next, we added the column names manually by passing the variable names as a list to the `columns` attribute of the dataframe.

To determine the frequency of each category in the `class` variable, we counted the number of cars per category using pandas `value_counts()` and divided the result by the total cars in the dataset, which is determined with the Python built-in `len` method. Python's `len` method counted the number of rows in the dataframe. We captured the returned percentage of cars per category, expressed as decimals, in the `label_freq` variable.

To make a plot of the category frequency, we sorted the categories in `label_freq` from that of most cars to that of the fewest cars using the pandas `sort_values()` method. Next, we used `plot.bar()` to produce a bar plot. With `axhline()`, from Matplotlib, we added a horizontal red line at the height of 0.05 to indicate the 5% percentage limit, under which we considered a category as rare. We added x and y labels and a title with `plt.xlabel()`, `plt.ylabel()`, and `plt.title()` from Matplotlib.

Identifying a linear relationship

Linear models assume that the independent variables, X, take a linear relationship with the dependent variable, Y. This relationship can be dictated by the following equation:

$$Y \approx \beta0 + \beta1X1 + \beta2X2 + \ldots + \beta nXn$$

Here, X specifies the independent variables and β are the coefficients that indicate a unit change in Y per unit change in X. Failure to meet this assumption may result in poor model performance.

Linear relationships can be evaluated by scatter plots and residual plots. Scatter plots output the relationship of the independent variable X and the target Y. Residuals are the difference between the linear estimation of Y using X and the real target:

$$error = target - predictions$$

If the relationship is linear, the residuals should follow a normal distribution centered at zero, while the values should vary homogeneously along the values of the independent variable. In this recipe, we will evaluate the linear relationship using both scatter and residual plots in a toy dataset.

How to do it...

Let's begin by importing the necessary libraries:

1. Import the required Python libraries and a linear regression class:

```
import pandas as pd
import numpy as np
import matplotlib.pyplot as plt
import seaborn as sns
from sklearn.linear_model import LinearRegression
```

To proceed with this recipe, let's create a toy dataframe with an x variable that follows a normal distribution and shows a linear relationship with a y variable.

2. Create an x variable with 200 observations that are normally distributed:

```
np.random.seed(29)
x = np.random.randn(200)
```

 Setting the seed for reproducibility using np.random.seed() will help you get the outputs shown in this recipe.

3. Create a y variable that is linearly related to x with some added random noise:

```
y = x * 10 + np.random.randn(200) * 2
```

4. Create a dataframe with the x and y variables:

```
data = pd.DataFrame([x, y]).T
data.columns = ['x', 'y']
```

5. Plot a scatter plot to visualize the linear relationship:

```
sns.lmplot(x="x", y="y", data=data, order=1)
plt.ylabel('Target')
plt.xlabel('Independent variable')
```

The preceding code results in the following output:

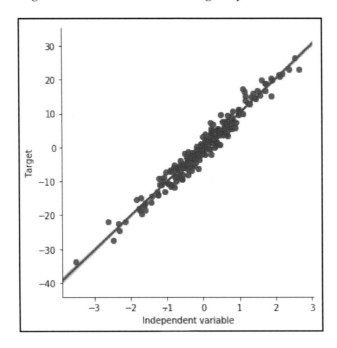

To evaluate the linear relationship using residual plots, we need to carry out a few more steps.

6. Build a linear regression model between x and y:

```
linreg = LinearRegression()
linreg.fit(data['x'].to_frame(), data['y'])
```

Scikit-learn predictor classes do not take pandas Series as arguments. Because data['x'] is a pandas Series, we need to convert it into a dataframe using to_frame().

Now, we need to calculate the residuals.

7. Make predictions of y using the fitted linear model:

```
predictions = linreg.predict(data['x'].to_frame())
```

8. Calculate the residuals, that is, the difference between the predictions and the real outcome, y:

```
residuals = data['y'] - predictions
```

9. Make a scatter plot of the independent variable x and the residuals:

```
plt.scatter(y=residuals, x=data['x'])
plt.ylabel('Residuals')
plt.xlabel('Independent variable x')
```

The output of the preceding code is as follows:

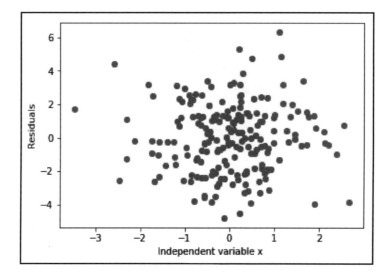

10. Finally, let's evaluate the distribution of the residuals:

```
sns.distplot(residuals, bins=30)
plt.xlabel('Residuals')
```

In the following output, we can see that the residuals are normally distributed and centered around zero:

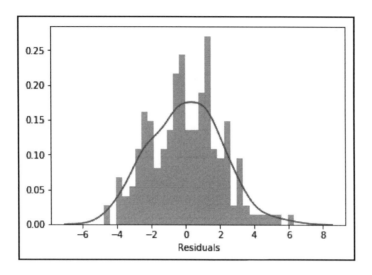

Check the accompanying Jupyter Notebook for examples of scatter and residual plots in variables from a real dataset which can be found at https://github.com/PacktPublishing/Python-Feature-Engineering-Cookbook/blob/master/Chapter01/Recipe-5-Identifying-a-linear-relationship.ipynb.

How it works...

In this recipe, we identified a linear relationship between an independent and a dependent variable using scatter and residual plots. To proceed with this recipe, we created a toy dataframe with an independent variable x that is normally distributed and linearly related to a dependent variable y. Next, we created a scatter plot between x and y, built a linear regression model between x and y, and obtained the predictions. Finally, we calculated the residuals and plotted the residuals versus the variable and the residuals histogram.

To generate the toy dataframe, we created an independent variable x that is normally distributed using NumPy's `random.randn()`, which extracts values at random from a normal distribution. Then, we created the dependent variable y by multiplying x 10 times and added random noise using NumPy's `random.randn()`. After, we captured x and y in a pandas dataframe using the pandas `DataFrame()` method and transposed it using the `T` method to return a 200 row x 2 column dataframe. We added the column names by passing them in a list to the `columns` dataframe attribute.

To create the scatter plot between x and y, we used the seaborn `lmplot()` method, which allows us to plot the data and fit and display a linear model on top of it. We specified the independent variable by setting `x='x'`, the dependent variable by setting `y='y'`, and the dataset by setting `data=data`. We created a model of order 1 that is a linear model, by setting the `order` argument to 1.

> Seaborn `lmplot()` allows you to fit many polynomial models. You can indicate the order of the model by utilizing the `order` argument. In this recipe, we fit a linear model, so we indicated `order=1`.

Next, we created a linear regression model between x and y using the `LinearRegression()` class from scikit-learn. We instantiated the model into a variable called `linreg` and then fitted the model with the `fit()` method with x and y as arguments. Because `data['x']` was a pandas Series, we converted it into a dataframe with the `to_frame()` method. Next, we obtained the predictions of the linear model with the `predict()` method.

To make the residual plots, we calculated the residuals by subtracting the predictions from y. We evaluated the distribution of the residuals using seaborn's `distplot()`. Finally, we plotted the residuals against the values of x using Matplotlib `scatter()` and added the axis labels by utilizing Matplotlib's `xlabel()` and `ylabel()` methods.

There's more...

In the GitHub repository of this book (`https://github.com/PacktPublishing/Python-Feature-Engineering-Cookbook`), there are additional demonstrations that use variables from a real dataset. In the Jupyter Notebook, you will find the example plots of variables that follow a linear relationship with the target, variables that are not linearly related.

See also

For more details on how to modify seaborn's `scatter` and `distplot`, take a look at the following links:

- `distplot()`: `https://seaborn.pydata.org/generated/seaborn.distplot.html`
- `lmplot()`: `https://seaborn.pydata.org/generated/seaborn.lmplot.html`

For more details about the scikit-learn linear regression algorithm, visit: `https://scikit-learn.org/stable/modules/generated/sklearn.linear_model.LinearRegression.html`.

Identifying a normal distribution

Linear models assume that the independent variables are normally distributed. Failure to meet this assumption may produce algorithms that perform poorly. We can determine whether a variable is normally distributed with histograms and Q-Q plots. In a Q-Q plot, the quantiles of the independent variable are plotted against the expected quantiles of the normal distribution. If the variable is normally distributed, the dots in the Q-Q plot should fall along a 45 degree diagonal. In this recipe, we will learn how to evaluate normal distributions using histograms and Q-Q plots.

How to do it...

Let's begin by importing the necessary libraries:

1. Import the required Python libraries and modules:

```
import pandas as pd
import numpy as np
import matplotlib.pyplot as plt
import seaborn as sns
import scipy.stats as stats
```

To proceed with this recipe, let's create a toy dataframe with a single variable, x, that follows a normal distribution.

2. Create a variable, x, with 200 observations that are normally distributed:

```
np.random.seed(29)
x = np.random.randn(200)
```

Setting the seed for reproducibility using `np.random.seed()` will help you get the outputs shown in this recipe.

3. Create a dataframe with the x variable:

```
data = pd.DataFrame([x]).T
data.columns = ['x']
```

4. Make a histogram and a density plot of the variable distribution:

```
sns.distplot(data['x'], bins=30)
```

The output of the preceding code is as follows:

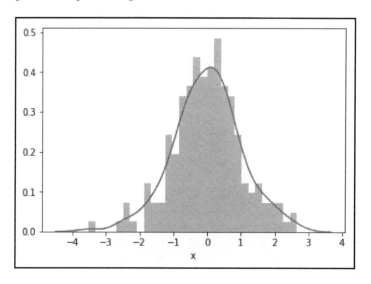

We can also create a histogram using the pandas `hist()` method, that is, `data['x'].hist(bins=30)`.

5. Create and display a Q-Q plot to assess a normal distribution:

```
stats.probplot(data['x'], dist="norm", plot=plt)
plt.show()
```

The output of the preceding code is as follows:

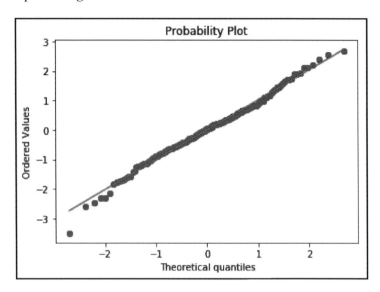

Since the variable is normally distributed, its values follow the theoretical quantiles and thus lie along the 45-degree diagonal.

How it works...

In this recipe, we determined whether a variable is normally distributed with a histogram and a Q-Q plot. To do so, we created a toy dataframe with a single independent variable, x, that is normally distributed, and then created a histogram and a Q-Q plot.

For the toy dataframe, we created a normally distributed variable, x, using the NumPy `random.randn()` method, which extracted 200 random values from a normal distribution. Next, we captured x in a dataframe using the pandas `DataFrame()` method and transposed it using the `T` method to return a 200 row x 1 column dataframe. Finally, we added the column name as a list to the dataframe's `columns` attribute.

To display the variable distribution as a histogram and density plot, we used seaborn's `distplot()` method. By setting the `bins` argument to `30`, we created 30 contiguous intervals for the histogram. To create the Q-Q plot, we used `stats.probplot()` from SciPy, which generated a plot of the quantiles for our x variable in the *y*-axis versus the quantiles of a theoretical normal distribution, which we indicated by setting the `dist` argument to `norm`, in the *x*-axis. We used Matplotlib to display the plot by setting the `plot` argument to `plt`. Since x was normally distributed, its quantiles followed the quantiles of the theoretical distribution, so that the dots of the variable values fell along the 45-degree line.

There's more...

For examples of Q-Q plots using real data, visit the Jupyter Notebook in this book's GitHub repository (`https://github.com/PacktPublishing/Python-Feature-Engineering-Cookbook/blob/master/Chapter01/Recipe-6-Identifying-a-normal-distribution.ipynb`).

See also

For more details about seaborn's `distplot` or SciPy's Q-Q plots, take a look at the following links:

- `distplot()`: `https://seaborn.pydata.org/generated/seaborn.distplot.html`
- `stats.probplot()`: `https://docs.scipy.org/doc/scipy/reference/generated/scipy.stats.probplot.html`

Distinguishing variable distribution

A probability distribution is a function that describes the likelihood of obtaining the possible values of a variable. There are many well-described variable distributions, such as the normal, binomial, or Poisson distributions. Some machine learning algorithms assume that the independent variables are normally distributed. Other models make no assumptions about the distribution of the variables, but a better spread of these values may improve their performance. In this recipe, we will learn how to create plots to distinguish the variable distributions in the entire dataset by using the Boston House Prices dataset from scikit-learn.

Getting ready

In this recipe, we will learn how to visualize the distributions of the variables in a dataset using histograms. For more details about different probability distributions, visit the following gallery: `https://www.itl.nist.gov/div898/handbook/eda/section3/eda366.htm`.

How to do it...

Let's begin by importing the necessary libraries:

1. Import the required Python libraries and modules:

```
import pandas as pd
import matplotlib.pyplot as plt
```

2. Load the Boston House Prices dataset from scikit-learn:

```
from sklearn.datasets import load_boston
boston_dataset = load_boston()
boston = pd.DataFrame(boston_dataset.data,
        columns=boston_dataset.feature_names)
```

3. Visualize the variable distribution with histograms:

```
boston.hist(bins=30, figsize=(12,12), density=True)
plt.show()
```

The output of the preceding code is shown in the following screenshot:

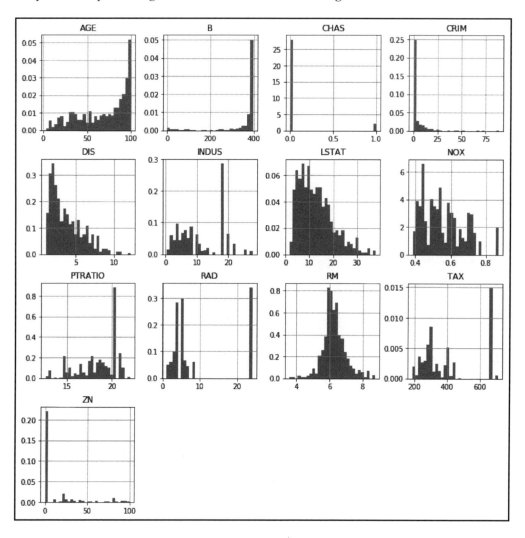

 Most of the numerical variables in the dataset are skewed.

How it works...

In this recipe, we used pandas `hist()` to plot the distribution of all the numerical variables in the Boston House Prices dataset from scikit-learn. To load the data, we imported the dataset from scikit-learn `datasets` and then used `load_boston()` to load the data. Next, we captured the data into a dataframe using pandas `DataFrame()`, indicating that the data is stored in the `data` attribute and the variable names in the `feature_names` attribute.

To display the histograms of all the numerical variables, we used pandas `hist()`, which calls `matplotlib.pyplot.hist()` on each variable in the dataframe, resulting in one histogram per variable. We indicated the number of intervals for the histograms using the `bins` argument, adjusted the figure size with `figsize`, and normalized the histogram by setting `density` to `True`. If the histogram is normalized, the sum of the area under the curve is `1`.

See also

For more details on how to modify a pandas histogram, visit `https://pandas.pydata.org/pandas-docs/stable/reference/api/pandas.DataFrame.hist.html`.

Highlighting outliers

An outlier is a data point that is significantly different from the remaining data. On occasions, outliers are very informative; for example, when looking for credit card transactions, an outlier may be an indication of fraud. In other cases, outliers are rare observations that do not add any additional information. These cases may also affect the performance of some machine learning models.

> *"An outlier is an observation which deviates so much from the other observations as to arouse suspicions that it was generated by a different mechanism." [D. Hawkins. Identification of Outliers, Chapman and Hall, 1980.]*

Getting ready

In this recipe, we will learn how to identify outliers using boxplots and the **inter-quartile range** (IQR) proximity rule. According to the IQR proximity rule, a value is an outlier if it falls outside these boundaries:

$$Upper\ boundary = 75th\ quantile + (IQR * 1.5)$$

$$Lower\ boundary = 25th\ quantile - (IQR * 1.5)$$

Here, IQR is given by the following equation:

$$IQR = 75th\ quantile - 25th\ quantile$$

 Typically, we calculate the IQR proximity rule boundaries by multiplying the IQR by 1.5. However, it is also common practice to find extreme values by multiplying the IQR by 3.

How to do it...

Let's begin by importing the necessary libraries and preparing the dataset:

1. Import the required Python libraries and the dataset:

```
import pandas as pd
import numpy as np
import matplotlib.pyplot as plt
import seaborn as sns
from sklearn.datasets import load_boston
```

2. Load the Boston House Prices dataset from scikit-learn and retain three of its variables in a dataframe:

```
boston_dataset = load_boston()
boston = pd.DataFrame(boston_dataset.data,
columns=boston_dataset.feature_names)[['RM', 'LSTAT', 'CRIM']]
```

3. Make a boxplot for the RM variable:

```
sns.boxplot(y=boston['RM'])
plt.title('Boxplot')
```

The output of the preceding code is as follows:

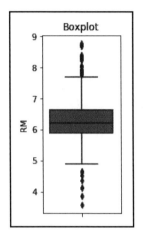

We can change the final size of the plot using the `figure()` method from
Matplotlib. We need to call this command before making the plot with
seaborn:

```
plt.figure(figsize=(3,6))
sns.boxplot(y=boston['RM'])
plt.title('Boxplot')
```

To find the outliers in a variable, we need to find the distribution boundaries
according to the IQR proximity rule, which we discussed in the *Getting ready*
section of this recipe.

4. Create a function that takes a dataframe, a variable name, and the factor to use in
   the IQR calculation and returns the IQR proximity rule boundaries:

```
def find_boundaries(df, variable, distance):

    IQR = df[variable].quantile(0.75) - df[variable].quantile(0.25)

    lower_boundary = df[variable].quantile(0.25) - (IQR * distance)
    upper_boundary = df[variable].quantile(0.75) + (IQR * distance)

    return upper_boundary, lower_boundary
```

5. Calculate and then display the IQR proximity rule boundaries for the RM variable:

```
upper_boundary, lower_boundary = find_boundaries(boston, 'RM', 1.5)
upper_boundary, lower_boundary
```

The `find_boundaries()` function returns the values above and below which we can consider a value to be an outlier, as shown here:

```
(7.730499999999999, 4.778500000000001)
```

If you want to find very extreme values, you can use 3 as the distance of `find_boundaries()` instead of 1.5.

Now, we need to find the outliers in the dataframe.

6. Create a boolean vector to flag observations outside the boundaries we determined in *step 5*:

```
outliers = np.where(boston['RM'] > upper_boundary, True,
                    np.where(boston['RM'] < lower_boundary, True, False))
```

7. Create a new dataframe with the outlier values and then display the top five rows:

```
outliers_df = boston.loc[outliers, 'RM']
outliers_df.head()
```

We can see the top five outliers in the RM variable in the following output:

```
97      8.069
98      7.820
162     7.802
163     8.375
166     7.929
Name: RM, dtype: float64
```

To remove the outliers from the dataset, execute `boston.loc[~outliers, 'RM']`.

How it works...

In this recipe, we identified outliers in the numerical variables of the Boston House Prices dataset from scikit-learn using boxplots and the IQR proximity rule. To proceed with this recipe, we loaded the dataset from scikit-learn and created a boxplot for one of its numerical variables as an example. Next, we created a function to identify the boundaries using the IQR proximity rule and used the function to determine the boundaries of the numerical RM variable. Finally, we identified the values of RM that were higher or lower than those boundaries, that is, the outliers.

To load the data, we imported the dataset from `sklearn.datasets` and used `load_boston()`. Next, we captured the data in a dataframe using pandas `DataFrame()`, indicating that the data was stored in the `data` attribute and that the variable names were stored in the `feature_names` attribute. To retain only the RM, LSTAT, and CRIM variables, we passed the column names in double brackets `[[]]` at the back of pandas `DataFrame()`.

To display the boxplot, we used seaborn's `boxplot()` method and passed the pandas Series with the RM variable as an argument. In the boxplot displayed after *step 3*, the IQR is delimited by the rectangle, and the upper and lower boundaries corresponding to either, the 75th quantile plus 1.5 times the IQR, or the 25th quantile minus 1.5 times the IQR. This is indicated by the whiskers. The outliers are the asterisks lying outside the whiskers.

To identify those outliers in our dataframe, in *step 4*, we created a function to find the boundaries according to the IQR proximity rule. The function took the dataframe and the variable as arguments and calculated the IQR and the boundaries using the formula described in the *Getting ready* section of this recipe. With the pandas `quantile()` method, we calculated the values for the 25th (0.25) and 75th quantiles (0.75). The function returned the upper and lower boundaries for the RM variable.

To find the outliers of RM, we used NumPy's `where()` method, which produced a boolean vector with `True` if the value was an outlier. Briefly, `where()` scanned the rows of the RM variable, and if the value was bigger than the upper boundary, it assigned `True`, whereas if the value was smaller, the second `where()` nested inside the first one and checked whether the value was smaller than the lower boundary, in which case it also assigned `True`, otherwise `False`. Finally, we used the `loc[]` method from pandas to capture only those values in the RM variable that were outliers in a new dataframe.

Comparing feature magnitude

Many machine learning algorithms are sensitive to the scale of the features. For example, the coefficients of linear models are directly informed by the scale of the feature. In addition, features with bigger value ranges tend to dominate over features with smaller ranges. Having features within a similar scale also helps algorithms converge faster, thus improving performance and training times. In this recipe, we will explore and compare feature magnitude by looking at statistical parameters such as the mean, median, standard deviation, and maximum and minimum values by leveraging the power of pandas.

Getting ready

For this recipe, you need to be familiar with common statistical parameters such as mean, quantiles, maximum and minimum values, and standard deviation. We will use the Boston House Prices dataset included in scikit-learn to do this.

How to do it...

Let's begin by importing the necessary libraries and loading the dataset:

1. Import the required Python libraries and classes:

```
import pandas as pd
from sklearn.datasets import load_boston
```

2. Load the Boston House Prices dataset from scikit-learn into a dataframe:

```
boston_dataset = load_boston()
data = pd.DataFrame(boston_dataset.data,
columns=boston_dataset.feature_names)
```

3. Print the main statistics for each variable in the dataset, that is, the mean, count, standard deviation, median, quantiles, and minimum and maximum values:

```
data.describe()
```

The following is the output of the preceding code when we run it from a Jupyter Notebook:

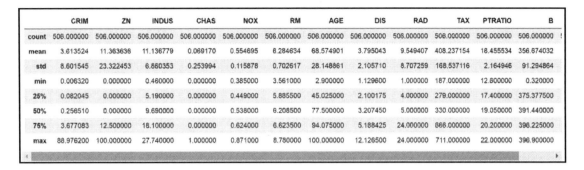

	CRIM	ZN	INDUS	CHAS	NOX	RM	AGE	DIS	RAD	TAX	PTRATIO	B
count	506.000000	506.000000	506.000000	506.000000	506.000000	506.000000	506.000000	506.000000	506.000000	506.000000	506.000000	506.000000
mean	3.613524	11.363636	11.136779	0.069170	0.554695	6.284634	68.574901	3.795043	9.549407	408.237154	18.455534	356.674032
std	8.601545	23.322453	6.860353	0.253994	0.115878	0.702617	28.148861	2.105710	8.707259	168.537116	2.164946	91.294864
min	0.006320	0.000000	0.460000	0.000000	0.385000	3.561000	2.900000	1.129600	1.000000	187.000000	12.600000	0.320000
25%	0.082045	0.000000	5.190000	0.000000	0.449000	5.885500	45.025000	2.100175	4.000000	279.000000	17.400000	375.377500
50%	0.256510	0.000000	9.690000	0.000000	0.538000	6.208500	77.500000	3.207450	5.000000	330.000000	19.050000	391.440000
75%	3.677083	12.500000	18.100000	0.000000	0.624000	6.623500	94.075000	5.188425	24.000000	666.000000	20.200000	396.225000
max	88.976200	100.000000	27.740000	1.000000	0.871000	8.780000	100.000000	12.126500	24.000000	711.000000	22.000000	396.900000

4. Calculate the value range of each variable, that is, the difference between the maximum and minimum value:

```
data.max() - data.min()
```

The following output shows the value ranges of the different variables:

```
CRIM        88.96988
ZN         100.00000
INDUS       27.28000
CHAS         1.00000
NOX          0.48600
RM           5.21900
AGE         97.10000
DIS         10.99690
RAD         23.00000
TAX        524.00000
PTRATIO      9.40000
B          396.58000
LSTAT       36.24000
dtype: float64
```

The value ranges of the variables are quite different.

How it works...

In this recipe, we used the `describe()` method from pandas to return the main statistical parameters of a distribution, namely, the mean, standard deviation, minimum and maximum values, 25th, 50th, and 75th quantiles, and the number of observations (count).

 We can also calculate these parameters individually using the pandas `mean()`, `count()`, `min()`, `max()`, `std()`, and `quantile()` methods.

Finally, we calculated the value range by subtracting the minimum from the maximum value in each variable using the pandas `max()` and `min()` methods.

Imputing Missing Data 2

Missing data refers to the absence of values for certain observations and is an unavoidable problem in most data sources. Scikit-learn does not support missing values as input, so we need to remove observations with missing data or transform them into permitted values. The act of replacing missing data with statistical estimates of missing values is called **imputation**. The goal of any imputation technique is to produce a complete dataset that can be used to train machine learning models. There are multiple imputation techniques we can apply to our data. The choice of imputation technique we use will depend on whether the data is missing at random, the number of missing values, and the machine learning model we intend to use. In this chapter, we will discuss several missing data imputation techniques.

This chapter will cover the following recipes:

- Removing observations with missing data
- Performing mean or median imputation
- Implementing mode or frequent category imputation
- Replacing missing values with an arbitrary number
- Capturing missing values in a bespoke category
- Replacing missing values with a value at the end of the distribution
- Implementing random sample imputation
- Adding a missing value indicator variable
- Performing multivariate imputation by chained equations
- Assembling an imputation pipeline with scikit-learn
- Assembling an imputation pipeline with Feature-engine

Technical requirements

In this chapter, we will use the Python libraries: pandas, NumPy and scikit-learn. I recommend installing the free Anaconda Python distribution (`https://www.anaconda.com/distribution/`), which contains all these packages.

> For details on how to install the Python Anaconda distribution, visit the *Technical requirements* section in `Chapter 1`, *Foreseeing Variable Problems When Building ML Models*.

We will also use the open source Python library called Feature-engine, which I created and can be installed using `pip`:

```
pip install feature-engine
```

To learn more about Feature-engine, visit the following sites:

- Home page: `www.trainindata.com/feature-engine`
- Docs: `https://feature-engine.readthedocs.io`
- GitHub: `https://github.com/solegalli/feature_engine/`

> Check that you have installed the right versions of the numerical Python libraries, which you can find in the `requirement.txt` file in the accompanying GitHub repository: `https://github.com/PacktPublishing/Python-Feature-Engineering-Cookbook`.

We will also use the **Credit Approval Data Set**, which is available in the UCI Machine Learning Repository (`https://archive.ics.uci.edu/ml/datasets/credit+approval`).

> Dua, D. and Graff, C. (2019). *UCI Machine Learning Repository* [`http://archive.ics.uci.edu/ml`]. Irvine, CA: University of California, School of Information and Computer Science.

To prepare the dataset, follow these steps:

1. Visit `http://archive.ics.uci.edu/ml/machine-learning-databases/credit-screening/`.

2. Click on `crx.data` to download the data:

← → C ⓘ Not secure | archive.ics.uci.edu/ml/machine-learning-databases/credit-screening/

Index of /ml/machine-learning-databases/credit-screening

- Parent Directory
- Index
- credit.lisp
- credit.names
- crx.data ⬅
- crx.names

Apache/2.4.6 (CentOS) OpenSSL/1.0.2k-fips SVN/1.7.14 Phusion_Passenger/4.0.53 mod_perl/2.0.10 Perl/v5.16.3 Server at archive.ics.uci.edu Port 80

3. Save `crx.data` to the folder where you will run the following commands.

   After you've downloaded the dataset, open a Jupyter Notebook or a Python IDE and run the following commands.

4. Import the required Python libraries:

```
import random
import pandas as pd
import numpy as np
```

5. Load the data with the following command:

```
data = pd.read_csv('crx.data', header=None)
```

6. Create a list with variable names:

```
varnames = ['A'+str(s) for s in range(1,17)]
```

7. Add the variable names to the dataframe:

```
data.columns = varnames
```

8. Replace the question marks (?) in the dataset with NumPy NaN values:

```
data = data.replace('?', np.nan)
```

9. Recast the numerical variables as `float` data types:

```
data['A2'] = data['A2'].astype('float')
data['A14'] = data['A14'].astype('float')
```

10. Recode the target variable as binary:

```
data['A16'] = data['A16'].map({'+':1, '-':0})
```

To demonstrate the recipes in this chapter, we will introduce missing data at random in four additional variables in this dataset.

11. Add some missing values at random positions in four variables:

```
random.seed(9001)
values = set([random.randint(0, len(data)) for p in range(0, 100)])
for var in ['A3', 'A8', 'A9', 'A10']:
    data.loc[values, var] = np.nan
```

With `random.randint()`, we extracted random digits between 0 and the number of observations in the dataset, which is given by `len(data)`, and used these digits as the indices of the dataframe where we introduce the NumPy NaN values.

Setting the seed, as specified in *step 11*, should allow you to obtain the results provided by the recipes in this chapter.

12. Save your prepared data:

```
data.to_csv('creditApprovalUCI.csv', index=False)
```

Now, you are ready to carry on with the recipes in this chapter.

Removing observations with missing data

Complete Case Analysis (CCA), also called list-wise deletion of cases, consists of discarding those observations where the values in **any** of the variables are missing. CCA can be applied to categorical and numerical variables. CCA is quick and easy to implement and has the advantage that it preserves the distribution of the variables, provided the data is missing at random and only a small proportion of the data is missing. However, if data is missing across many variables, CCA may lead to the removal of a big portion of the dataset.

How to do it...

Let's begin by loading `pandas` and the dataset:

1. First, we'll import the `pandas` library:

   ```
   import pandas as pd
   ```

2. Let's load the Credit Approval Data Set:

   ```
   data = pd.read_csv('creditApprovalUCI.csv')
   ```

3. Let's calculate the percentage of missing values for each variable and sort them in ascending order:

   ```
   data.isnull().mean().sort_values(ascending=True)
   ```

   The output of the preceding code is as follows:

   ```
   A11     0.000000
   A12     0.000000
   A13     0.000000
   A15     0.000000
   A16     0.000000
   A4      0.008696
   A5      0.008696
   A6      0.013043
   A7      0.013043
   A1      0.017391
   A2      0.017391
   A14     0.018841
   A3      0.133333
   A8      0.133333
   A9      0.133333
   A10     0.133333
   dtype:  float64
   ```

4. Now, we'll remove the observations with missing data in **any** of the variables:

   ```
   data_cca = data.dropna()
   ```

   To remove observations where data is missing in a subset of variables, we can execute `data.dropna(subset=['A3', 'A4'])`. To remove observations if data is missing in **all** the variables, we can execute `data.dropna(how='all')`.

5. Let's print and compare the size of the original and complete case datasets:

```
print('Number of total observations: {}'.format(len(data)))
print('Number of observations with complete cases:
{}'.format(len(data_cca)))
```

Here, we removed more than 100 observations with missing data, as shown in the following output:

```
Number of total observations: 690
Number of observations with complete cases: 564
```

We can use the code from *step 3* to corroborate the absence of missing data in the complete case dataset.

How it works...

In this recipe, we determined the percentage of missing data for each variable in the Credit Approval Data Set and removed all observations with missing information to create a complete case dataset.

First, we loaded the data from a CSV file into a dataframe with the pandas `read_csv()` method. Next, we used the pandas `isnull()` and `mean()` methods to determine the percentage of missing observations for each variable. We discussed these methods in the *Quantifying missing data* recipe in `Chapter 1`, *Foreseeing Variable Problems When Building ML Models*. With pandas `sort_values()`, we ordered the variables from the one with the fewest missing values to the one with the most.

To remove observations with missing values in **any** of the variables, we used the pandas `dropna()` method, thereby obtaining a complete case dataset. Finally, we calculated the number of observations we removed using the Python built-in method `len`, which returned the number of rows in the original and complete case datasets. Using `format`, we included the `len` output within the `{}` in the `print` statement, thereby displaying the number of missing observations next to the text.

See also

To learn more about `dropna()`, go to `https://pandas.pydata.org/pandas-docs/stable/reference/api/pandas.DataFrame.dropna.html`.

Performing mean or median imputation

Mean or median imputation consists of replacing missing values with the variable mean or median. This can only be performed in numerical variables. The mean or the median is calculated using a train set, and these values are used to impute missing data in train and test sets, as well as in future data we intend to score with the machine learning model. Therefore, we need to store these mean and median values. Scikit-learn and Feature-engine transformers learn the parameters from the train set and store these parameters for future use. So, in this recipe, we will learn how to perform mean or median imputation using the scikit-learn and Feature-engine libraries and pandas for comparison.

Use mean imputation if variables are normally distributed and median imputation otherwise. Mean and median imputation may distort the distribution of the original variables if there is a high percentage of missing data.

How to do it...

Let's begin this recipe:

1. First, we'll import `pandas` and the required functions and classes from scikit-learn and Feature-engine:

    ```
    import pandas as pd
    from sklearn.model_selection import train_test_split
    from sklearn.impute import SimpleImputer
    from feature_engine.missing_data_imputers import MeanMedianImputer
    ```

2. Let's load the dataset:

    ```
    data = pd.read_csv('creditApprovalUCI.csv')
    ```

3. In mean and median imputation, the mean or median values should be calculated using the variables in the train set; therefore, let's separate the data into train and test sets and their respective targets:

    ```
    X_train, X_test, y_train, y_test = train_test_split(
        data.drop('A16', axis=1), data['A16'], test_size=0.3,
        random_state=0)
    ```

You can check the size of the returned datasets using pandas' shape:
`X_train.shape, X_test.shape`.

4. Let's check the percentage of missing values in the train set:

```
X_train.isnull().mean()
```

The following output shows the percentage of missing values for each variable:

```
A1    0.008282
A2    0.022774
A3    0.140787
A4    0.008282
A5    0.008282
A6    0.008282
A7    0.008282
A8    0.140787
A9    0.140787
A10   0.140787
A11   0.000000
A12   0.000000
A13   0.000000
A14   0.014493
A15   0.000000
dtype: float64
```

5. Let's replace the missing values with the median in five numerical variables using pandas:

```
for var in ['A2', 'A3', 'A8', 'A11', 'A15']:
    value = X_train[var].median()
    X_train[var] = X_train[var].fillna(value)
    X_test[var] = X_test[var].fillna(value)
```

Note how we calculate the median using the train set and then use this value to replace the missing data in the train and test sets.

To impute missing data with the mean, we use pandas' `mean()`: `value = X_train[var].mean()`.

If you run the code in *step 4* after imputation, the percentage of missing values for the A2, A3, A8, A11, and A15 variables should be 0.

The pandas' `fillna()` returns a new dataset with imputed values by default. We can set the `inplace` argument to `True` to replace missing data in the original dataframe: `X_train[var].fillna(inplace=True)`.

Now, let's impute missing values by the median using scikit-learn so that we can store learned parameters.

6. To do this, let's separate the original dataset into train and test sets, keeping only the numerical variables:

```
X_train, X_test, y_train, y_test = train_test_split(
    data[['A2', 'A3', 'A8', 'A11', 'A15']], data['A16'],
    test_size=0.3, random_state=0)
```

`SimpleImputer()` from scikit-learn will impute **all** variables in the dataset. Therefore, if we use mean or median imputation and the dataset contains categorical variables, we will get an error.

7. Let's create a median imputation transformer using `SimpleImputer()` from scikit-learn:

```
imputer = SimpleImputer(strategy='median')
```

To perform mean imputation, we should set the `strategy` to `mean`:
`imputer = SimpleImputer(strategy = 'mean')`.

8. Let's fit the `SimpleImputer()` to the train set so that it learns the median values of the variables:

```
imputer.fit(X_train)
```

9. Let's inspect the learned median values:

```
imputer.statistics_
```

The imputer stores median values in the `statistics_` attribute, as shown in the following output:

```
array([28.835,  2.75 ,  1.  ,  0.  ,  6.  ])
```

10. Let's replace missing values with medians:

```
X_train = imputer.transform(X_train)
X_test = imputer.transform(X_test)
```

`SimpleImputer()` returns NumPy arrays. We can transform the array into a dataframe using `pd.DataFrame(X_train, columns = ['A2', 'A3', 'A8', 'A11', 'A15'])`. Be mindful of the order of the variables.

Finally, let's perform median imputation using `MeanMedianImputer()` from Feature-engine. First, we need to load and divide the dataset, just like we did in *step 2* and *step 3*. Next, we need to create an imputation transformer.

11. Let's set up a median imputation transformer using `MeanMedianImputer()` from Feature-engine specifying the variables to impute:

```
median_imputer = MeanMedianImputer(imputation_method='median',
                     variables=['A2', 'A3', 'A8', 'A11', 'A15'])
```

To perform mean imputation, change the imputation method, as follows: `MeanMedianImputer(imputation_method='mean')`.

12. Let's fit the median imputer so that it learns the median values for each of the specified variables:

```
median_imputer.fit(X_train)
```

13. Let's inspect the learned medians:

```
median_imputer.imputer_dict_
```

With the previous command, we can visualize the median values stored in a dictionary in the `imputer_dict_` attribute:

```
{'A2': 28.835, 'A3': 2.75, 'A8': 1.0, 'A11': 0.0, 'A15': 6.0}
```

14. Finally, let's replace the missing values with the median:

```
X_train = median_imputer.transform(X_train)
X_test = median_imputer.transform(X_test)
```

Feature-engine's `MeanMedianImputer()` returns a dataframe. You can check that the imputed variables do not contain missing values using `X_train[['A2','A3', 'A8', 'A11', 'A15']].isnull().mean()`.

How it works...

We replaced the missing values in the Credit Approval Data Set with the median estimates of the variables using pandas, scikit-learn, and Feature-engine. Since the mean or median values should be learned from the train set variables, we divided the dataset into train and test sets. To do so, in *step 3*, we used scikit-learn's `train_test_split()` function, which takes the dataset with predictor variables, the target, the percentage of observations to retain in the test set, and a `random_state` value for reproducibility as arguments. To obtain a dataset with predictor variables only, we used pandas `drop()` with the target variable A16 as an argument. To obtain the target, we sliced the dataframe on the target column, A16. By doing this, we obtained a train set with 70% of the original observations and a test set with 30% of the original observations.

We calculated the percentage of missing data for each variable using pandas `isnull()`, followed by pandas `mean()`, which we described in the *Quantifying missing data* recipe in `Chapter 1`, *Foreseeing Variable Problems When Building ML Models*. To impute missing data with pandas in multiple numerical variables, in *step 5* we created a `for` loop over the A2, A3, A8, A11, and A15 variables. For each variable, we calculated the median with pandas' `median()` in the train set and used this value to replace the missing values with pandas' `fillna()` in the train and test sets.

To replace the missing values using scikit-learn, we divided the Credit Approval data into train and test sets, keeping only the numerical variables. Next, we created an imputation transformer using `SimpleImputer()` and set the `strategy` argument to median. With the `fit()` method, `SimpleImputer()` learned the median of each variable in the train set and stored them in its `statistics_` attribute. Finally, we replaced the missing values using the `transform()` method of `SimpleImputer()` in the train and test sets.

To replace missing values via Feature-engine, we set up `MeanMedianImputer()` with `imputation_method` set to `median` and passed the names of the variables to impute in a list to the `variables` argument. With the `fit()` method, the transformer learned and stored the median values of the specified variables in a dictionary in its `imputer_dict_` attribute. With the `transform()` method, the missing values were replaced by the median in the train and test sets.

`SimpleImputer()` from scikit-learn operates on the entire dataframe and returns NumPy arrays. In contrast, `MeanMedianImputer()` from Feature-engine can take an entire dataframe as input and yet it will only impute the specified variables, returning a pandas dataframe.

There's more...

Scikit-learn's `SimpleImputer()` imputes all the variables in the dataset but, with scikit-learn's `ColumnTransformer()`, we can select specific variables we want to impute. For details on how to use `ColumnTransformer()` with `SimpleImputer()`, see the *Assembling an imputation pipeline with scikit-learn* recipe or check out the Jupyter Notebook for this recipe in the accompanying GitHub repository: `https://github.com/PacktPublishing/Python-Feature-Engineering-Cookbook`.

See also

To learn more about scikit-learn transformers, take a look at the following websites:

- `SimpleImputer()`: `https://scikit-learn.org/stable/modules/generated/sklearn.impute.SimpleImputer.html#sklearn.impute.SimpleImputer`
- `ColumnTransformer()`: `https://scikit-learn.org/stable/modules/generated/sklearn.compose.ColumnTransformer.html`
- `Stackoverflow`: `https://stackoverflow.com/questions/54160370/how-to-use-sklearn-column-transformer`

To learn more about mean or median imputation with Feature-engine, go to `https://feature-engine.readthedocs.io/en/latest/imputers/MeanMedianImputer.html`.

Implementing mode or frequent category imputation

Mode imputation consists of replacing missing values with the mode. We normally use this procedure in categorical variables, hence the **frequent category imputation** name. Frequent categories are estimated using the train set and then used to impute values in train, test, and future datasets. Thus, we need to learn and store these parameters, which we can do using scikit-learn and Feature-engine's transformers; in the following recipe, we will learn how to do so.

If the percentage of missing values is high, frequent category imputation may distort the original distribution of categories.

How to do it...

To begin, let's make a few imports and prepare the data:

1. Let's import pandas and the required functions and classes from scikit-learn and Feature-engine:

```
import pandas as pd
from sklearn.model_selection import train_test_split
from sklearn.impute import SimpleImputer
from feature_engine.missing_data_imputers import
FrequentCategoryImputer
```

2. Let's load the dataset:

```
data = pd.read_csv('creditApprovalUCI.csv')
```

3. Frequent categories should be calculated using the train set variables, so let's separate the data into train and test sets and their respective targets:

```
X_train, X_test, y_train, y_test = train_test_split(
    data.drop('A16', axis=1), data['A16'], test_size=0.3,
    random_state=0)
```

Remember that you can check the percentage of missing values in the train set with X_train.isnull().mean().

4. Let's replace missing values with the frequent category, that is, the mode, in four categorical variables:

```
for var in ['A4', 'A5', 'A6', 'A7']:
    value = X_train[var].mode()[0]
    X_train[var] = X_train[var].fillna(value)
    X_test[var] = X_test[var].fillna(value)
```

Note how we calculate the mode in the train set and use that value to replace the missing data in the train and test sets.

The pandas' `fillna()` returns a new dataset with imputed values by default. Instead of doing this, we can replace missing data in the original dataframe by executing `X_train[var].fillna(inplace=True)`.

Now, let's impute missing values by the most frequent category using scikit-learn.

5. First, let's separate the original dataset into train and test sets and only retain the categorical variables:

```
X_train, X_test, y_train, y_test = train_test_split(
    data[['A4', 'A5', 'A6', 'A7']], data['A16'], test_size=0.3,
    random_state=0)
```

6. Let's create a frequent category imputer with `SimpleImputer()` from scikit-learn:

```
imputer = SimpleImputer(strategy='most_frequent')
```

`SimpleImputer()` from scikit-learn will learn the mode for numerical and categorical variables alike. But in practice, mode imputation is done for categorical variables only.

7. Let's fit the imputer to the train set so that it learns the most frequent values:

```
imputer.fit(X_train)
```

8. Let's inspect the most frequent values learned by the imputer:

```
imputer.statistics_
```

The most frequent values are stored in the `statistics_` attribute of the imputer, as follows:

```
array(['u', 'g', 'c', 'v'], dtype=object)
```

9. Let's replace missing values with frequent categories:

```
X_train = imputer.transform(X_train)
X_test = imputer.transform(X_test)
```

Note that `SimpleImputer()` will return a NumPy array and not a pandas dataframe.

Finally, let's impute missing values using Feature-engine. First, we need to load and separate the data into train and test sets, just like we did in *step 2* and *step 3* in this recipe.

10. Next, let's create a frequent category imputer with `FrequentCategoryImputer()` from Feature-engine, specifying the categorical variables that should have missing data removed:

```
mode_imputer = FrequentCategoryImputer(variables=['A4', 'A5', 'A6', 'A7'])
```

`FrequentCategoryImputer()` will select all categorical variables in the train set by default; that is, unless we pass a list of variables to impute.

11. Let's fit the imputation transformer to the train set so that it learns the most frequent categories:

```
mode_imputer.fit(X_train)
```

12. Let's inspect the learned frequent categories:

```
mode_imputer.imputer_dict_
```

We can see the dictionary with the most frequent values in the following output:

```
{'A4': 'u', 'A5': 'g', 'A6': 'c', 'A7': 'v'}
```

13. Finally, let's replace the missing values with frequent categories:

```
X_train = mode_imputer.transform(X_train)
X_test = mode_imputer.transform(X_test)
```

`FrequentCategoryImputer()` returns a pandas dataframe with the imputed values.

Remember that you can check that the categorical variables do not contain missing values by using `X_train[['A4', 'A5', 'A6', 'A7']].isnull().mean()`.

How it works...

In this recipe, we replaced the missing values of the categorical variables in the Credit Approval Data Set with the most frequent categories using pandas, scikit-learn, and Feature-engine. Frequent categories should be learned from the train set, so we divided the dataset into train and test sets using `train_test_split()` from scikit-learn, as described in the *Performing mean or median imputation* recipe.

To impute missing data with pandas in multiple categorical variables, in *step 4* we created a `for` loop over the categorical variables A4 to A7, and for each variable, we calculated the most frequent value using the pandas `mode()` method in the train set. Then, we used this value to replace the missing values with pandas `fillna()` in the train and test sets. Pandas `fillna()` returned a pandas Series without missing values, which we reassigned to the original variable in the dataframe.

To replace missing values using scikit-learn, we divided the data into train and test sets but only kept categorical variables. Next, we set up `SimpleImputer()` and specified `most_frequent` as the imputation method in the `strategy`. With the `fit()` method, `imputer` learned and stored frequent categories in its `statistics_` attribute. With the `transform()` method, the missing values in the train and test sets were replaced with the learned statistics, returning NumPy arrays.

Finally, to replace the missing values via Feature-engine, we set up `FrequentCategoryImputer()`, specifying the variables to impute in a list. With `fit()`, the `FrequentCategoryImputer()` learned and stored frequent categories in a dictionary in the `imputer_dict_` attribute. With the `transform()` method, missing values in the train and test sets were replaced with stored parameters, which allowed us to obtain pandas dataframes without missing data.

 Note that, unlike `SimpleImputer()` from scikit-learn, `FrequentCategoryImputer()` will only impute categorical variables and ignores numerical ones.

See also

To learn more about scikit-learn's `SimpleImputer()` go to `https://scikit-learn.org/stable/modules/generated/sklearn.impute.SimpleImputer.html#sklearn.impute.SimpleImputer`.

To learn more about Feature-engine's `FrequentCategoryImputer()`, go to `https://feature-engine.readthedocs.io/en/latest/imputers/FrequentCategoryImputer.html`.

Replacing missing values with an arbitrary number

Arbitrary number imputation consists of replacing missing values with an arbitrary value. Some commonly used values include 999, 9999, or -1 for positive distributions. This method is suitable for numerical variables. A similar method for categorical variables will be discussed in the *Capturing missing values in a bespoke category* recipe.

When replacing missing values with an arbitrary number, we need to be careful not to select a value close to the mean or the median, or any other common value of the distribution.

 Arbitrary number imputation can be used when data is not missing at random, when we are building non-linear models, and when the percentage of missing data is high. This imputation technique distorts the original variable distribution.

In this recipe, we will impute missing data by arbitrary numbers using pandas, scikit-learn, and Feature-engine.

How to do it...

Let's begin by importing the necessary tools and loading and preparing the data:

1. Import `pandas` and the required functions and classes from scikit-learn and Feature-engine:

```
import pandas as pd
from sklearn.model_selection import train_test_split
from sklearn.impute import SimpleImputer
from feature_engine.missing_data_imputers import
ArbitraryNumberImputer
```

2. Let's load the dataset:

```
data = pd.read_csv('creditApprovalUCI.csv')
```

3. Let's separate the data into train and test sets:

```
X_train, X_test, y_train, y_test = train_test_split(
    data.drop('A16', axis=1), data['A16'], test_size=0.3,
    random_state=0)
```

Normally, we select arbitrary values that are bigger than the maximum value of the distribution.

4. Let's find the maximum value of four numerical variables:

```
X_train[['A2','A3', 'A8', 'A11']].max()
```

The following is the output of the preceding code block:

```
A2      76.750
A3      26.335
A8      20.000
A11     67.000
dtype:  float64
```

5. Let's replace the missing values with 99 in the numerical variables that we specified in *step 4*:

```
for var in ['A2','A3', 'A8', 'A11']:
    X_train[var].fillna(99, inplace=True)
    X_test[var].fillna(99, inplace=True)
```

 We chose 99 as the arbitrary value because it is bigger than the maximum value of these variables.

We can check the percentage of missing values using X_train[['A2','A3', 'A8', 'A11']].isnull().mean(), which should be 0 after *step 5*.

Now, we'll impute missing values with an arbitrary number using scikit-learn instead.

6. First, let's separate the data into train and test sets while keeping only the numerical variables:

```
X_train, X_test, y_train, y_test = train_test_split(
    data[['A2', 'A3', 'A8', 'A11']], data['A16'], test_size=0.3,
    random_state=0)
```

7. Let's set up `SimpleImputer()` so that it replaces any missing values with `99`:

```
imputer = SimpleImputer(strategy='constant', fill_value=99)
```

If your dataset contains categorical variables, `SimpleImputer()` will add `99` to those variables as well if any values are missing.

8. Let's fit the imputer to the train set:

```
imputer.fit(X_train)
```

9. Let's replace the missing values with `99`:

```
X_train = imputer.transform(X_train)
X_test = imputer.transform(X_test)
```

Note that `SimpleImputer()` will return a NumPy array. Be mindful of the order of the variables if you're transforming the array back into a dataframe.

To finish, let's impute missing values using Feature-engine. First, we need to load the data and separate it into train and test sets, just like we did in *step 2* and *step 3*.

10. Next, let's create an imputation transformer with Feature-engine's `ArbitraryNumberImputer()` in order to replace any missing values with `99` and specify the variables from which missing data should be imputed:

```
imputer = ArbitraryNumberImputer(arbitrary_number=99,
                        variables=['A2','A3', 'A8', 'A11'])
```

`ArbitraryNumberImputer()` will automatically select **all** numerical variables in the train set; that is, unless we specify which variables to impute in a list.

11. Let's fit the arbitrary number imputer to the train set:

```
imputer.fit(X_train)
```

12. Finally, let's replace the missing values with `99`:

```
X_train = imputer.transform(X_train)
X_test = imputer.transform(X_test)
```

The variables specified in *step 10* should now have missing data replaced with the number `99`.

How it works...

In this recipe, we replaced missing values in numerical variables in the Credit Approval Data Set with an arbitrary number, `99`, using pandas, scikit-learn, and Feature-engine. We loaded the data and divided it into train and test sets using `train_test_split()` from scikit-learn, as described in the *Performing mean or median imputation* recipe.

To determine which arbitrary value to use, we inspected the maximum values of four numerical variables using the pandas `max()` method. Next, we chose a value, `99`, that was bigger than the maximum values of the selected variables. In *step 5*, we used a `for` loop over the numerical variables to replace any missing data with the pandas `fillna()` method while passing `99` as an argument and setting the `inplace` argument to `True` in order to replace the values in the original dataframe.

To replace missing values using scikit-learn, we called `SimpleImputer()`, set `strategy` to `constant`, and specified `99` as the arbitrary value in the `fill_value` argument. Next, we fitted the imputer to the train set with the `fit()` method and replaced missing values using the `transform()` method in the train and test sets. `SimpleImputer()` returned a NumPy array with the missing data replaced by `99`.

Finally, we replaced missing values with `ArbitraryValueImputer()` from Feature-engine, specifying a value, `99`, in the `arbitrary_number` argument. We also included the variables to impute in a list to the `variables` argument. Next, we applied the `fit()` method. `ArbitraryNumberimputer()` checked that the selected variables were numerical after applying the `fit()` method. With the `transform()` method, the missing values in the train and test sets were replaced with `99`, thus returning dataframes without missing values in selected variables.

There's more...

Scikit-learn released the `ColumnTransformer()` object, which allows us to select specific variables so that we can apply a certain imputation method. To learn how to use `ColumnTransformer()`, check out the *Assembling an imputation pipeline with scikit-learn* recipe.

See also

To learn more about Feature-engine's `ArbitraryValueImputer()`, go to `https://feature-engine.readthedocs.io/en/latest/imputers/ArbitraryValueImputer.html`.

Capturing missing values in a bespoke category

Missing data in categorical variables can be treated as a different category, so it is common to replace missing values with the **Missing** string. In this recipe, we will learn how to do so using pandas, scikit-learn, and Feature-engine.

How to do it...

To proceed with the recipe, let's import the required tools and prepare the dataset:

1. Import `pandas` and the required functions and classes from scikit-learn and Feature-engine:

```
import pandas as pd
from sklearn.model_selection import train_test_split
from sklearn.impute import SimpleImputer
from feature_engine.missing_data_imputers import
CategoricalVariableImputer
```

2. Let's load the dataset:

```
data = pd.read_csv('creditApprovalUCI.csv')
```

3. Let's separate the data into train and test sets:

```
X_train, X_test, y_train, y_test = train_test_split(
    data.drop('A16', axis=1), data['A16'], test_size=0.3,
    random_state=0)
```

4. Let's replace missing values in four categorical variables by using the `Missing` string:

```
for var in ['A4', 'A5', 'A6', 'A7']:
    X_train[var].fillna('Missing', inplace=True)
    X_test[var].fillna('Missing', inplace=True)
```

Alternatively, we can replace missing values with the `Missing` string using scikit-learn as follows.

5. First, let's separate the data into train and test sets while keeping only categorical variables:

```
X_train, X_test, y_train, y_test = train_test_split(
    data[['A4', 'A5', 'A6', 'A7']], data['A16'], test_size=0.3,
    random_state=0)
```

6. Let's set up `SimpleImputer()` so that it replaces missing data with the `Missing` string and fit it to the train set:

```
imputer = SimpleImputer(strategy='constant', fill_value='Missing')
imputer.fit(X_train)
```

`SimpleImputer()` from scikit-learn will replace missing values with `Missing` in both numerical and categorical variables. Be careful of this behavior or you will end up accidentally casting your numerical variables as **objects**.

7. Let's replace the missing values:

```
X_train = imputer.transform(X_train)
X_test = imputer.transform(X_test)
```

Remember that `SimpleImputer()` returns a NumPy array, which you can transform into a dataframe using `pd.DataFrame(X_train, columns = ['A4', 'A5', 'A6', 'A7'])`.

To finish, let's impute missing values using Feature-engine. First, we need to separate the dataset, just like we did in *step 3* of this recipe.

8. Next, let's set up the `CategoricalVariableImputer()` from Feature-engine, which replaces missing values with the `Missing` string, specifying the categorical variables to impute, and then fit the transformer to the train set:

    ```
    imputer = CategoricalVariableImputer(variables=['A4', 'A5', 'A6',
    'A7'])
    imputer.fit(X_train)
    ```

If we don't pass a list with categorical variables, `FrequentCategoryImputer()` will select **all** categorical variables in the train set.

9. Finally, let's replace the missing values:

    ```
    X_train = imputer.transform(X_train)
    X_test = imputer.transform(X_test)
    ```

Remember that you can check that missing values have been replaced with pandas' `isnull()`, followed by `sum()`.

How it works...

In this recipe, we replaced the missing values in categorical variables in the Credit Approval Data Set by using the `Missing` string using pandas, scikit-learn, and Feature-engine. First, we loaded the data and divided it into train and test sets using `train_test_split()`, as described in the *Performing mean or median imputation* recipe. To impute missing data with pandas, we used the `fillna()` method, passed the `Missing` string as an argument and set `inplace=True` to replace the values directly in the original dataframe.

To replace missing values using scikit-learn, we called `SimpleImputer()`, set `strategy` to `constant`, and added the `Missing` string to the `fill_value` argument. Next, we fitted the imputer to the train set and replaced missing values using the `transform()` method in the train and test sets, which returned NumPy arrays.

Finally, we replaced missing values with `FrequentCategoryImputer()` from Feature-engine, specifying the variables to impute in a list. With the `fit()` method, `FrequentCategoryImputer()` checked that the variables were categorical, and with `transform()` missing values were replaced with the `Missing` string in both train and test sets, thereby returning pandas dataframes.

Note that, unlike `SimpleImputer()`, `CategoricalVariableImputer()` will not impute numerical variables.

See also

To learn more about Feature-engine's `CategoricalVariableImputer()`, go to `https://feature-engine.readthedocs.io/en/latest/imputers/CategoricalVariableImputer.html`.

Replacing missing values with a value at the end of the distribution

Replacing missing values with a value at the end of the variable distribution is equivalent to replacing them with an arbitrary value, but instead of identifying the arbitrary values manually, these values are automatically selected as those at the very end of the variable distribution. The values that are used to replace missing information are estimated using the mean plus or minus three times the standard deviation if the variable is normally distributed, or the **inter-quartile range (IQR)** proximity rule otherwise. According to the IQR proximity rule, missing values will be replaced with the 75th quantile + (IQR * 1.5) at the right tail or by the 25th quantile - (IQR * 1.5) at the left tail. The IQR is given by the 75th quantile - the 25th quantile.

 Some users will also identify the minimum or maximum values of the variable and replace missing data as a factor of these values, for example, three times the maximum value.

The value that's used to replace missing information should be learned from the train set and stored to impute train, test, and future data. Feature-engine offers this functionality. In this recipe, we will implement end-of-tail imputation using pandas and Feature-engine.

 End-of-tail imputation may distort the distribution of the original variables, so it may not be suitable for linear models.

How to do it...

To complete this recipe, we need to import the necessary tools and load the data:

1. Let's import pandas, the `train_test_split` function from scikit-learn, and the `EndTailImputer` function from Feature-engine:

```
import pandas as pd
from sklearn.model_selection import train_test_split
from feature_engine.missing_data_imputers import EndTailImputer
```

2. Let's load the dataset:

```
data = pd.read_csv('creditApprovalUCI.csv')
```

The values at the end of the distribution should be calculated from the variables in the train set.

3. Let's separate the data into train and test sets:

```
X_train, X_test, y_train, y_test = train_test_split(
    data.drop('A16', axis=1), data['A16'], test_size=0.3,
    random_state=0)
```

Remember that you can check the percentage of missing values using `X_train.isnull().mean()`.

4. Let's loop over five numerical variables, calculate the IQR, determine the value of the 75th quantile plus 1.5 times the IQR, and replace the missing observations in the train and test sets with that value:

```
for var in ['A2', 'A3', 'A8', 'A11', 'A15']:

    IQR = X_train[var].quantile(0.75) - X_train[var].quantile(0.25)
    value = X_train[var].quantile(0.75) + 1.5 * IQR

    X_train[var] = X_train[var].fillna(value)
    X_test[var] = X_test[var].fillna(value)
```

If we want to use the Gaussian approximation instead of the IQR proximity rule, we can calculate the value to replace missing data using `value = X_train[var].mean() + 3*X_train[var].std()`. Some users also calculate the value as `X_train[var].max()*3`.

Note how we calculated the value to impute the missing data using the variables in the train set and then used this to impute train and test sets.

We can also place replace missing data with values at the left tail of the distribution using `value = X_train[var].quantile(0.25) - 1.5 * IQR` or `value = X_train[var].mean() - 3*X_train[var].std()`.

To finish, let's impute missing values using Feature-engine. First, we need to load and separate the data into train and test sets, just like in *step 2* and *step 3* of this recipe.

5. Next, let's set up `EndTailImputer()` so that we can estimate a value at the right tail using the IQR proximity rule and specify the variables we wish to impute:

```
imputer = EndTailImputer(distribution='skewed', tail='right',
                    variables=['A2', 'A3', 'A8', 'A11', 'A15'])
```

To use mean and standard deviation to calculate the replacement values, we need to set `distribution='gaussian'`. We can use `'left'` or `'right'` in the `tail` argument to specify the side of the distribution where we'll place the missing values.

6. Let's fit the `EndTailImputer()` to the train set so that it learns the parameters:

```
imputer.fit(X_train)
```

7. Let's inspect the learned values:

```
imputer.imputer_dict_
```

We can see a dictionary with the values in the following output:

```
{'A2': 88.18,
 'A3': 27.31,
 'A8': 11.504999999999999,
 'A11': 12.0,
 'A15': 1800.0}
```

8. Finally, let's replace the missing values:

```
X_train = imputer.transform(X_train)
X_test = imputer.transform(X_test)
```

Remember that you can corroborate that the missing values were replaced after *step 4* and *step 8* by using `X_train[['A2','A3', 'A8', 'A11', 'A15']].isnull().mean()`.

How it works...

In this recipe, we replaced the missing values in numerical variables with a value at the end of the distribution using pandas and Feature-engine. These values were calculated using the IQR proximity rule or the mean and standard deviation. First, we loaded the data and divided it into train and test sets using `train_test_split()`, as described in the *Performing mean or median imputation* recipe.

To impute missing data with pandas, we calculated the values at the end of the distributions using the IQR proximity rule or the mean and standard deviation according to the formulas we described in the introduction to this recipe. We determined the quantiles using pandas `quantile()` and the mean and standard deviation using pandas `mean()` and `std()`. Next, we used pandas' `fillna()` to replace the missing values.

We can set the `inplace` argument of `fillna()` to `True` to replace missing values in the original dataframe, or leave it as `False` to return a new Series with the imputed values.

Finally, we replaced missing values with `EndTailImputer()` from Feature-engine. We set the `distribution` to `'skewed'` to calculate the values with the IQR proximity rule and the `tail` to `'right'` to place values at the right tail. We also specified the variables to impute in a list to the `variables` argument.

If we don't specify a list of numerical variables in the argument variables, `EndTailImputer()` will select **all** numerical variables in the train set.

With the `fit()` method, `imputer` learned and stored the values in a dictionary in the `imputer_dict_` attribute. With the `transform()` method, the missing values were replaced, returning dataframes.

See also

To learn more about Feature-engine's `EndTailImputer()`, go to `https://feature-engine.readthedocs.io/en/latest/imputers/EndTailImputer.html`.

Implementing random sample imputation

Random sampling imputation consists of extracting random observations from the pool of available values in the variable. Random sampling imputation preserves the original distribution, which differs from the other imputation techniques we've discussed in this chapter and is suitable for numerical and categorical variables alike. In this recipe, we will implement random sample imputation with pandas and Feature-engine.

How to do it...

Let's begin by importing the required libraries and tools and preparing the dataset:

1. Let's import `pandas`, the `train_test_split` function from scikit-learn, and `RandomSampleImputer` from Feature-engine:

   ```
   import pandas as pd
   from sklearn.model_selection import train_test_split
   from feature_engine.missing_data_imputers import
   RandomSampleImputer
   ```

2. Let's load the dataset:

   ```
   data = pd.read_csv('creditApprovalUCI.csv')
   ```

3. The random values that will be used to replace missing data should be extracted from the train set, so let's separate the data into train and test sets:

   ```
   X_train, X_test, y_train, y_test = train_test_split(
       data.drop('A16', axis=1), data['A16'], test_size=0.3,
       random_state=0)
   ```

   First, we will run the commands line by line to understand their output. Then, we will execute them in a loop to impute several variables. In random sample imputation, we extract as many random values as there is missing data in the variable.

4. Let's calculate the number of missing values in the A2 variable:

```
number_na = X_train['A2'].isnull().sum()
```

5. If you print the number_na variable, you will obtain 11 as output, which is the number of missing values in A2. Thus, let's extract 11 values at random from A2 for the imputation:

```
random_sample_train = X_train['A2'].dropna().sample(number_na,
                                        random_state=0)
```

6. We can only use one pandas Series to replace values in another pandas Series if their indexes are identical, so let's re-index the extracted random values so that they match the index of the missing values in the original dataframe:

```
random_sample_train.index = X_train[X_train['A2'].isnull()].index
```

7. Now, let's replace the missing values in the original dataset with randomly extracted values:

```
X_train.loc[X_train['A2'].isnull(), 'A2'] = random_sample_train
```

8. Now, let's combine *step 4* to *step 7* in a loop to replace the missing data in the variables in various train and test sets:

```
for var in ['A1', 'A3', 'A4', 'A5', 'A6', 'A7', 'A8']:

    # extract a random sample
    random_sample_train = X_train[var].dropna().sample(
        X_train[var].isnull().sum(), random_state=0)

    random_sample_test = X_train[var].dropna().sample(
        X_test[var].isnull().sum(), random_state=0)

    # re-index the randomly extracted sample
    random_sample_train.index = X_train[
            X_train[var].isnull()].index
    random_sample_test.index = X_test[X_test[var].isnull()].index

    # replace the NA
    X_train.loc[X_train[var].isnull(), var] = random_sample_train
    X_test.loc[X_test[var].isnull(), var] = random_sample_test
```

Note how we always extract values from the train set, but we calculate the number of missing values and the index using the train or test sets, respectively.

To finish, let's impute missing values using Feature-engine. First, we need to separate the data into train and test, just like we did in *step 3* of this recipe.

9. Next, let's set up `RandomSamplemputer()` and fit it to the train set:

```
imputer = RandomSampleImputer()
imputer.fit(X_train)
```

`RandomSampleImputer()` will replace the values in all variables in the dataset by default.

We can specify the variables to impute by passing variable names in a list to the imputer using `imputer = RandomSampleImputer(variables = ['A2', 'A3'])`.

10. Finally, let's replace the missing values:

```
X_train = imputer.transform(X_train)
X_test = imputer.transform(X_test)
```

To obtain reproducibility between code runs, we can set the `random_state` to a number when we initialize the `RandomSampleImputer()`. It will use the `random_state` at each run of the `transform()` method.

How it works...

In this recipe, we replaced missing values in the numerical and categorical variables of the Credit Approval Data Set with values extracted at random from the same variables using pandas and Feature-engine. First, we loaded the data and divided it into train and test sets using `train_test_split()`, as described in the *Performing mean or median imputation* recipe.

To perform random sample imputation using pandas, we calculated the number of missing values in the variable using pandas `isnull()`, followed by `sum()`. Next, we used pandas `dropna()` to drop missing information from the original variable in the train set so that we extracted values from observations with data using pandas `sample()`. We extracted as many observations as there was missing data in the variable to impute. Next, we re-indexed the pandas Series with the randomly extracted values so that we could assign those to the missing observations in the original dataframe. Finally, we replaced the missing values with values extracted at random using pandas' `loc`, which takes the location of the rows with missing data and the name of the column to which the new values are to be assigned as arguments.

We also carried out random sample imputation with `RandomSampleImputer()` from Feature-engine. With the `fit()` method, the `RandomSampleImputer()` stores a copy of the train set. With `transform()`, the imputer extracts values at random from the stored dataset and replaces the missing information with them, thereby returning complete pandas dataframes.

See also

To learn more about Feature-engine's `RandomSampleImputer()`, go to `https://feature-engine.readthedocs.io/en/latest/imputers/RandomSampleImputer.html`. Pay particular attention to the different ways in which you can set the seed to ensure reproducibility.

Adding a missing value indicator variable

A missing indicator is a binary variable that specifies whether a value was missing for an observation (1) or not (0). It is common practice to replace missing observations by the mean, median, or mode while flagging those missing observations with a missing indicator, thus covering two angles: if the data was missing at random, this would be contemplated by the mean, median, or mode imputation, and if it wasn't, this would be captured by the missing indicator. In this recipe, we will learn how to add missing indicators using NumPy, scikit-learn, and Feature-engine.

Getting ready

For an example of the implementation of missing indicators, along with mean imputation, check out the *Winning the KDD Cup Orange Challenge with Ensemble Selection* article, which was the winning solution in the KDD 2009 cup: http://www.mtome.com/Publications/CiML/CiML-v3-book.pdf.

How to do it...

Let's begin by importing the required packages and preparing the data:

1. Let's import the required libraries, functions and classes:

```
import pandas as pd
import numpy as np
from sklearn.model_selection import train_test_split
from sklearn.impute import MissingIndicator
from feature_engine.missing_data_imputers import
AddNaNBinaryImputer
```

2. Let's load the dataset:

```
data = pd.read_csv('creditApprovalUCI.csv')
```

3. Let's separate the data into train and test sets:

```
X_train, X_test, y_train, y_test = train_test_split(
    data.drop('A16', axis=1), data['A16'], test_size=0.3,
    random_state=0)
```

4. Using NumPy, we'll add a missing indicator to the numerical and categorical variables in a loop:

```
for var in ['A1', 'A3', 'A4', 'A5', 'A6', 'A7', 'A8']:
    X_train[var + '_NA'] = np.where(X_train[var].isnull(), 1, 0)
    X_test[var + '_NA'] = np.where(X_test[var].isnull(), 1, 0)
```

Note how we name the new missing indicators using the original variable name, plus _NA.

5. Let's inspect the result of the preceding code block:

```
X_train.head()
```

We can see the newly added variables at the end of the dataframe:

	A1	A2	A3	A4	A5	A6	A7	A8	A9	A10	...	A13	A14	A15	A1_NA	A3_NA	A4_NA	A5_NA	A6_NA	A7_NA	A8_NA
596	a	46.08	3.000	u	g	c	v	2.375	t	t	...	g	396.0	4159	0	0	0	0	0	0	0
303	a	15.92	2.875	u	g	q	v	0.085	f	f	...	g	120.0	0	0	0	0	0	0	0	0
204	b	36.33	2.125	y	p	w	v	0.085	t	t	...	g	50.0	1187	0	0	0	0	0	0	0
351	b	22.17	0.585	y	p	ff	ff	0.000	f	f	...	g	100.0	0	0	0	0	0	0	0	0
118	b	57.83	7.040	u	g	m	v	14.000	t	t	...	g	360.0	1332	0	0	0	0	0	0	0

The mean of the new variables and the percentage of missing values in the original variables should be the same, which you can corroborate by executing `X_train['A3'].isnull().mean()`, `X_train['A3_NA'].mean()`.

Now, let's add missing indicators using Feature-engine instead. First, we need to load and divide the data, just like we did in *step 2* and *step 3* of this recipe.

6. Next, let's set up a transformer that will add binary indicators to all the variables in the dataset using `AddNaNBinaryImputer()` from Feature-engine:

```
imputer = AddNaNBinaryImputer()
```

We can specify the variables which should have missing indicators by passing the variable names in a list: `imputer = AddNaNBinaryImputer(variables = ['A2', 'A3'])`. Alternatively, the imputer will add indicators to all the variables.

7. Let's fit `AddNaNBinaryImputer()` to the train set:

```
imputer.fit(X_train)
```

8. Finally, let's add the missing indicators:

```
X_train = imputer.transform(X_train)
X_test = imputer.transform(X_test)
```

We can inspect the result using `X_train.head()`; it should be similar to the output of *step 5* in this recipe.

We can also add missing indicators using scikit-learn's `MissingIndicator()` class. To do this, we need to load and divide the dataset, just like we did in *step 2* and *step 3*.

9. Next, we'll set up a `MissingIndicator()`. Here, we will add indicators only to variables with missing data:

```
indicator = MissingIndicator(features='missing-only')
```

10. Let's fit the transformer so that it finds the variables with missing data in the train set:

```
indicator.fit(X_train)
```

Now, we can concatenate the missing indicators that were created by `MissingIndicator()` to the train set.

11. First, let's create a column name for each of the new missing indicators with a list comprehension:

```
indicator_cols = [c+'_NA' for c in
X_train.columns[indicator.features_]]
```

The `features_` attribute contains the indices of the features for which missing indicators will be added. If we pass these indices to the train set column array, we can get the variable names.

12. Next, let's concatenate the original train set with the missing indicators, which we obtain using the `transform` method:

```
X_train = pd.concat([
    X_train.reset_index(),
    pd.DataFrame(indicator.transform(X_train),
                 columns = indicator_cols)], axis=1)
```

Scikit-learn transformers return NumPy arrays, so to concatenate them into a dataframe, we must cast it as a dataframe using pandas `DataFrame()`.

The result of the preceding code block should contain the original variables, plus the indicators.

How it works...

In this recipe, we added missing value indicators to categorical and numerical variables in the Credit Approval Data Set using NumPy, scikit-learn, and Feature-engine. To add missing indicators using NumPy, we used the `where()` method, which created a new vector after scanning all the observations in a variable, assigning the value of 1 if there was a missing observation or 0 otherwise. We captured the indicators in columns with the name of the original variable, plus _NA.

To add a missing indicator with Feature-engine, we created an instance of `AddNaNBinaryImputer()` and fitted it to the train set. Then, we used the `transform()` method to add missing indicators to the train and test sets. Finally, to add missing indicators with scikit-learn, we created an instance of `MissingIndicator()` so that we only added indicators to variables with missing data. With the `fit()` method, the transformer identified variables with missing values. With `transform()`, it returned a NumPy array with binary indicators, which we captured in a dataframe and then concatenated to the original dataframe.

There's more...

We can add missing indicators using scikit-learn's `SimpleImputer()` by setting the `add_indicator` argument to `True`. For example, `imputer = SimpleImputer(strategy='mean', add_indicator=True)` will return a NumPy array with missing indicators, **plus** the missing values in the original variables were replaced by the mean after using the `fit()` and `transform()` methods.

See also

To learn more about the transformers that were discussed in this recipe, take a look at the following links:

- Scikit-learn's `MissingIndicator()`: https://scikit-learn.org/stable/modules/generated/sklearn.impute.MissingIndicator.html
- Scikit-learn's `SimpleImputer()`: https://scikit-learn.org/stable/modules/generated/sklearn.impute.SimpleImputer.html
- Feature-engine's `AddNaNBinaryImputer()`: https://feature-engine.readthedocs.io/en/latest/imputers/AddNaNBinaryImputer.html

Performing multivariate imputation by chained equations

Multivariate imputation methods, as opposed to univariate imputation, use the entire set of variables to estimate the missing values. In other words, the missing values of a variable are modeled based on the other variables in the dataset. **Multivariate imputation by chained equations** (**MICE**) is a multiple imputation technique that models each variable with missing values as a function of the remaining variables and uses that estimate for imputation. MICE has the following basic steps:

1. A simple univariate imputation is performed for every variable with missing data, for example, median imputation.
2. One specific variable is selected, say, var_1, and the missing values are set back to missing.
3. A model that's used to predict var_1 is built based on the remaining variables in the dataset.
4. The missing values of var_1 are replaced with the new estimates.
5. Repeat *step 2* to *step 4* for each of the remaining variables.

Once all the variables have been modeled based on the rest, a cycle of imputation is concluded. *Step 2* to *step 4* are performed multiple times, typically 10 times, and the imputation values after each round are retained. The idea is that, by the end of the cycles, the distribution of the imputation parameters should have converged.

Each variable with missing data can be modeled based on the remaining variable by using multiple approaches, for example, linear regression, Bayes, decision trees, k-nearest neighbors, and random forests.

In this recipe, we will implement MICE using scikit-learn.

Getting ready

To learn more about MICE, take a look at the following links:

- *A multivariate technique for multiplying imputing missing values using a sequence of regression models*: http://citeseerx.ist.psu.edu/viewdoc/download?doi=10.1.1.405.4540rep=rep1type=pdf

- *Multiple Imputation by Chained Equations: What is it and how does it work?*: `https://www.ncbi.nlm.nih.gov/pmc/articles/PMC3074241/`

- *Scikit-learn*: `https://scikit-learn.org/stable/modules/impute.html`

In this recipe, we will perform MICE imputation using `IterativeImputer()` from scikit-learn: `https://scikit-learn.org/stable/modules/generated/sklearn.impute.IterativeImputer.html#sklearn.impute.IterativeImputer`.

To follow along with this recipe, prepare the Credit Approval Data Set, as specified in the *Technical requirements* section of this chapter.

 For this recipe, make sure you are using scikit-learn version 0.21.2 or above.

How to do it...

To complete this recipe, let's import the required libraries and load the data:

1. Let's import the required Python libraries and classes:

```
import pandas as pd
from sklearn.model_selection import train_test_split
from sklearn.linear_model import BayesianRidge
from sklearn.experimental import enable_iterative_imputer
from sklearn.impute import IterativeImputer
```

2. Let's load the dataset with some numerical variables:

```
variables = ['A2','A3','A8', 'A11', 'A14', 'A15', 'A16']
data = pd.read_csv('creditApprovalUCI.csv', usecols=variables)
```

The models that will be used to estimate missing values should be built on the train data and used to impute values in the train, test, and future data:

3. Let's divide the data into train and test sets:

```
X_train, X_test, y_train, y_test = train_test_split(
    data.drop('A16', axis=1),data['A16' ], test_size=0.3,
    random_state=0)
```

4. Let's create a MICE `imputer` using Bayes regression as an `estimator`, specifying the number of iteration cycles and setting `random_state` for reproducibility:

```
imputer = IterativeImputer(estimator = BayesianRidge(),
max_iter=10, random_state=0)
```

`IterativeImputer()` contains other useful arguments. For example, we can specify the first imputation strategy using the `initial_strategy` parameter and specify how we want to cycle over the variables either randomly, or from the one with the fewest missing values to the one with the most.

5. Let's fit `IterativeImputer()` to the train set so that it trains the estimators to predict the missing values in each variable:

```
imputer.fit(X_train)
```

6. Finally, let's fill in missing values in both train and test set:

```
X_train = imputer.transform(X_train)
X_test = imputer.transform(X_test)
```

Remember that scikit-learn returns NumPy arrays and not dataframes.

How it works...

In this recipe, we performed MICE using `IterativeImputer()` from scikit-learn. First, we loaded data using pandas `read_csv()` and separated it into train and test sets using scikit-learn's `train_test_split()`. Next, we created a multivariate imputation object using the `IterativeImputer()` from scikit-learn. We specified that we wanted to estimate missing values using Bayes regression and that we wanted to carry out 10 rounds of imputation over the entire dataset. We fitted `IterativeImputer()` to the train set so that each variable was modeled based on the remaining variables in the dataset. Next, we transformed the train and test sets with the `transform()` method in order to replace missing data with their estimates.

There's more...

Using `IterativeImputer()` from scikit-learn, we can model variables using multiple algorithms, such as Bayes, k-nearest neighbors, decision trees, and random forests. Perform the following steps to do so:

1. Import the required Python libraries and classes:

```
import pandas as pd
import matplotlib.pyplot as plt
from sklearn.model_selection import train_test_split
from sklearn.linear_model import BayesianRidge
from sklearn.tree import DecisionTreeRegressor
from sklearn.ensemble import ExtraTreesRegressor
from sklearn.neighbors import KNeighborsRegressor
```

2. Load the data and separate it into train and test sets:

```
variables = ['A2','A3','A8', 'A11', 'A14', 'A15', 'A16']
data = pd.read_csv('creditApprovalUCI.csv', usecols=variables)

X_train, X_test, y_train, y_test = train_test_split(
    data.drop('A16', axis=1), data['A16'], test_size=0.3,
        random_state=0)
```

3. Build MICE imputers using different modeling strategies:

```
imputer_bayes = IterativeImputer(
    estimator=BayesianRidge(),
    max_iter=10,
    random_state=0)

imputer_knn = IterativeImputer(
    estimator=KNeighborsRegressor(n_neighbors=5),
    max_iter=10,
    random_state=0)

imputer_nonLin = IterativeImputer(
    estimator=DecisionTreeRegressor(
        max_features='sqrt', random_state=0),
    max_iter=10,
    random_state=0)

imputer_missForest = IterativeImputer(
    estimator=ExtraTreesRegressor(
        n_estimators=10, random_state=0),
```

```
                    max_iter=10,
                    random_state=0)
```

Note how, in the preceding code block, we create four different MICE `imputers`, each with a different machine learning algorithm which will be used to model every variable based on the remaining variables in the dataset.

4. Fit the MICE imputers to the train set:

```
imputer_bayes.fit(X_train)
imputer_knn.fit(X_train)
imputer_nonLin.fit(X_train)
imputer_missForest.fit(X_train)
```

5. Impute missing values in the train set:

```
X_train_bayes = imputer_bayes.transform(X_train)
X_train_knn = imputer_knn.transform(X_train)
X_train_nonLin = imputer_nonLin.transform(X_train)
X_train_missForest = imputer_missForest.transform(X_train)
```

Remember that scikit-learn transformers return NumPy arrays.

6. Convert the NumPy arrays into dataframes:

```
predictors = [var for var in variables if var !='A16']
X_train_bayes = pd.DataFrame(X_train_bayes, columns = predictors)
X_train_knn = pd.DataFrame(X_train_knn, columns = predictors)
X_train_nonLin = pd.DataFrame(X_train_nonLin, columns = predictors)
X_train_missForest = pd.DataFrame(X_train_missForest, columns =
predictors)
```

7. Plot and compare the results:

```
fig = plt.figure()
ax = fig.add_subplot(111)

X_train['A3'].plot(kind='kde', ax=ax, color='blue')
X_train_bayes['A3'].plot(kind='kde', ax=ax, color='green')
X_train_knn['A3'].plot(kind='kde', ax=ax, color='red')
X_train_nonLin['A3'].plot(kind='kde', ax=ax, color='black')
X_train_missForest['A3'].plot(kind='kde', ax=ax, color='orange')

# add legends
lines, labels = ax.get_legend_handles_labels()
```

```
labels = ['A3 original', 'A3 bayes', 'A3 knn', 'A3 Trees', 'A3
missForest']
ax.legend(lines, labels, loc='best')
plt.show()
```

The output of the preceding code is as follows:

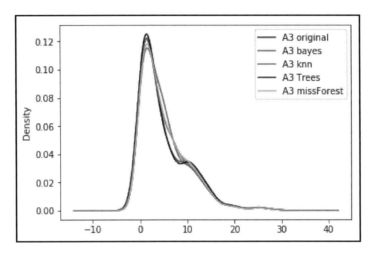

In the preceding plot, we can see that the different algorithms return slightly different distributions of the original variable.

Assembling an imputation pipeline with scikit-learn

Datasets often contain a mix of numerical and categorical variables. In addition, some variables may contain a few missing data points, while others will contain quite a big proportion. The mechanisms by which data is missing may also vary among variables. Thus, we may wish to perform different imputation procedures for different variables. In this recipe, we will learn how to perform different imputation procedures for different feature subsets using scikit-learn.

How to do it...

To proceed with the recipe, let's import the required libraries and classes and prepare the dataset:

1. Let's import pandas and the required classes from scikit-learn:

```
import pandas as pd
from sklearn.compose import ColumnTransformer
from sklearn.pipeline import Pipeline
from sklearn.impute import SimpleImputer
from sklearn.model_selection import train_test_split
```

2. Let's load the dataset:

```
data = pd.read_csv('creditApprovalUCI.csv')
```

3. Let's divide the data into train and test sets:

```
X_train, X_test, y_train, y_test = train_test_split(
    data.drop('A16', axis=1), data['A16'], test_size=0.3,
        random_state=0)
```

4. Let's group a subset of columns to which we want to apply different imputation techniques in lists:

```
features_num_arbitrary = ['A3', 'A8']
features_num_median = ['A2', 'A14']
features_cat_frequent = ['A4', 'A5', 'A6', 'A7']
features_cat_missing = ['A1', 'A9', 'A10']
```

5. Let's create different imputation transformers using `SimpleImputer()` within the `scikit-learn` pipeline:

```
imputer_num_arbitrary = Pipeline(steps=[
    ('imputer', SimpleImputer(strategy='constant', fill_value=99)),
])
imputer_num_median = Pipeline(steps=[
    ('imputer', SimpleImputer(strategy='median')),
])
imputer_cat_frequent = Pipeline(steps=[
    ('imputer', SimpleImputer(strategy='most_frequent')),
])
imputer_cat_missing = Pipeline(steps=[
    ('imputer', SimpleImputer(strategy='constant',
fill_value='Missing')),
])
```

We have covered all these imputation strategies in dedicated recipes throughout this chapter.

6. Now, let's assemble the pipelines with the imputers within `ColumnTransformer()` and assign them to the different feature subsets we created in *step 4*:

```
preprocessor = ColumnTransformer(transformers=[
    ('imp_num_arbitrary', imputer_num_arbitrary,
                        features_num_arbitrary),
    ('imp_num_median', imputer_num_median, features_num_median),
    ('imp_cat_frequent', imputer_cat_frequent,
features_cat_frequent),
    ('imp_cat_missing', imputer_cat_missing, features_cat_missing),
    ], remainder='passthrough')
```

7. Next, we need to fit the preprocessor to the train set so that the imputation parameters are learned:

```
preprocessor.fit(X_train)
```

8. Finally, let's replace the missing values in the train and test sets:

```
X_train = preprocessor.transform(X_train)
X_test = preprocessor.transform(X_test)
```

Remember that scikit-learn transformers return NumPy arrays. The beauty of this procedure is that we can save the preprocessor in one object to perpetuate all the parameters that are learned by the different transformers.

How it works...

In this recipe, we carried out different imputation techniques over different variable groups using scikit-learn's `SimpleImputer()` and `ColumnTransformer()`.

After loading and dividing the dataset, we created four lists of features. The first list contained numerical variables to impute with an arbitrary value. The second list contained numerical variables to impute by the median. The third list contained categorical variables to impute by a frequent category. Finally, the fourth list contained categorical variables to impute with the `Missing` string.

Next, we created multiple imputation objects using `SimpleImputer()` in a scikit-learn pipeline. To assemble each `Pipeline()`, we gave each step a name with a string. In our example, we used `imputer`. Next to this, we created the imputation object with `SimpleImputer()`, varying the strategy for the different imputation techniques.

Next, we arranged pipelines with different imputation strategies within `ColumnTransformer()`. To set up `ColumnTransformer()`, we gave each step a name with a string. Then, we added one of the created pipelines and the list with the features which should be imputed with said pipeline.

Next, we fitted `ColumnTransformer()` to the train set, where the imputers learned the values to be used to replace missing data from the train set. Finally, we imputed the missing values in the train and test sets, using the `transform()` method of `ColumnTransformer()` to obtain complete NumPy arrays.

See also

To learn more about scikit-learn transformers and how to use them, take a look at the following links:

- `SimpleImputer()`: https://scikit-learn.org/stable/modules/generated/sklearn.impute.SimpleImputer.html#sklearn.impute.SimpleImputer
- `ColumnTransformer()`: https://scikit-learn.org/stable/modules/generated/sklearn.compose.ColumnTransformer.html
- Stack Overflow: https://stackoverflow.com/questions/54160370/how-to-use-sklearn-column-transformer

Assembling an imputation pipeline with Feature-engine

Feature-engine is an open source Python library that allows us to easily implement different imputation techniques for different feature subsets. Often, our datasets contain a mix of numerical and categorical variables, with few or many missing values. Therefore, we normally perform different imputation techniques on different variables, depending on the nature of the variable and the machine learning algorithm we want to build. With Feature-engine, we can assemble multiple imputation techniques in a single step, and in this recipe, we will learn how to do this.

How to do it...

Let's begin by importing the necessary Python libraries and preparing the data:

1. Let's import pandas and the required function and class from scikit-learn, and the missing data imputation module from Feature-engine:

```
import pandas as pd
from sklearn.model_selection import train_test_split
from sklearn.pipeline import Pipeline
import feature_engine.missing_data_imputers as mdi
```

2. Let's load the dataset:

```
data = pd.read_csv('creditApprovalUCI.csv')
```

3. Let's divide the data into train and test sets:

```
X_train, X_test, y_train, y_test = train_test_split(
    data.drop('A16', axis=1), data['A16'], test_size=0.3,
        random_state=0)
```

4. Let's create lists with the names of the variables that we want to apply specific imputation techniques to:

```
features_num_arbitrary = ['A3', 'A8']
features_num_median = ['A2', 'A14']
features_cat_frequent = ['A4', 'A5', 'A6', 'A7']
features_cat_missing = ['A1', 'A9', 'A10']
```

5. Let's assemble an arbitrary value imputer, a median imputer, a frequent category imputer, and an imputer to replace any missing values with the `Missing` string within a scikit-learn pipeline:

```
pipe = Pipeline(steps=[
    ('imp_num_arbitrary', mdi.ArbitraryNumberImputer(
        variables = features_num_arbitrary)),
    ('imp_num_median', mdi.MeanMedianImputer(
        imputation_method = 'median',
variables=features_num_median)),
    ('imp_cat_frequent', mdi.FrequentCategoryImputer(
        variables = features_cat_frequent)),
    ('imp_cat_missing', mdi.CategoricalVariableImputer(
        variables=features_cat_missing))
    ])
```

Note how we pass the feature lists we created in *step 4* to the imputers.

6. Let's fit the pipeline to the train set so that each imputer learns and stores the imputation parameters:

```
pipe.fit(X_train)
```

7. Finally, let's replace missing values in the train and test sets:

```
X_train = pipe.transform(X_train)
X_test = pipe.transform(X_test)
```

We can store the pipeline after fitting it as an object to perpetuate the use of the learned parameters.

How it works...

In this recipe, we performed different imputation techniques on different variable groups from the Credit Approval Data Set by utilizing Feature-engine within a single scikit-learn pipeline.

After loading and dividing the dataset, we created four lists of features. The first list contained numerical variables to impute with an arbitrary value. The second list contained numerical variables to impute by the median. The third list contained categorical variables to impute with a frequent category. Finally, the fourth list contained categorical variables to impute with the `Missing` string.

Next, we assembled the different Feature-engine imputers within a single scikit-learn pipeline. With `ArbitraryNumberImputer()`, we imputed missing values with the number 999; with `MeanMedianImputer()`, we performed median imputation; with `FrequentCategoryImputer()`, we replaced the missing values with the mode; and with `CategoricalVariableImputer()`, we replaced the missing values with the `Missing` string. We specified a list of features to impute within each imputer.

When assembling a scikit-learn pipeline, we gave each step a name using a string, and next to it we set up each of the Feature-engine imputers, specifying the feature subset **within** each imputer.

With the `fit()` method, the imputers learned and stored parameters and with `transform()` the missing values were replaced, returning complete pandas dataframes.

We can store the scikit-learn pipeline with Feature-engine's transformers as one object in order to perpetuate the learned parameters.

See also

To learn more about Feature-engine, take a look at the following links:

- Feature-engine: www.trainindata.com/feature-engine
- Docs: https://feature-engine.readthedocs.io/en/latest/
- GitHub repository: https://github.com/solegalli/feature_engine/

Encoding Categorical Variables 3

Categorical variables are those values which are selected from a group of categories or labels. For example, the variable **Gender** with the values of **male** or **female** is categorical, and so is the variable **marital status** with the values of **never married**, **married**, **divorced**, or **widowed**. In some categorical variables, the labels have an intrinsic order, for example, in the variable **Student's grade**, the values of **A**, **B**, **C**, or **Fail** are ordered, **A** being the highest grade and **Fail** the lowest. These are called ordinal categorical variables. Variables in which the categories do not have an intrinsic order are called nominal categorical variables, such as the variable **City**, with the values of **London**, **Manchester**, **Bristol**, and so on.

The values of categorical variables are often encoded as strings. Scikit-learn, the open source Python library for machine learning, does not support strings as values, therefore, we need to transform those strings into numbers. The act of replacing strings with numbers is called **categorical encoding**. In this chapter, we will discuss multiple categorical encoding techniques.

This chapter will cover the following recipes:

- Creating binary variables through one-hot encoding
- Performing one-hot encoding of frequent categories
- Replacing categories with ordinal numbers
- Replacing categories with counts or frequency of observations
- Encoding with integers in an ordered manner
- Encoding with the mean of the target
- Encoding with the Weight of Evidence
- Grouping rare or infrequent categories
- Performing binary encoding
- Performing feature hashing

Technical requirements

In this chapter, we will use the following Python libraries: pandas, NumPy, Matplotlib, and scikit-learn. I recommend installing the free Anaconda Python distribution, which contains all of these packages.

 For details on how to install the Anaconda Python distribution, visit the *Technical requirements* section in `Chapter 1`, *Foreseeing Variable Problems in Building ML Models*.

We will also use the open source Python library's `feature-engine` and category encoders, which can be installed using `pip`:

```
pip install feature-engine
pip install category_encoders
```

To learn more about Feature-engine, visit the following sites:

- Home page: `https://www.trainindata.com/feature-engine`
- GitHub: `https://github.com/solegalli/feature_engine/`
- Documentation: `https://feature-engine.readthedocs.io`

To learn more about category encoders, visit the following:

- Documentation: `https://contrib.scikit-learn.org/categorical-encoding/`

 To run the recipes successfully, check that you have the same or higher versions of the Python libraries indicated in the `requirement.txt` file in the accompanying GitHub repository at `https://github.com/PacktPublishing/Python-Feature-Engineering-Cookbook`.

We will use the Credit Approval Dataset available in the UCI Machine Learning Repository, available at `https://archive.ics.uci.edu/ml/datasets/credit+approval`.

 Dua, D. and Graff, C. (2019). UCI Machine Learning Repository [`http://archive.ics.uci.edu/ml`]. `Irvine, CA: University of California, School of Information and Computer Science.`

To prepare the dataset, follow these steps:

1. Visit `http://archive.ics.uci.edu/ml/machine-learning-databases/credit-screening/`.

2. Click on `crx.data` to download the data:

3. Save `crx.data` to the folder from which you will run the following commands.

    After downloading the data, open up a Jupyter Notebook or a Python IDE and run the following commands.

4. Import the required libraries:

```
import random
import pandas as pd
import numpy as np
```

5. Load the data:

```
data = pd.read_csv('crx.data', header=None)
```

6. Create a list with the variable names:

```
varnames = ['A'+str(s) for s in range(1,17)]
```

7. Add the variable names to the dataframe:

```
data.columns = varnames
```

8. Replace the question marks in the dataset with NumPy NaN values:

```
data = data.replace('?', np.nan)
```

9. Re-cast numerical variables to `float` types:

```
data['A2'] = data['A2'].astype('float')
data['A14'] = data['A14'].astype('float')
```

10. Re-code the target variable as binary:

```
data['A16'] = data['A16'].map({'+':1, '-':0})
```

11. Make lists with categorical and numerical variables:

```
cat_cols = [c for c in data.columns if data[c].dtypes=='O']
num_cols = [c for c in data.columns if data[c].dtypes!='O']
```

12. Fill in the missing data:

```
data[num_cols] = data[num_cols].fillna(0)
data[cat_cols] = data[cat_cols].fillna('Missing')
```

13. Save the prepared data:

```
data.to_csv('creditApprovalUCI.csv', index=False)
```

You can find a Jupyter Notebook with these commands in the accompanying GitHub repository at https://github.com/PacktPublishing/Python-Feature-Engineering-Cookbook.

Creating binary variables through one-hot encoding

In one-hot encoding, we represent a categorical variable as a group of binary variables, where each binary variable represents one category. The binary variable indicates whether the category is present in an observation (1) or not (0). The following table shows the one-hot encoded representation of the **Gender** variable with the categories of **Male** and **Female**:

Gender	Female	Male
Female	1	0
Male	0	1
Male	0	1
Female	1	0
Female	1	0

As shown in the table, from the **Gender** variable, we can derive the binary variable of **Female**, which shows the value of **1** for females, or the binary variable of **Male**, which takes the value of **1** for the males in the dataset.

For the categorical variable of **Color** with the values of **red**, **blue**, and **green**, we can create three variables called red, blue, and green. These variables will take the value of **1** if the observation is red, blue, or green, respectively, or 0 otherwise.

A categorical variable with k unique categories can be encoded in k-1 binary variables. For **Gender**, k is 2 as it contains two labels (male and female), therefore, we need to create only one binary variable ($k - 1 = 1$) to capture all of the information. For the color variable, which has three categories ($k=3$; red, blue, and green), we need to create two ($k - 1 = 2$) binary variables to capture all the information, so that the following occurs:

- If the observation is red, it will be captured by the variable **red** (red = 1, blue = 0).
- If the observation is blue, it will be captured by the variable **blue** (red = 0, blue = 1).
- If the observation is green, it will be captured by the combination of **red** and **blue** (red = 0, blue = 0).

There are a few occasions in which we may prefer to encode the categorical variables with k binary variables:

- When training decision trees, as they do not evaluate the entire feature space at the same time
- When selecting features recursively
- When determining the importance of each category within a variable

In this recipe, we will learn how to perform one-hot encoding using pandas, scikit-learn, and Feature-engine.

Getting ready

To run the recipe in our example dataset, download and prepare the dataset as indicated in the *Technical requirements* section. Alternatively, you can try the recipe on any dataset you like. Make sure that you have **already imputed missing data** with any of the recipes from `Chapter 2`, *Imputing Missing Data*.

The parameters to use in the categorical encoding should be learned from the train set and then used to encode the test set. Therefore, in all our recipes, we will first divide the dataset into train and test sets.

How to do it...

Let's first make the necessary imports and get the data ready:

1. Import pandas and the required function and class from scikit-learn:

```
import pandas as pd
from sklearn.model_selection import train_test_split
from sklearn.preprocessing import OneHotEncoder
```

2. Let's load the Credit Approval dataset:

```
data = pd.read_csv('creditApprovalUCI.csv')
```

3. Let's separate the data into train and test sets:

```
X_train, X_test, y_train, y_test = train_test_split(
    data.drop(labels=['A16'], axis=1), data['A16'], test_size=0.3,
        random_state=0)
```

4. Let's inspect the unique categories of the A4 variable:

```
X_train['A4'].unique()
```

We see the unique values of A4 in the output of the preceding step:

```
array(['u', 'y', 'Missing', 'l'], dtype=object)
```

5. Let's encode A4 into *k-1* binary variables using pandas and then inspect the first five rows of the resulting dataframe:

```
tmp = pd.get_dummies(X_train['A4'], drop_first=True)
tmp.head()
```

The pandas' get_dummies() function ignores missing data, unless we specifically indicate otherwise, in which case it will return missing data as an additional category: tmp = pd.get_dummies(X_train['A4'], drop_first=True, **dummy_na=True**). To encode the variable into *k* binaries, use instead drop_first=**False**.

We can see the output of *step 5*, where each label is now a binary variable:

```
      l   u   y
596   0   1   0
303   0   1   0
204   0   0   1
351   0   0   1
118   0   1   0
```

6. To encode all categorical variables at the same time, let's first make a list with their names:

```
vars_categorical = ['A1', 'A4', 'A5', 'A6', 'A7', 'A9', 'A10',
'A12', 'A13']
```

7. Now, let's encode all of the categorical variables into *k-1* binaries each, capturing the result in a new dataframe:

```
X_train_enc = pd.get_dummies(X_train[vars_categorical],
drop_first=True)
X_test_enc = pd.get_dummies(X_test[vars_categorical],
drop_first=True)
```

8. Let's inspect the first five rows of the binary variables created from the train set:

```
X_train_enc.head()
```

The pandas' `get_dummies()` function captures the variable name, say, A1, and places an underscore followed by the category name to identify the resulting binary variables.

We can see the binary variables in the output of the preceding code block:

	A1_a	A1_b	A4_l	A4_u	A4_y	A5_g	A5_gg	A5_p	A6_aa	A6_c
...	A7_j	\								
596	1	0	0	1	0	1	0	0	0	1
...	0									
303	1	0	0	1	0	1	0	0	0	0
...	0									
204	0	1	0	0	1	0	0	1	0	0
...	0									
351	0	1	0	0	1	0	0	1	0	0
...	0									
118	0	1	0	1	0	1	0	0	0	0
...	0									

```
   A7_n  A7_o  A7_v  A7_z  A9_t  A10_t  A12_t  A13_p  A13_s
```

596	0	0	1	0	1	1	1	0	0
303	0	0	1	0	0	0	0	0	0
204	0	0	1	0	1	1	0	0	0
351	0	0	0	0	0	0	0	0	0
118	0	0	1	0	1	1	1	0	0

The pandas' `get_dummies()` function will create one binary variable per found category. Hence, if there are more categories in the train set than in the test set, `get_dummies()` will return more columns in the transformed train set than in the transformed test set.

Now, let's do one-hot encoding using scikit-learn.

9. Let's create a `OneHotEncoder` transformer that encodes into *k-1* binary variables and returns a NumPy array:

```
encoder = OneHotEncoder(categories='auto', drop='first',
    sparse=False)
```

10. Let's fit the encoder to a slice of the train set with the categorical variables so it identifies the categories to encode:

```
encoder.fit(X_train[vars_categorical])
```

Scikit-learn's `OneHotEncoder()` function will only encode the categories learned from the train set. If there are new categories in the test set, we can instruct the encoder to ignore them or to return an error with the `handle_unknown='ignore'` argument or the `handle_unknown='error'` argument, respectively.

11. Now, let's create the NumPy arrays with the binary variables for train and test sets:

```
X_train_enc = encoder.transform(X_train[vars_categorical])
X_test_enc = encoder.transform(X_test[vars_categorical])
```

Unfortunately, the feature names are not preserved in the NumPy array, therefore, identifying which feature was derived from which variable is not straightforward.

How it works...

In this recipe, we performed a one-hot encoding of categorical variables using pandas and scikit-learn.

We loaded the dataset and separated it into train and test sets using scikit-learn's `train_test_split()` function. Next, we used pandas' `get_dummies()` function on the `A4` variable, setting `drop_first=True` to drop the first binary variable and hence obtain *k-1* binary variables. Next, we used `get_dummies()` on all of the categorical variables of the dataset, which returned a dataframe with binary variables representing the categories of the different features.

> One-hot encoding expands the feature space. We created, from 9 original categorical variables, 36 binary ones.

Finally, we performed one-hot encoding using `OneHotEncoder()` from scikit-learn, setting the `categories='auto'` argument so that the transformer learns the categories to encode from the train set; `drop='first'` so that the transformer drops the first binary variable, returning *k-1* binary features per categorical variable; and `sparse=False` so that the transformer returns a NumPy array (the default is to return a sparse matrix). With the `fit()` method, `OneHotEncoder()` learned the categories to encode from the train set and with the `transform()` method, it returned the binary variables in a NumPy array.

The beauty of pandas' `get_dummies()` function is that it returns feature names that clearly indicate which variable and which category each feature represents. On the downside, `get_dummies()` does not persist the information learned from the train set to the test set. Contrarily, scikit-learn's `OneHotEncoder()` function can persist the information from the train set, but it returns a NumPy array, where the information about the meaning of the features is lost.

> Scikit-learn's `OneHotEncoder()` function will create binary indicators from all variables in the dataset, so be mindful not to pass numerical variables when fitting or transforming your datasets.

There's more...

We can also implement one-hot encoding with Feature-engine. Feature-engine has multiple advantages: first, it allows us to select the variables to encode directly in the transformer. Second, it returns a pandas dataframe with clear variable names, and third, it preserves the information learned from the train set, therefore returning the same number of columns in both train and test sets. With that, Feature-engine overcomes the limitations of pandas' `get_dummies()` method and scikit-learn's `OneHotEncoder()` class.

To perform one-hot encoding with Feature-engine, we import pandas, then load and divide the data into train and test as we did in *step 1* to *step 3* of the main recipe. Next, follow these steps:

1. Let's import `OneHotCategoricalEncoder()` from Feature-engine:

```
from feature_engine.categorical_encoders import
OneHotCategoricalEncoder
```

2. Next, let's set up the encoder to return *k-1* binary variables:

```
ohe_enc = OneHotCategoricalEncoder(top_categories=None,
        drop_last=True)
```

With `top_categories=None`, we indicate that we want to encode **all** of the categories present in the categorical variables.

Feature-engine detects the categorical variables automatically. To encode only a subset of the categorical variables, we can pass the variable names in a list: `ohe_enc = OneHotCategoricalEncoder(variables=['A1', 'A4'])`.

3. Let's fit the encoder to the train set so that it learns the categories and variables to encode:

```
ohe_enc.fit(X_train)
```

4. Let's encode the categorical variables in train and test sets, and display the first five rows of the encoded train set:

```
X_train_enc = ohe_enc.transform(X_train)
X_test_enc = ohe_enc.transform(X_test)
X_train.head()
```

Feature-engine's `OneHotCategoricalEncoder()` returns the binary variables and removes the original categorical variable from the dataset.

We can inspect the result of the preceding code block in the following screenshot:

	A2	A3	A8	A11	A14	A15	A1_a	A1_b	A4_u	A4_y	...	A7_z	A7_bb	A7_j	A7_Missing	A7_n	A9_t	A10_t	A12_t	A13_g	A13_s
596	46.08	3.000	2.375	8	396.0	4159	1	0	1	0	...	0	0	0	0	0	1	1	1	1	0
303	15.92	2.875	0.085	0	120.0	0	1	0	1	0	...	0	0	0	0	0	0	0	0	1	0
204	36.33	2.125	0.085	1	50.0	1187	0	1	0	1	...	0	0	0	0	0	1	1	0	1	0
351	22.17	0.585	0.000	0	100.0	0	0	1	0	1	...	0	0	0	0	0	0	0	0	1	0
118	57.83	7.040	14.000	6	360.0	1332	0	1	1	0	...	0	0	0	0	0	1	1	1	1	0

Note how the categorical variable **A4** was replaced by **A4_u**, **A4_y**, and so on.

See also

To learn more about the classes and transformers discussed in this recipe, follow these links:

- pandas `get_dummies()`: `https://pandas.pydata.org/pandas-docs/stable/reference/api/pandas.get_dummies.html`
- Scikit-learn's `OneHotEncoder()`: `https://scikit-learn.org/stable/modules/generated/sklearn.preprocessing.OneHotEncoder.html`
- Feature-Engine's `OneHotCategoricalEncoder()`: `https://feature-engine.readthedocs.io/en/latest/encoders/OneHotCategoricalEncoder.html`

See also `OneHotEncoder` from the Category Encoders package: `https://contrib.scikit-learn.org/categorical-encoding/onehot.html`.

Performing one-hot encoding of frequent categories

One-hot encoding represents each category of a categorical variable with a binary variable. Hence, one-hot encoding of highly cardinal variables or datasets with multiple categorical features can expand the feature space dramatically. To reduce the number of binary variables, we can perform one-hot encoding **of the most frequent categories** only. One-hot encoding of top categories is equivalent to treating the remaining, less frequent categories as a single, unique category, which we will discuss in the *Grouping rare or infrequent categories* recipe toward the end of this chapter.

 For more details on variable cardinality and frequency, visit the *Determining cardinality in categorical variables* recipe and the *Pinpointing rare categories in categorical variables* recipe in `Chapter 1`, *Foreseeing Variable Problems in Building ML Models*.

In this recipe, we will learn how to implement one-hot encoding of the most popular categories using pandas and Feature-engine.

Getting ready

In the winning solution of the KDD 2009 cup, `http://www.mtome.com/Publications/CiML/CiML-v3-book.pdf`, the authors limit one-hot encoding to the 10 most frequent categories of each variable. Check the *Winning the KDD Cup Orange Challenge with Ensemble Selection* article for more details. The number of top categories to encode is arbitrarily set by the user. In this recipe, we will encode the **five** most frequent categories.

How to do it...

Let's first import the necessary Python libraries and get the dataset ready:

1. Import the required Python libraries, functions, and classes:

```
import pandas as pd
import numpy as np
from sklearn.model_selection import train_test_split
from feature_engine.categorical_encoders import
OneHotCategoricalEncoder
```

2. Let's load the dataset and divide into train and test sets:

```
data = pd.read_csv('creditApprovalUCI.csv')

X_train, X_test, y_train, y_test = train_test_split(
    data.drop(labels=['A16'], axis=1), # predictors
    data['A16'], # target
    test_size=0.3, # percentage of observations in test set
    random_state=0) # seed to ensure reproducibility
```

The most frequent categories need to be determined in the train set. As with any machine learning algorithm, this is to avoid overfitting and information leakage.

3. Let's inspect the unique categories of the A6 variable:

```
X_train['A6'].unique()
```

The unique values of A6 are displayed in the following output:

```
array(['c', 'q', 'w', 'ff', 'm', 'i', 'e', 'cc', 'x', 'd', 'k',
'j', 'Missing, 'aa', 'r'], dtype=object)
```

4. Let's count the number of observations per category of A6, sort them in decreasing order, and then display the five most frequent categories:

```
X_train['A6'].value_counts().sort_values(ascending=False).head(5)
```

We can see the five most frequent categories and the number of observations per category in the output of *step 4*:

```
c       93
q       56
w       48
i       41
ff      38
```

5. Now, let's capture the most frequent categories of A6 in a list using the code in *step 4* inside a list comprehension:

```
top_5 = [cat for cat in X_train['A6'].value_counts().sort_values(
    ascending=False).head(5).index]
```

6. Now, let's add a binary variable per top category in the train and test sets:

```
for category in top_5:
    X_train['A6' + '_' + category] = np.where(X_train['A6'] ==
category, 1, 0)
    X_test['A6' + '_' + category] = np.where(X_test['A6'] ==
category, 1, 0)
```

7. Let's output the top 10 rows of the original and encoded variable, A6, in the train set:

```
print(X_train[['A6'] + ['A6'+'_'+c for c in top_5]].head(10))
```

We can see, in the output of *step 7*, the original A6 variable, followed by the new binary variables and some of their values:

	A6	A6_c	A6_q	A6_w	A6_i	A6_ff
596	c	1	0	0	0	0
303	q	0	1	0	0	0
204	w	0	0	1	0	0
351	ff	0	0	0	0	1
118	m	0	0	0	0	0
247	q	0	1	0	0	0
652	i	0	0	0	1	0
513	e	0	0	0	0	0
230	cc	0	0	0	0	0
250	e	0	0	0	0	0

We can simplify this procedure, that is, the one-hot encoding of frequent categories, with Feature-engine. First, let's load and divide the dataset as we did in *step 2*.

8. Let's set up the one-hot encoder to encode the five most frequent categories of the variables A6 and A7:

```
ohe_enc = OneHotCategoricalEncoder(top_categories=5,
variables=['A6', 'A7'], drop_last=False)
```

Feature-engine's `OneHotCategoricalEncoder()` will encode all of the categorical variables in the dataset by default, unless we specify the variables to encode as in *step 8*.

9. Let's fit the encoder to the train set so that it learns and stores the most frequent categories of A6 and A7:

```
ohe_enc.fit(X_train)
```

10. Finally, let's encode A6 and A7 in the train and test sets:

```
X_train_enc = ohe_enc.transform(X_train)
X_test_enc = ohe_enc.transform(X_test)
```

You can see the new binary variables in the dataframe executing X_train_enc.head(). You can also find the top five categories learned by the encoder executing ohe_enc.encoder_dict_.

Feature-engine replaces the original variable with the binary ones returned by one-hot encoding, leaving the dataset ready to use in machine learning.

How it works...

In this recipe, we performed one-hot encoding of the five most popular categories using pandas, NumPy and Feature-engine.

First, we loaded the data and, with train_test_split(), we separated the dataset into train and test sets, indicating the predictors by dropping the target from the dataset with pandas' drop(), and the target, A16, as a pandas Series. We also set the percentage of observations for the test set and set random_state for reproducibility.

In the first part of the recipe, we worked with the categorical A6 variable. We first displayed its unique categories with pandas' unique() method and observed that it contained multiple categories. Next, we counted the number of observations in the train set, per category of A6 using pandas' value_counts() method and sorted the categories from the one with most observations to the one with the least using pandas' sort_values() method, and captured the five most popular categories in a list using list comprehension syntax. Finally, we looped over each top category, and with NumPy's where() method, created binary variables by placing a 1 if the observation showed the category, or 0 otherwise. We named the new variables using the original variable name, A6, plus an underscore followed by the category name.

To perform a one-hot encoding of the five most popular categories of variables A6 and A7 with Feature-engine, we used OneHotCategoricalEncoder(), indicating 5 in the top_categories argument, and passing the variable names in a list to the variables argument. With fit(), the encoder learned the top categories from the train set and stored them in its attribute encoder_dict_, and then with transform(), OneHotCategoricalEncoder() replaced the original variables with the set of binary ones.

There's more...

You can also perform one-hot encoding of the five most popular categories using scikit-learn's OneHotEncoder() function. To do this, you need to pass a list of lists or an array of values to the categories argument where each list or each row of the array holds the top five categories expected in the relevant variable. You can find more details on the scikit-learn website at https://scikit-learn.org/stable/modules/generated/sklearn.preprocessing.OneHotEncoder.html.

Replacing categories with ordinal numbers

Ordinal encoding consists of replacing the categories with digits from 1 to *k* (or 0 to *k-1*, depending on the implementation), where *k* is the number of distinct categories of the variable. The numbers are assigned arbitrarily. Ordinal encoding is better suited for non-linear machine learning models, which can navigate through the arbitrarily assigned digits to try and find patterns that relate to the target.

In this recipe, we will perform ordinal encoding using pandas, scikit-learn, and Feature-engine.

How to do it...

Let's first import the necessary Python libraries and prepare the dataset:

1. Import pandas and the required function and classes:

```
import pandas as pd
from sklearn.model_selection import train_test_split
from sklearn.preprocessing import OrdinalEncoder
from feature_engine.categorical_encoders import
OrdinalCategoricalEncoder
```

2. Let's load the dataset and divide it into train and test sets:

```
data = pd.read_csv('creditApprovalUCI.csv')

X_train, X_test, y_train, y_test = train_test_split(
    data.drop(labels=['A16'], axis=1), data['A16'],test_size=0.3,
        random_state=0)
```

3. Let's encode the `A7` variable for this demonstration. First, let's make a dictionary of category to integer pairs and then display the result:

```
ordinal_mapping = {k: i for i, k in enumerate(
    X_train['A7'].unique(), 0) }
ordinal_mapping
```

We can see the digits that will replace each unique category in the following output:

```
{'v': 0,
 'ff': 1,
 'h': 2,
 'dd': 3,
 'z': 4,
 'bb': 5,
 'j': 6,
 'Missing': 7,
 'n': 8,
 'o': 9}
```

4. Now, let's replace the categories with numbers in the original variables:

```
X_train['A7'] = X_train['A7'].map(ordinal_mapping)
X_test['A7'] = X_test['A7'].map(ordinal_mapping)
```

With `print(X_train['A7'].head(10))`, we can display the result of the preceding operation:

```
596    0
303    0
204    0
351    1
118    0
247    2
652    0
513    3
230    0
250    4
Name: A7, dtype: int64
```

First, we need to divide the data into train and test sets as we did in *step 2*. Next we do the following:.

5. First, let's make a list with the categorical variables to encode:

```
vars_categorical = ['A1', 'A4', 'A5', 'A6', 'A7', 'A9', 'A10',
'A12', 'A13']
```

6. Let's start the ordinal encoder:

```
le = OrdinalEncoder()
```

7. Let's fit the encoder to the slice of the train set with the categorical variables so that it creates and stores representations of categories to digits:

```
le.fit(X_train[vars_categorical])
```

 Scikit-learn's `OrdinalEncoder()` function will encode the entire dataset. To encode only a selection of variables, we need to slice the dataframe as we did in *step 7*. Alternatively, we can use scikit-learn's `ColumnTransformer()`. You can find more details in the *See also* section.

8. Now let's encode the categorical variables in the train and test sets:

```
X_train_enc = le.transform(X_train[vars_categorical])
X_test_enc = le.transform(X_test[vars_categorical])
```

 Remember that scikit-learn returns a NumPy array.

Now let's do ordinal encoding with Feature-engine. First, let's load and divide the dataset as we did in *step 2*.

9. Let's create an ordinal encoder that replaces categories with numbers **arbitrarily** and encodes the categorical variables specified in *step 5*:

```
ordinal_enc = OrdinalCategoricalEncoder(
        encoding_method='arbitrary', variables=vars_categorical)
```

10. Let's fit the encoder to the train set so that it learns and stores the category-to-digit mappings:

```
ordinal_enc.fit(X_train)
```

> The category to digit mappings are stored in the `encoder_dict_` attribute and can be accessed by executing `ordinal_enc.encoder_dict_`.

11. Finally, let's encode the categorical variables in the train and test sets:

```
X_train = ordinal_enc.transform(X_train)
X_test = ordinal_enc.transform(X_test)
```

Feature-engine returns pandas dataframes where the values of the original variables are replaced with numbers, leaving the dataframe ready to use in machine learning models.

How it works...

In this recipe, we replaced each category in a categorical variable with an integer, assigned arbitrarily, using pandas, scikit-learn, or Feature-engine.

We loaded the dataset and divided it into train and test sets as described in the previous recipe. We worked first with the categorical A7 variable. With pandas `unique()`, we displayed the unique values of A7 and using Python's list comprehension syntax, we created a dictionary of key-value pairs, where each key was one of the unique categories, and each value was a digit that would replace the category. Finally, we used pandas' `map()` method to replace the strings in A7 with the integers indicated in the dictionary.

To carry out ordinal encoding with scikit-learn, we used `OrdinalEncoder()` function. With the `fit()` method, the transformer assigned an integer to each category of each variable in the train set. With the `transform()` method, the categories were replaced with integers, returning a NumPy array.

To perform ordinal encoding with Feature-engine, we used `OrdinalCategoricalEncoder()` and indicated that the numbers should be assigned arbitrarily in `encoding_method`. We indicated the variables to encode in the list of the `variables` argument. With the `fit()` method, the encoder assigned integers to categories, which were stored in the `encoder_dict_` attribute. These mappings were then used during the `transform()` method, to replace categories with numbers in the train and test sets, returning dataframes.

There's more...

We can smooth the implementation of *step 3* and *step 4* of the main recipe across multiple variables:

1. To do so, we capture *step 3* and *step 4* into functions, and apply those functions to every categorical variable, as follows:

```
def find_category_mappings(df, variable):
    return {k: i for i, k in enumerate(df[variable].unique(), 0)}

def integer_encode(train, test, variable, ordinal_mapping):
    X_train[variable] = X_train[variable].map(ordinal_mapping)
    X_test[variable] = X_test[variable].map(ordinal_mapping)

for variable in vars_categorical:
        mappings = find_category_mappings(X_train, variable)
        integer_encode(X_train, X_test, variable, mappings)
```

The preceding code block replaces strings in all categorical variables with integers, leaving the data ready for use with machine learning models.

See also

We can also perform ordinal encoding with the Category Encoders package: `https://contrib.scikit-learn.org/categorical-encoding/ordinal.html`.

Scikit-learn's transformers operate over the entire dataset, but we can select columns using `ColumnTransformer()`: `https://scikit-learn.org/stable/modules/generated/sklearn.compose.ColumnTransformer.html`.

With scikit-learn, we can also perform ordinal encoding one variable at a time using `LabelEncoder()`: `https://scikit-learn.org/stable/modules/generated/sklearn.preprocessing.LabelEncoder.html`.

Finally, you can find more details and example outputs of the various steps of the recipe in the accompanying GitHub repository: `https://github.com/PacktPublishing/Python-Feature-Engineering-Cookbook`.

Replacing categories with counts or frequency of observations

In count or frequency encoding, we replace the categories with the count or the percentage of observations with that category. That is, if 10 out of 100 observations show the category **blue** for the variable **color**, we would replace **blue** with 10 when doing count encoding, or by 0.1 if performing frequency encoding. These techniques, which capture the representation of each label in a dataset, are very popular in data science competitions. The assumption is that the number of observations per category is somewhat predictive of the target.

 Note that if two different categories are present in the same percentage of observations, they will be replaced by the same value, which may lead to information loss.

In this recipe, we will perform count and frequency encoding using pandas and Feature-engine.

How to do it...

Let's begin with the recipe by making some imports and preparing the data:

1. Import pandas and the required functions and classes:

```
import pandas as pd
from sklearn.model_selection import train_test_split
from feature_engine.categorical_encoders import
CountFrequencyCategoricalEncoder
```

2. Let's load the dataset and divide it into train and test sets:

```
data = pd.read_csv('creditApprovalUCI.csv')

X_train, X_test, y_train, y_test = train_test_split(
    data.drop(labels=['A16'], axis=1), data['A16'],test_size=0.3,
        random_state=0)
```

3. Let's count the number of observations per category of the A7 variable and capture it in a dictionary:

```
count_map = X_train['A7'].value_counts().to_dict()
```

To replace by **frequency** instead of count, we should divide the count per category by the total number of observations before creating the dictionary: `frequency_map = (X_train['A6'].value_counts() / len(X_train) ).to_dict().`

If we print the dictionary executing `print(count_map)`, we observe the count of observations per category:

```
{'v': 277,
 'h': 101,
 'ff': 41,
 'bb': 39,
 'z': 7,
 'dd': 5,
 'j': 5,
 'n': 3,
 'o': 1}
```

4. Let's replace the categories in A7 with the counts:

```
X_train['A7'] = X_train['A7'].map(count_map)
X_test['A7'] = X_test['A7'].map(count_map)
```

Go ahead and inspect the data executing `X_train.head()` to corroborate that the categories have been replaced by the counts.

Now, let's do count encoding using Feature-engine. First, let's load and divide the dataset as we did in *step 2*.

5. Let's create an encoder that replaces categories in **all** categorical variables by the count of observations:

```
count_enc = CountFrequencyCategoricalEncoder(
        encoding_method='count', variables=None)
```

`CountFrequencyCategoricalEncoder()` will automatically detect and encode **all** categorical variables in the train set. To encode only a subset of the categorical variables, we can pass the variable names in a list to the `variables` argument.

To replace the categories by frequency instead, we need to change `encoding_method` to `'frequency'`.

6. Let's fit the encoder to the train set so that it counts and stores the number of observations per category per variable:

```
count_enc.fit(X_train)
```

The dictionaries with the category-to-counts pairs are stored in the `encoder_dict_` attribute and can be displayed by executing `count_enc.encoder_dict_`.

7. Finally, let's replace the categories with counts in the train and test sets:

```
X_train_enc = count_enc.transform(X_train)
X_test_enc = count_enc.transform(X_test)
```

If there are categories in the test set that were not present in the train set, the transformer will replace those with `np.nan` and return a warning to make you aware. A good idea to prevent this behavior is to group infrequent labels as we describe in the *Grouping rare or infrequent categories* recipe.

The encoder returns pandas dataframes with the strings of the categorical variables replaced with the counts of observations, leaving the variables ready to use in machine learning models.

How it works...

In this recipe, we replaced categories by the number of observations per category using pandas and Feature-engine.

First, we loaded the dataset and divided it into train and test sets. Using pandas' `value_counts()` method, we determined the number of observations per category of the A7 variable, and with pandas' `to_dict()` method, we captured these values in a dictionary, where each key is a unique category, and each value the number of observations for that category. With pandas' `map()` method and this dictionary, we replaced the categories with counts in both train and test sets.

To perform count encoding with Feature-engine, we called `CountFrequencyCategoricalEncoder()` and set the `encoding_method` argument to `'count'`. We left the `variables` argument as `None` so that the encoder automatically finds all of the categorical variables in the dataset. With the `fit()` method, the transformer found the categorical variables and learned and stored the category to count pairs per variable as dictionaries in the `encoder_dict_` attribute. With the `transform()` method, the transformer replaced the categories with the counts in both the train and test sets, returning pandas dataframes.

There's more...

We can smooth the implementation of *step 3* and *step 4* of the main recipe across multiple variables. To do so, we capture *step 3* and *step 4* in functions, and next, we apply the functions to every categorical variable, as follows:

```python
def count_mappings(df, variable):
    return df[variable].value_counts().to_dict()

def frequency_mappings(df, variable):
    return (df[variable].value_counts() / len(df)).to_dict()

def encode(train, test, variable, mapping):
    X_train[variable] = X_train[variable].map(mapping)
    X_test[variable] = X_test[variable].map(mapping)

vars_categorical = [
    'A1', 'A4', 'A5', 'A6', 'A7', 'A9', 'A10', 'A12', 'A13']

for variable in vars_categorical:
    mappings = count_mappings(X_train, variable)
    encode(X_train, X_test, variable, mappings)
```

The preceding code block replaces strings in all categorical variables by the observation counts, leaving the data ready for use with machine learning models.

Encoding with integers in an ordered manner

In the *Replacing categories with ordinal numbers* recipe, we replaced categories with integers, which were assigned arbitrarily. This encoding works well with non-linear machine learning algorithms that can navigate through the arbitrarily assigned digits to try and find patterns that relate them to the target. However, this encoding method may not work so well with linear models.

We can instead assign integers to the categories given the target values. To do this, we do the following:

1. Calculate the mean value of the target per category.
2. Order the categories from the one with the lowest to the one with the highest target mean value.
3. Assign digits to the ordered categories, starting with 0 to the first category all of the way up to $k-1$ to the last category, where k is the number of distinct categories.

This encoding technique creates a monotonic relationship between the categorical variable and the response and therefore makes the variables more adequate for use in linear models.

In this recipe, we will encode categories following the target value using pandas and Feature-engine.

How to do it...

Let's first import the necessary Python libraries and get the dataset ready:

1. Import the required Python libraries, functions, and classes:

```
import pandas as pd
import matplotlib.pyplot as plt
from sklearn.model_selection import train_test_split
from feature_engine.categorical_encoders import
OrdinalCategoricalEncoder
```

2. Let's load the dataset and divide it into train and test sets:

```
data = pd.read_csv('creditApprovalUCI.csv')

X_train, X_test, y_train, y_test = train_test_split(data,
        data['A16'], test_size=0.3, random_state=0)
```

Note that to encode with integers based on the target with pandas, we need to keep the target in the `X_train` and `X_test` datasets.

To better understand the monotonic relationship concept, let's plot the relationship of the categories of the A7 variable with the target before and after the encoding.

3. Let's plot the mean target response per category of the A7 variable:

```
X_train.groupby(['A7'])['A16'].mean().plot()
plt.title('Relationship between A7 and the target')
plt.ylabel('Mean of target')
plt.show()
```

We can see the non-monotonic relationship between categories of A7 and the target, A16, in the following screenshot:

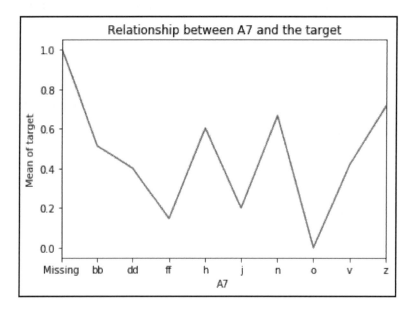

4. Now, let's calculate the mean target value per category in A7, then let's sort the categories from that with the lowest to that with the highest target value, and finally, let's retain the ordered category names:

```
ordered_labels =
X_train.groupby(['A7'])['A16'].mean().sort_values().index
```

To better understand the preceding line of code, execute the pandas methods one at a time in a Jupyter Notebook and familiarize yourself with the output. You can also see the output of each individual method in the Jupyter Notebook in the accompanying GitHub repository at https:// github.com/PacktPublishing/Python-Feature-Engineering-Cookbook.

To display the output of the preceding line of code, we can execute print(ordered_labels):

```
Index(['o', 'ff', 'j', 'dd', 'v', 'bb', 'h', 'n', 'z', 'Missing'],
dtype='object', name='A7')
```

5. Let's create a dictionary of category to integer pairs, using the ordered list we created in *step 4*:

```
ordinal_mapping = {k: i for i, k in enumerate(ordered_labels, 0)}
```

We can visualize the result of the preceding code executing print(ordinal_mapping):

```
{'o': 0,
 'ff': 1,
 'j': 2,
 'dd': 3,
 'v': 4,
 'bb': 5,
 'h': 6,
 'n': 7,
 'z': 8,
 'Missing': 9}
```

6. Let's use the dictionary created in *step 5* to replace the categories in A7 in the train and test sets:

```
X_train['A7'] = X_train['A7'].map(ordinal_mapping)
X_test['A7'] = X_test['A7'].map(ordinal_mapping)
```

Note that if the test set contains a category not present in the train set, the preceding code will introduce `np.nan`.

7. Let's plot the mean target value per category in the encoded variable:

```
X_train.groupby(['A7'])['A16'].mean().plot()
plt.title('Relationship between A7 and the target')
plt.ylabel('Mean of target')
plt.show()
```

The encoded variable shows a monotonic relationship with the target—the higher the mean target value, the higher the digit assigned to the category:

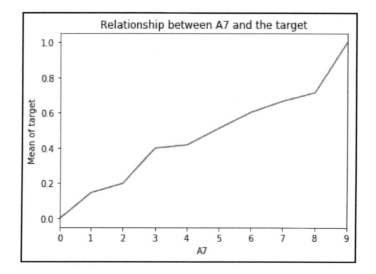

Now, let's perform ordered ordinal encoding using Feature-engine.

8. First, let's load and divide the dataset into train and test:

```
X_train, X_test, y_train, y_test = train_test_split(
    data.drop(labels=['A16'], axis=1), data['A16'], test_size=0.3,
        random_state=0)
```

Note that to encode with integers based on the target with Feature-engine, we **don't need to** keep the target in the X_train and X_test datasets.

9. Next, let's create an encoder that assigns digits to categories according to the target mean value, and encodes all categorical variables in the dataset:

```
ordinal_enc = OrdinalCategoricalEncoder(encoding_method='ordered',
    variables=None)
```

OrdinalCategoricalEncoder() will detect and encode all categorical variables automatically. Alternatively, we can indicate which variables to encode by passing their names in a list to the variables argument.

10. Let's fit the encoder to the train set so that it finds the categorical variables, and then it creates and stores the category and digit pairs for each categorical feature:

```
ordinal_enc.fit(X_train, y_train)
```

When fitting the encoder, we need to pass the train set and the **target**, like with many scikit-learn predictor classes.

11. Finally, let's replace the categories with numbers in the train and test sets:

```
X_train_enc = ordinal_enc.transform(X_train)
X_test_enc = ordinal_enc.transform(X_test)
```

A list of the categorical variables is stored in the variables attribute of OrdinalCategoricalEncoder() and the dictionaries with the category-to-digit mappings in the encoder_dict_ attribute.

Go ahead and check the monotonic relationship between other encoded categorical variables and the target using the code in *step 7* and changing the variable name in the groupby() method.

How it works...

In this recipe, we replaced the categories with integers according to the target mean value using pandas and Feature-engine.

We first loaded the dataset and divided it into train and test sets. In the first part of the recipe, we worked with the categorical `A7` variable. We plotted the mean target value per `A7` category. With pandas' `groupby()` method, we grouped the data per category of `A7`, and next with pandas' `mean()` method, we determined the mean value of the target, `A16`, for each of the categories of `A7`. We followed up with pandas' `plot()` method to create a plot of category versus target mean value. We added a title and *y* labels with Matplotlib's `title()` and `ylabel()` methods.

To perform the encoding, we first determined the mean target value per category of `A7`, using pandas' `groupby()` method followed by pandas' `mean()` method, as described in the preceding paragraph. Next, we ordered the categories with pandas' `sort_values()` method from the one with the lowest to the one with the highest target mean response. The output of this operation was a pandas Series, with the categories as indices and the target mean as values. With pandas' `index`, we captured the ordered categories in an array, and next, with a Python dictionary comprehension, we created a dictionary of category-to-integer pairs. Finally, we used this dictionary to replace the category by integers using pandas' `map()` method in train and test sets.

To perform the encoding with Feature-engine, we called `OrdinalCategoricalEncoder()` and indicated `'ordered'` in the `encoding_method` argument, and left the argument variables as `None`, so that the encoder automatically detects all categorical variables in the dataset. With the `fit()` method, the encoder found and stored the categorical variables to encode, and next, assigned digits to their categories, according to the target mean value. Variables to encode and dictionaries with category-to-digit pairs were stored in the `variables` and `encoder_dict_` attributes, respectively. Finally, using the `transform()` method, the transformer replaced the categories with digits in the train and test sets, returning pandas dataframes.

See also

For more details on Feature-engine's `OrdinalCategoricalEncoder()`, visit `https://feature-engine.readthedocs.io/en/latest/encoders/OrdinalCategoricalEncoder.html`.

Encoding with the mean of the target

Mean encoding or target encoding implies replacing the categories with the average target value for that category. For example, if we have a **City** variable, with the categories of **London**, **Manchester**, and **Bristol**, and we want to predict the default rate; if the default rate for **London** is 30%, we replace **London** with 0.3; if the default rate for **Manchester** is 20%, we replace **Manchester** with 0.2; and so on. The same can be done with a continuous target.

As with any machine learning algorithm, the parameters for target encoding, that is, the mean target value per category, need to be learned from the train set only and used to replace categories in the train and test sets.

In this recipe, we will perform mean encoding using pandas and Feature-engine.

How to do it...

Let's first import the necessary Python libraries and get the dataset ready:

1. Import pandas and the required functions and classes:

    ```
    import pandas as pd
    from sklearn.model_selection import train_test_split
    from feature_engine.categorical_encoders import
    MeanCategoricalEncoder
    ```

2. Let's load the dataset and divide it into train and test sets:

    ```
    data = pd.read_csv('creditApprovalUCI.csv')

    X_train, X_test, y_train, y_test = train_test_split(
            data, data['A16'], test_size=0.3, random_state=0)
    ```

Note that, to encode with integers based on the target with pandas, we need to keep the target in the X_train and X_test datasets.

3. Let's determine the mean target value per category of the A7 variable and then store them in a dictionary:

```
ordered_labels = X_train.groupby(['A7'])['A16'].mean().to_dict()
```

We can display the content of the dictionary by executing `print(ordered_labels)`:

```
{'Missing': 1.0,
 'bb': 0.5128205128205128,
 'dd': 0.4,
 'ff': 0.14634146341463414,
 'h': 0.6039603960396039,
 'j': 0.2,
 'n': 0.6666666666666666,
 'o': 0.0,
 'v': 0.4187725631768953,
 'z': 0.7142857142857143}
```

4. Let's replace the categories with the mean target value using the dictionary created in *step 3* in the train and test sets:

```
X_train['A7'] = X_train['A7'].map(ordered_labels)
X_test['A7'] = X_test['A7'].map(ordered_labels)
```

Go ahead and inspect the new values of A7 by executing `X_train['A7'].head()`.

Now, let's perform target encoding with Feature-engine.

5. First, let's load and divide the dataset into train and test sets:

```
X_train, X_test, y_train, y_test = train_test_split(
    data.drop(labels=['A16'], axis=1), data['A16'],
    test_size=0.3, random_state=0)
```

Note that, to encode with integers based on the target with Feature-engine, we **don't need to** keep the target in the X_train and X_test datasets.

6. Let's now create a target mean encoder to encode all categorical variables:

```
mean_enc = MeanCategoricalEncoder(variables=None)
```

MeanCategoricalEncoder() will find and encode **all** categorical variables by default. Alternatively, we can indicate the variables to encode passing their names in a list to the `variables` argument.

7. Let's fit the transformer to the train set so that it learns and stores the mean target value per category per variable:

```
mean_enc.fit(X_train, y_train)
```

To fit `MeanCategoricalEncoder()`, we need to pass both the train set and the target, as we do with many scikit-learn predictor classes.

8. Finally, let's encode the train and test sets:

```
X_train_enc = mean_enc.transform(X_train)
X_test_enc = mean_enc.transform(X_test)
```

The category-to-number pairs are stored as a dictionary of dictionaries in the `encoder_dict_` attribute. To display the stored parameters, execute `mean_enc.encoder_dict_`.

Feature-engine returns pandas dataframes with the categorical variables ready to use in machine learning models.

How it works...

In this recipe, we replaced the categories with the mean target value using pandas and Feature-engine.

We first loaded the dataset and divided it into train and test sets. Next, we calculated the mean of the target per category. With pandas' `groupby()` method over the categorical A7 variable, followed by pandas' `mean()` method over the target A16 variable, we created a pandas Series with the categories as indices and the target mean as values. With pandas' `to_dict()` method, we converted this Series into a dictionary. Finally, we used this dictionary to replace the categories in the train and test sets using pandas' `map()` method.

To perform the encoding with Feature-engine, we called
`OrdinalCategoricalEncoder()` and set `encoding_method` to `'ordered'`. With
the `fit()` method, the transformer found and stored the categorical variables, and then
learned and stored the category to mean target value pairs, as a dictionary of dictionaries in
its `encoder_dict_` attribute. Finally, with the `transform()` method, categories were
replaced with numbers in train and test sets, returning pandas dataframes.

See also

You can find a different implementation of target encoding in the Category Encoders
Python package: `https://contrib.scikit-learn.org/categorical-encoding/`
`targetencoder.html`.

To learn more about Feature-engine's `MeanCategoricalEncoder()`, visit: `https://`
`feature-engine.readthedocs.io/en/latest/encoders/MeanCategoricalEncoder.html`.

Finally, you can find more details of the intermediate outputs of the steps in the recipe in
the Jupyter Notebook in the accompanying GitHub repository: `https://github.com/`
`PacktPublishing/Python-Feature-Engineering-Cookbook`.

Encoding with the Weight of Evidence

The **Weight of Evidence (WoE)** was developed primarily for credit and financial industries
to facilitate variable screening and exploratory analysis and to build more predictive linear
models to evaluate the risk of loan default; that is, to predict how likely money lent to a
person or institution is to be lost.

The WoE is computed from the basic odds ratio:

$$WoE = log(\frac{p(Y=1)}{p(Y=0)})$$

Here, *p(Y=1)* is the probability of an event occurring. Therefore, the WoE takes the
following values:

- *WoE = 0* if *p(1) / p(0) = 1*, that is, if the outcome is random
- *WoE > 0* if *p(1) > p(0)*
- *WoE < 0* if *p(0) > p(1)*

This allows for a direct visualization of the predictive power of the category in the variable: the higher the WoE, the more likely the event will occur, and in fact, if the WOE is positive, the event is likely to occur.

Logistic regression models a binary response, *Y*, based off *X* predictor variables, assuming that there is a linear relationship between *X* and the log of odds of *Y*:

$$log(\frac{p(Y=1)}{p(Y=0)}) = b0 + b1X1 + b2X2 + \ldots + bnXn$$

Here, log (*p(Y=1)/p(Y=0)*) is the log of odds. As you can see, the WoE encodes the categories in the same scale, that is, the log of odds, as the outcome of the logistic regression. Therefore, by using WoE, the predictors are prepared and coded in the same scale, and the parameters in the logistic regression, that is, the coefficients, can be directly compared.

In this recipe, we will perform WoE encoding using pandas and Feature-engine.

How to do it...

Let's begin with the recipe by making some imports and preparing the data:

1. Import pandas and the required functions and classes:

```
import pandas as pd
from sklearn.model_selection import train_test_split
from feature_engine.categorical_encoders import
WoERatioCategoricalEncoder
```

2. Let's load the dataset and divide it into train and test sets:

```
data = pd.read_csv('creditApprovalUCI.csv')

X_train, X_test, y_train, y_test = train_test_split(
        data, data['A16'],test_size=0.3, random_state=0)
```

3. Let's create a pandas Series with the probability of the target being 1, that is, *p(1)*, for each category in A1:

```
p1 = X_train.groupby(['A1'])['A16'].mean()
```

4. Let's create a pandas Series with the probability of the target being 0, that is, *p(0)*, for each category in `A1`:

```
p0 = 1 - p1
```

By definition, the probability of the target being 1 plus the probability of the target being 0 is 1.

5. Now, let's create a dictionary with the WoE per category:

```
woe = dict(np.log(p1 / p0))
```

We can display the dictionary with the category to WoE pairs executing `print(woe)`:

```
{'Missing': 0.0, 'a': -0.11122563511022437, 'b':
-0.24600937605121306}
```

6. Finally, let's replace the categories of `A1` by the WoE:

```
X_train['A1'] = X_train['A1'].map(woe)
X_test['A1'] = X_test['A1'].map(woe)
```

Now, let's perform WoE encoding using Feature-engine.

7. First, let's load and divide the dataset into train and test sets:

```
X_train, X_test, y_train, y_test = train_test_split(
    data.drop(labels=['A16'], axis=1), data['A16'],
    test_size=0.3, random_state=0)
```

8. Next, let's create a WoE encoder to encode three categorical variables, `A1`, `A10`, and `A12`:

```
woe_enc = WoERatioCategoricalEncoder(encoding_method='woe',
    variables=['A1', 'A10', 'A12'])
```

Feature-engine's `WoERatioCategoricalEncoder()` will return an error if *p(0) = 0* for any category because the division by 0 is not defined. To avoid this error, group infrequent categories, as we discuss in the *Grouping rare or infrequent categories* recipe.

9. Let's fit the transformer to the train set so that it learns and stores the WoE of the different categories:

```
woe_enc.fit(X_train, y_train)
```

We can display the dictionaries with the categories to WoE pairs by executing `woe_enc.encoder_dict_`.

10. Finally, let's encode the three categorical variables in the train and test sets:

```
X_train_enc = woe_enc.transform(X_train)
X_test_enc = woe_enc.transform(X_test)
```

The Feature-engine transformer returns pandas dataframes with the encoded categorical variables ready to use in machine learning models.

How it works...

In this recipe, we replaced the categories with the WoE using pandas and Feature-engine.

We first loaded the dataset and divided it into train and test sets. Next, we calculated the mean target value per category using pandas' `groupby()` method over the categorical A1 variable and pandas' `mean()` method over the target A16 variable. This is equivalent to the probability of the target being 1, that is, p(1), per category. The output of these operations was a pandas Series with the categories as indices and the target mean as values. Next, we subtracted this pandas Series from 1 to create another pandas Series with the probability of the target being 0, that is, p(0), per category. Next, we created a third pandas Series with the logarithm of the ratio of the first and the second pandas Series, that is, the logarithm of the ratio of p(1) and p(0) per category. With the built-in Python `dict()` method, we captured the category-to-WoE value pairs in a dictionary. Finally, we used this dictionary to replace the categories in the train and test sets using pandas' `map()` method.

To perform WoE encoding with Feature-engine, we used `WoERatioCategoricalEncoder()` and indicated `'woe'` in `encoding_method`. We also passed a list with categorical variables to encode to the `variables` argument. With the `fit()` method, the transformer learned and stored the category to WoE pairs. Finally, with `transform()`, the categories of the three selected variables were replaced by the WoE values, returning pandas dataframes.

See also

You can find an alternative implementation of the WoE in the Category Encoders package: `https://contrib.scikit-learn.org/categorical-encoding/woe.html`.

To learn more about Feature-engine's `WoERatioCategoricalEncoder()`, visit: `https://feature-engine.readthedocs.io/en/latest/encoders/WoERatioCategoricalEncoder.html`.

Grouping rare or infrequent categories

Rare values are those categories that are present only in a small percentage of the observations. There is no rule of thumb to determine how small is a small percentage, but typically, any value below 5 % can be considered rare. Infrequent labels often appear only on the train set or only on the test set, therefore making the algorithms prone to overfitting or unable to score an observation. To avoid these complications, we can group infrequent categories into a new category called **Rare** or **Other**.

 For details on how to identify rare labels, visit the *Pinpointing rare categories in categorical variables* recipe in `Chapter 1`, *Foreseeing Variable Problems in Building ML Models*.

In this recipe, we will group infrequent categories using pandas and Feature-engine.

How to do it...

Let's first import the necessary Python libraries and get the dataset ready:

1. Import the required Python libraries, functions, and classes:

```
import numpy as np
import pandas as pd
from sklearn.model_selection import train_test_split
from feature_engine.categorical_encoders import
RareLabelCategoricalEncoder
```

2. Let's load the dataset and divide it into train and test sets:

```
data = pd.read_csv('creditApprovalUCI.csv')

X_train, X_test, y_train, y_test = train_test_split(
    data.drop(labels=['A16'], axis=1), data['A16'],test_size=0.3,
    random_state=0)
```

3. Let's determine the percentage of observations per category in the A7 variable:

```
X_train['A7'].value_counts() / len(X_train)
```

We can see the percentage of observations per category of A7, expressed as decimals, in the following output:

```
v           0.573499
h           0.209110
ff          0.084886
bb          0.080745
z           0.014493
dd          0.010352
j           0.010352
Missing     0.008282
n           0.006211
o           0.002070
Name: A7, dtype: float64
```

If we consider as rare those labels present in less than 5% of the observations, then z, dd, j, Missing, n, and o are rare categories.

4. Let's create a function that takes a dataframe and variable name, determines the percentage of observations per category, and then retains those categories where the percentage is above a minimum value:

```
def find_frequent_labels(df, variable, tolerance):
    temp = df[variable].value_counts()  / len(df)
    frequent = [x for x in temp.loc[temp>tolerance].index.values]
    return frequent
```

5. Let's find the categories in A7 present in more than 5% of the observations, using the function created in *step 4*:

```
frequent_cat = find_frequent_labels(X_train, 'A7', 0.05)
```

If we execute print(frequent_cat), we will see the frequent categories of A7:

```
['v', 'h', 'ff', 'bb']
```

6. Let's replace rare labels, that is, those present in <= 5% of the observations, with the Rare string:

```
X_train['A7'] = np.where(X_train['A7'].isin(frequent_cat),
    X_train['A7'], 'Rare')
X_test['A7'] = np.where(X_test['A7'].isin(frequent_cat),
    X_test['A7'], 'Rare')
```

7. Let's determine the percentage of observations in the encoded variable:

```
X_train['A7'].value_counts() / len(X_train)
```

We can see that the infrequent labels have now been *re-grouped* in the Rare category:

```
v        0.573499
h        0.209110
ff       0.084886
bb       0.080745
Rare     0.051760
Name: A7, dtype: float64
```

Now, let's group rare labels using Feature-engine. First, we load and divide the dataset into train and test sets as we did in *step 2*.

8. Let's create a rare label encoder that groups categories present in less than 5% of the observations, provided that the categorical variable has more than four distinct values:

```
rare_encoder = RareLabelCategoricalEncoder(tol=0.05,
    n_categories=4)
```

9. Let's fit the encoder so that it finds the categorical variables and then learns their most frequent categories:

```
rare_encoder.fit(X_train)
```

We can display the frequent categories per variable by executing rare_encoder.encoder_dict_.

10. Finally, let's group rare labels in train and test sets:

```
X_train_enc = rare_encoder.transform(X_train)
X_test_enc = rare_encoder.transform(X_test)
```

Now that we have grouped rare labels, we are ready to encode the categorical variables as we describe in the other recipes in this chapter.

How it works...

In this recipe, we grouped infrequent categories using pandas and Feature-engine.

We first loaded the dataset and divided it into train and test sets. Next, we determined the percentage of observations per category of the A7 variable. With pandas' `value_counts()` method, we counted the observations per category of A7 and then divided these values by the total number of observations, determined using Python's built-in `len` method, to obtain the percentage of observations per category.

Next, we created a function that took as arguments a dataframe, a categorical variable, and a tolerance, which is the minimum frequency for a category **not** to be considered rare. In the function, we used pandas' `value_counts()` method and Python's `len()` function to create a pandas Series with the categories in the index and the frequency of observations as values. Next, with a list comprehension over the preceding pandas Series, we captured the categories with a frequency higher than the indicated tolerance. In the list comprehension, we first sliced the Series selecting only the categories above the indicated tolerance with pandas' `loc` method, and next, using pandas' `index`, we retained the category names in a list.

With the preceding function, we captured the frequent categories of A7 in a list and then, using NumPy's `where()` method, we searched each row of A7, and if the observation was one of the frequent categories in the list, which we checked using pandas' `isin()` method, it was kept; otherwise, its original value was replaced with `'Rare'`.

We automated the preceding steps for multiple categorical variables using Feature-engine. To do this, we called Feature-engine's `RareLabelCategoricalEncoder()` categorical encoder, and indicated first the minimum frequency to retain a category by setting `tol` to `0.05`, and second, that we only wanted to group rare labels if the variable had at least four different categories by setting `n_categories` to 4. With the `fit()` method, the transformer identified the categorical variables and then it learned and stored the frequent categories per variable. With the `transform()` method, we replaced categories not present in those lists with the string, `Rare`.

See also

To learn more about Feature-engine's `RareLabelcategoricalEncoder()` categorical encoder, visit: `https://feature-engine.readthedocs.io/en/latest/encoders/RareLabelCategoricalEncoder.html`.

Performing binary encoding

Binary encoding is an alternative categorical encoding technique that uses binary code, that is, a sequence of zeroes and ones, to represent the different categories of the variable. How does it work? First, the categories are arbitrarily replaced by ordinal numbers, as shown in the intermediate step of the following table. Then, those numbers are converted into binary code. For example, the integer 1 can be represented as the sequence 01, the integer 2 as 10, the integer 3 as 00, and 4 as 11. The digits in the two positions of the binary string become the columns, which are the encoded representation of the original variable:

Color	Intermediate step	1st	2nd
Blue	1	0	1
Red	2	1	0
Green	3	0	0
Yellow	4	1	1

Binary encoding encodes the data in fewer dimensions than one-hot encoding. In our example, the color variable would be encoded into *k-1* categories, that is, three variables by one-hot encoding, but with binary encoding, we can represent the variable with only two variables. More generally, we determine the number of binary features needed to encode a variable as *log2(number of distinct categories)*; in our example, *log2(4) = 2* binary features. Also, the derived features are binary, which is suitable for linear models. But, the derived features **lack human interpretability**, therefore, the use of this technique in organizations is questionable.

In this recipe, we will learn how to perform binary encoding using the Category Encoders Python package.

Getting ready

In this recipe, we will implement binary encoding using the open source package, Category Encoders, which you can install with pip as described in the *Technical requirements* section.

How to do it...

Let's first import the necessary Python libraries and get the dataset ready:

1. Import the required Python library, function, and class:

    ```
    import pandas as pd
    from sklearn.model_selection import train_test_split
    from category_encoders import BinaryEncoder
    ```

2. Let's load the dataset and divide it into train and test sets:

    ```
    data = pd.read_csv('creditApprovalUCI.csv')

    X_train, X_test, y_train, y_test = train_test_split(
        data.drop(labels=['A16'], axis=1), data['A16'],test_size=0.3,
        random_state=0)
    ```

3. Let's inspect the unique categories in A7:

    ```
    X_train['A7'].unique()
    ```

    We can see in the output of the preceding code block that A7 has 10 different categories:

    ```
    array(['v', 'ff', 'h', 'dd', 'z', 'bb', 'j', 'Missing', 'n', 'o'],
    dtype=object)
    ```

4. Let's create a binary encoder to encode A7:

    ```
    encoder = BinaryEncoder(cols=['A7'], drop_invariant=True)
    ```

BinaryEncoder(), as well as other encoders from the Category Encoders package, allow us to select the variables to encode. We simply pass the column names in a list to the cols argument.

5. Let's fit the transformer to the train set so that it calculates how many binary variables it needs and creates the variable to binary code representations:

    ```
    encoder.fit(X_train)
    ```

6. Finally, let's encode A7 in the train and test sets:

    ```
    X_train_enc = encoder.transform(X_train)
    X_test_enc = encoder.transform(X_test)
    ```

We can display the top rows of the transformed train set by
executing `print(X_train_enc.head())`, which returns the following output:

	A1	A2	A3	A4	A5	A6	**A7_1**	**A7_2**	**A7_3**	**A7_4**	A8	A9	A10	A11
596	a	46.08	3.000	u	g	c	0	0	0	1	2.375	t	t	8
303	a	15.92	2.875	u	g	q	0	0	0	1	0.085	f	f	0
204	b	36.33	2.125	y	p	w	0	0	0	1	0.085	t	t	1
351	b	22.17	0.585	y	p	ff	0	0	1	0	0.000	f	f	0
118	b	57.83	7.040	u	g	m	0	0	0	1	14.000	t	t	6

	A12	A13	A14	A15	A16
596	t	g	396.0	4159	1
303	f	g	120.0	0	0
204	f	g	50.0	1187	1
351	f	g	100.0	0	0
118	t	g	360.0	1332	1

Binary encoding returned four binary variables for A7, which are A7_1, A7_2, A7_3, and
A7_4, instead of the nine that would have been returned by one-hot encoding.

How it works...

In this recipe, we performed binary encoding using the Category Encoders package. We
first loaded the dataset and divided it into train and test sets using `train_test_split()`
from scikit-learn. Next, we used `BinaryEncoder()` to encode the A7 variable. With the
`fit()` method, `BinaryEncoder()` created a mapping from category to set of binary
columns, and with the `transform()` method, the encoder encoded the A7 variable in both
the train and test sets.

With one-hot encoding, we would have created nine binary variables (*k-1*
= *10 unique categories - 1 = 9*) to encode all of the information in A7. With
binary encoding instead, we can represent the variable in less dimensions:
log2(10)=3.3, that is, we need only four binary variables.

See also

For more information about `BinaryEncoder()`, visit: `https://contrib.scikit-learn.org/categorical-encoding/binary.html`.

For a nice example of the output of binary encoding, check out the following `https://stats.stackexchange.com/questions/325263/binary-encoding-vs-one-hot-encoding`.

For a comparative study of categorical encoding techniques for neural networks classifiers, visit: `https://www.researchgate.net/publication/320465713_A_Comparative_Study_of_Categorical_Variable_Encoding_Techniques_for_Neural_Network_Classifiers`.

Performing feature hashing

With feature hashing, the categories of a variable are converted into a series of binary vectors using a hashing function. How does this work? First, we determine, **arbitrarily**, the number of binary vectors to represent the category. For example, let's say we would like to use five vectors. Next, we need a hash function that will take a category and return a number between 0 and $n-1$, where n is the number of binary vectors. In our example, the hash function should return a value between 0 and 4. Let's say our hash function returns the value of **3** for the category **blue**. That means that our category **blue** will be represented by a 0 in the vectors 0, 1, 2, and 4 and 1 in the vector 3: [0,0,0,1,0]. Any hash function can be used as long as it returns a number between 0 and $n-1$.

An example of a hash function is the module or remainder. In our example, it would be the remainder of 5.

In this recipe, we will perform feature hashing using the open source package, Category Encoders.

For more details on feature hashing, visit any of the recommended reads in the *See also* section at the end of this recipe.

Getting ready

In this recipe, we will implement feature hashing using the open source package, Category Encoders, which you can install with `pip` as described in the *Technical requirements* section.

How to do it...

Let's first import the necessary Python libraries and get the dataset ready:

1. Import the required Python library, function, and class:

```
import pandas as pd
from sklearn.model_selection import train_test_split
from category_encoders import HashingEncoder
```

2. Let's load the dataset and divide it into train and test sets:

```
data = pd.read_csv('creditApprovalUCI.csv')

X_train, X_test, y_train, y_test = train_test_split(
    data.drop(labels=['A16'], axis=1), data['A16'],test_size=0.3,
random_state=0)
```

3. Let's inspect the unique categories in A7:

```
X_train['A7'].unique()
```

We can see in the output of the preceding code block that A7 has 10 different categories:

```
array(['v', 'ff', 'h', 'dd', 'z', 'bb', 'j', 'Missing', 'n', 'o'],
dtype=object)
```

4. Let's create a hashing encoder to encode A7 into four binary vectors:

```
encoder = HashingEncoder(cols=['A7'], n_components=4)
```

5. Let's fit the encoder to the train set so that it creates and stores the category to vectors mappings:

```
encoder.fit(X_train)
```

6. Finally, let's now encode A7 in the train and test sets:

```
X_train_enc = encoder.transform(X_train)
X_test_enc = encoder.transform(X_test)
```

We can display the top rows of the transformed train set by executing `print(X_train_enc.head())`, which returns the following output:

	col_0	col_1	col_2	col_3	A1	A2	A3	A4	A5	A6	A8	A9	A10
\													
596	0	0	1	0	a	46.08	3.000	u	g	c	2.375	t	t
303	0	0	1	0	a	15.92	2.875	u	g	q	0.085	f	f
204	0	0	1	0	b	36.33	2.125	y	p	w	0.085	t	t
351	0	1	0	0	b	22.17	0.585	y	p	ff	0.000	f	f
118	0	0	1	0	b	57.83	7.040	u	g	m	14.000	t	t

	A11	A12	A13	A14	A15	A16
596	8	t	g	396.0	4159	1
303	0	f	g	120.0	0	0
204	1	f	g	50.0	1187	1
351	0	f	g	100.0	0	0
118	6	t	g	360.0	1332	1

Note how the encoded variable is returned as four binary vectors at the beginning of the dataframe (`cols_0` to `col_3`), and the original `A7` variable is removed.

> Feature hashing can return the **same encoding** for different categories. To minimize this behavior, you can try and encode the variable in more components.

How it works...

In this recipe, we performed feature hashing using the Category Encoders package. We first loaded the dataset and divided it into train and test sets using `train_test_split()` from scikit-learn. Next, we set up `HashingEncoder()` to encode the `A7` variable into four components. With the `fit()` method, `HashingEncoder()` created a mapping from the category to a set of binary vectors and with the `transform()` method, the encoder encoded the `A7` variable in both the train and test sets.

> With one-hot encoding, we would have needed nine binary variables to encode `A7`. With feature hashing, we can represent the variable in a smaller feature space, that is, with fewer derived features. The number of features is determined by the user.

See also

For more information about `HashingEncoder()`, visit: `https://contrib.scikit-learn.org/categorical-encoding/hashing.html`.

For more details on feature hashing, visit the following:

- `https://alex.smola.org/papers/2009/Weinbergeretal09.pdf`
- `https://towardsdatascience.com/understanding-feature-engineering-part-2-categorical-data-f54324193e63` **(recommended read)**
- `http://www.willmcginnis.com/2016/01/16/even-further-beyond-one-hot-hashing/`
- `https://www.quora.com/Can-you-explain-feature-hashing-in-an-easily-understandable-way`

4
Transforming Numerical Variables

Linear and logistic regression assume that the variables are normally distributed. If they are not, we can often apply a mathematical transformation to change their distribution into Gaussian, and sometimes even unmask linear relationships between variables and their targets. This means that transforming variables may improve the performance of linear machine learning models. Commonly used mathematical transformations include the logarithm, reciprocal, power, square and cube root transformations, as well as the Box-Cox and Yeo-Johnson transformations. In this chapter, we will learn how to implement all of these operations on the variables in our dataset using the NumPy, SciPy, scikit-learn, and Feature-engine libraries.

This chapter will cover the following recipes:

- Transforming variables with the logarithm
- Transforming variables with the reciprocal function
- Using square and cube root to transform variables
- Using power transformations on numerical variables
- Performing Box-Cox transformation on numerical variables
- Performing Yeo-Johnson transformation on numerical variables

Technical requirements

In this chapter, we will use the pandas, NumPy, Matplotlib, SciPy and scikit-learn Python libraries. These libraries are bundled in the free Anaconda Python distribution (https://www.anaconda.com/distribution/), which you can install as described in the *Technical Requirements* section of `Chapter 1`, *Foreseeing Variable Problems when Building ML Models*.

We will also use the open source Python library Feature-engine, which can be installed using `pip`:

```
pip install feature-engine
```

We will use the Boston House Prices dataset from scikit-learn, which contains **no missing data**. When trying the recipes in your own dataset, make sure you impute the missing values with any of the techniques we covered in `Chapter 2`, *Imputing Missing Data*.

Transforming variables with the logarithm

The logarithm function is commonly used to transform variables. It has a strong effect on the shape of the variable distribution and can only be applied to positive variables. In this recipe, we will learn how to perform logarithmic transformation using NumPy, scikit-learn, and Feature-engine. We will also create a diagnostic plot function to evaluate the effect of the transformation on the variable distribution.

How to do it...

Let's begin by importing the libraries and classes we need and getting the dataset ready:

1. Import the required Python libraries, classes, and functions:

```
import numpy as np
import pandas as pd
import matplotlib.pyplot as plt
import scipy.stats as stats
from sklearn.datasets import load_boston
from sklearn.preprocessing import FunctionTransformer
from feature_engine.variable_transformers import LogTransformer
```

2. Let's load the Boston House Prices dataset into a pandas dataframe:

```
boston_dataset = load_boston()
data = pd.DataFrame(boston_dataset.data,
columns=boston_dataset.feature_names)
```

3. To evaluate the effect of the transformation on the variable distribution, we'll create a function that takes a dataframe and a variable name as inputs and plots a histogram next to a Q-Q plot:

```
def diagnostic_plots(df, variable):
    plt.figure(figsize=(15,6))
    plt.subplot(1, 2, 1)
    df[variable].hist(bins=30)
    plt.subplot(1, 2, 2)
    stats.probplot(df[variable], dist="norm", plot=plt)
    plt.show()
```

For more details on Q-Q plots, take a look at the *Identifying a normal distribution* recipe of `Chapter 1`, *Foreseeing Variable Problems when Building ML Models*.

4. Now, let's plot the distribution of the LSTAT variable:

```
diagnostic_plots(data, 'LSTAT')
```

The following output shows that LSTAT is not normally distributed:

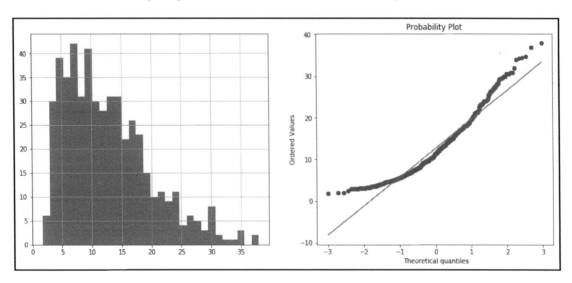

Now, let's transform the data with the logarithm.

5. First, let's make a copy of the original dataframe using pandas `copy()`:

```
data_tf = data.copy()
```

We've created a copy so that we can modify the values in the copy and not in the original dataframe, which we need for the rest of the recipe.

If we execute `data_tf = data` instead of using pandas `copy()`, `data_tf` will not be a copy of the dataframe; instead, it will be another view of the same data. Therefore, changes that are made in `data_tf` will be reflected in `data` as well.

6. Let's apply the logarithmic transformation with NumPy to a subset of positive variables to capture the transformed variables in the new dataframe:

```
data_tf[['LSTAT', 'NOX', 'DIS', 'RM']] = np.log(data[['LSTAT',
'NOX', 'DIS', 'RM']])
```

7. Let's check the distribution of `LSTAT` **after** the transformation with the diagnostic function we created in *step 3*:

```
diagnostic_plots(data_tf, 'LSTAT')
```

We can see the effect of the transformation in the following output:

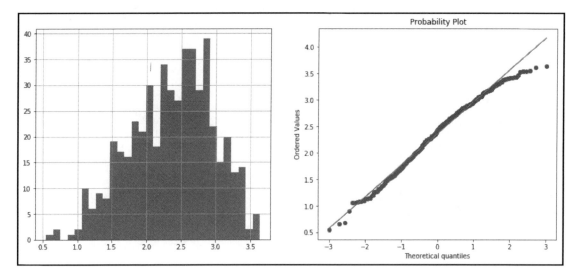

Now, let's apply the logarithmic transformation with scikit-learn.

8. Let's create a transformer using the `FunctionTransformer()` from scikit-learn:

```
transformer = FunctionTransformer(np.log)
```

> `FunctionTransformer()` doesn't need to be fit before transforming the data since there are no parameters to be learned from the train set.

9. Let's transform a subset of positive variables:

```
data_tf = transformer.transform(data[['LSTAT', 'NOX', 'DIS', 'RM']])
```

Note that `data_tf` is a NumPy array with **only** the transformed variables.

> We can transform the NumPy array into a pandas dataframe by executing `data_tf = pd.DataFrame(data_tf, columns = ['LSTAT', 'NOX', 'DIS', 'RM'])` and then check that the transformation was successful with the diagnostic function of *step 3*.

Now, let's do logarithm transformation with Feature-engine.

10. Let's create a transformer using `LogTransformer()` and fit it to the dataset:

```
lt = LogTransformer(variables = ['LSTAT', 'NOX', 'DIS', 'RM'])
lt.fit(data)
```

> If the `variables` argument is left as `None`, `LogTransformer()` identifies and applies the logarithm to **all the numerical variables** in the dataset. Alternatively, we can indicate which variables we want to transform, just like we did in *step 10*.

11. Finally, let's transform the data:

```
data_tf = lt.transform(data)
```

The transformer will only transform the variables indicated in *step 10*. Note that `data_tf` is a pandas dataframe that contains all of the original variables, where only the `LSTAT`, `NOX`, `DIS`, and `RM` variables were transformed by the logarithm.

How it works...

In this recipe, we applied the logarithm transformation to a subset of positive variables in the Boston House Prices using NumPy, scikit-learn, and Feature-engine. For details on how to load the dataset, take a look at the *Distinguishing variable distributions* recipe of Chapter 1, *Foreseeing Variable Problems When Building ML Models*.

To compare the effect of the transformation on the variable distribution, we created a diagnostic function to plot a histogram next to a Q-Q plot using the probplot() method from scipy.stats and pandas hist(), which we described in the *Identifying a normal distribution* recipe of Chapter 1, *Foreseeing Variable Problems when Building ML Models*. With plt.figure() and figsize, we adjusted the size of the figure and, with plt.subplot(), we organized the two plots in 1 row with 2 columns, that is, one plot next to the other. The number in the third position within plt.subpot() indicated the place of the plot: the histogram in position 1 and the Q-Q plot in position 2, that is, left and right, respectively.

We plotted a histogram and a Q-Q plot for the LSTAT variable before the transformation and observed that LSTAT was not normally distributed: most observations were at the left of the histogram and the values deviated from the 45-degree line in the Q-Q plot at both ends of the distribution.

To apply the logarithm using NumPy, we used the log() method on a slice of the dataframe with four positive variables. To corroborate that the transformation worked, we plotted a histogram and Q-Q plot of the transformed LSTAT. We observed that the values were more centered in the histogram and that, in the Q-Q plot, they only deviated from the 45-degree line toward the higher values.

Next, we used the FunctionTransformer() from scikit-learn, which applies any user-defined function to a dataset and returns the result of the operation in a NumPy array. We passed NumPy's log() as an argument to FunctionTransfomer() and, with the transform() method, we transformed a slice of the dataframe with the positive variables.

Finally, we used Feature-engine's LogTransformer() to apply the logarithmic transformation, indicating the variables to transform into a list as an argument. The fit() method of the transformer checked that the variables were numerical and the transform() method called NumPy's log() to transform the indicated variables.

See also

For more details about the methods and transformers that were used in this recipe, take a look at the following links:

- NumPy's `log()`: `https://docs.scipy.org/doc/numpy/reference/generated/numpy.log.html`
- Scikit-learn's `FunctionTransformer()`: `https://scikit-learn.org/stable/modules/generated/sklearn.preprocessing.FunctionTransformer.html`.
- Feature-engine's `LogTransformer()`: `https://feature-engine.readthedocs.io/en/latest/vartransformers/LogTransformer.html`

Transforming variables with the reciprocal function

The reciprocal function, defined as 1/x, is a strong transformation with a very drastic effect on the variable distribution. It isn't defined for the value 0, but it can be applied to negative numbers. In this recipe, we will implement the reciprocal transformation using NumPy, scikit-learn, and Feature-engine and compare its effect with a diagnostic function.

How to do it...

Let's begin by importing the libraries and getting the dataset ready:

1. Import the required Python libraries, methods, and classes:

```
import numpy as np
import pandas as pd
import matplotlib.pyplot as plt
import scipy.stats as stats
from sklearn.datasets import load_boston
from sklearn.preprocessing import FunctionTransformer
from feature_engine.variable_transformers import
ReciprocalTransformer
```

2. Let's load the Boston House Prices dataset:

```
boston_dataset = load_boston()
data = pd.DataFrame(boston_dataset.data,
columns=boston_dataset.feature_names)
```

3. To evaluate the effect of the transformation on the variable distribution, we'll create a function that takes a dataframe and a variable name as inputs and plots a histogram next to a Q-Q plot:

```
def diagnostic_plots(df, variable):
    plt.figure(figsize=(15,6))
    plt.subplot(1, 2, 1)
    df[variable].hist(bins=30)
    plt.subplot(1, 2, 2)
    stats.probplot(df[variable], dist="norm", plot=plt)
    plt.show()
```

4. Now, let's plot the distribution of the `DIS` variable:

```
diagnostic_plots(data, 'DIS')
```

`DIS` is not normally distributed, as shown in the following output:

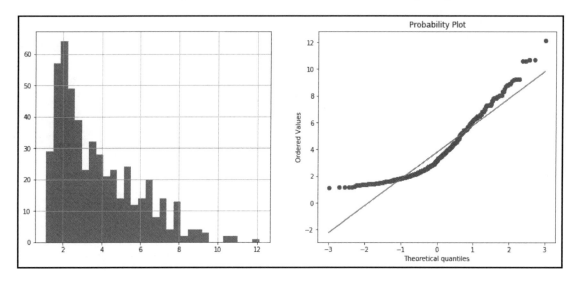

Now, let's apply the reciprocal transformation with NumPy.

5. First, let's make a copy of the original dataframe using pandas `copy()` so that we can modify the values in the copy and not in the original dataframe, which we need for the rest of this recipe:

```
data_tf = data.copy()
```

Remember that executing `data_tf = data`, instead of using pandas `copy()`, creates an additional view of the same data. Therefore, changes that are made in `data_tf` will be reflected in the data as well.

6. Using NumPy, we'll apply the reciprocal transformation to a group of variables:

```
data_tf[['LSTAT', 'NOX', 'DIS', 'RM']] =
np.reciprocal(data[['LSTAT', 'NOX', 'DIS', 'RM']])
```

7. Let's check the distribution of the `DIS` variable **after** the transformation with the diagnostic function we created in *step 3*:

```
diagnostic_plots(data_tf, 'DIS')
```

The transformed `DIS` distribution can be seen in the plots that are returned by the preceding code block:

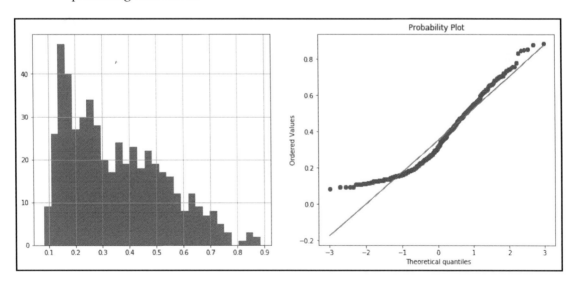

Now, let's apply reciprocal transformation with scikit-learn.

8. Let's create a transformer using `FunctionTransformer()` by passing `np.reciprocal` as an argument:

```
transformer = FunctionTransformer(np.reciprocal)
```

`FunctionTransformer()` doesn't need to be fit before transforming the data since there are no parameters to be learned from the train set.

9. Now, let's transform a group of variables from the dataset:

```
data_tf = transformer.transform(data[['LSTAT', 'NOX', 'DIS', 'RM']])
```

Note that `data_tf` is a NumPy array with **only** the transformed variables.

If we want to retain the original variables in the final output, we can create a copy of the original dataframe, like we did in *step 5*, and then execute `data_tf[['LSTAT', 'NOX', 'DIS', 'RM']] = transformer.transform(data[['LSTAT', 'NOX', 'DIS', 'RM']])`.

Now, let's apply the reciprocal transformation with Feature-engine.

10. Here, we'll call `ReciprocalTransformer()`, indicate the variables to transform, and then fit it to the dataset:

```
rt = ReciprocalTransformer(variables = ['LSTAT', 'NOX', 'DIS', 'RM'])
rt.fit(data)
```

If the `variables` argument is `None`, the transformer identifies and applies the reciprocal function to **all the numerical variables** in the dataset. If some of the variables contain the value zero, this will return an error.

11. Let's transform the selected variables in our dataset:

```
data_tf = rt.transform(data)
```

`ReciprocalTransformer()` will return a pandas dataframe with the original variables, where the variables indicated in 10 are transformed with the reciprocal function.

How it works...

In this recipe, we applied the reciprocal transformation to a group of variables using NumPy, scikit-learn, and Feature-engine. To determine the effect of the transformation, we created a diagnostic function to plot a histogram next to a Q-Q plot for a given variable. For more details on *step 1* to *step 3*, check out the *Transforming variables with the logarithm* recipe, earlier in this chapter.

Utilizing the diagnostic plot function, we plotted the histogram and Q-Q plot of the DIS variable and observed that it wasn't normally distributed: most of its values were at the left of the histogram and they deviated from the 45-degree line at both ends of the distribution in the Q-Q plot.

To apply the reciprocal transformation with NumPy, we used the `reciprocal()` method on a slice of the dataset with the variables to be transformed. Then, we utilized the diagnostic plot function to plot the histogram and Q-Q plot of the transformed DIS variable. We observed that the transformed DIS was not normally distributed, but there was an improvement in the value spread across a greater range: more values were now toward the center of the histogram and deviated from the 45-degree red line toward the higher values of the distribution in the Q-Q plot.

To apply the reciprocal transformation using scikit-learn's `FunctionTransformer()`, we called the transformer and passed NumPy's `reciprocal()` as an argument. The `transform()` method returned in a NumPy array **only** the transformed variables.

Finally, we used Feature-engine's `ReciprocalTransformer()` and specified the variables to transform in a list. The `fit()` method checked that the variables were numerical, while the `transform()` method called NumPy `reciprocal()` to transform the variables, returning a pandas dataframe. The returned dataframe contained all the variables in the original data, where the variables indicated in the list that were transformed with the reciprocal function.

See also

For more details about the methods and transformers that were used in this recipe, take a look at the following links:

- NumPy's `reciprocal()`: `https://docs.scipy.org/doc/numpy/reference/generated/numpy.reciprocal.html`
- Scikit-learn's `FunctionTransformer()`: `https://scikit-learn.org/stable/modules/generated/sklearn.preprocessing.FunctionTransformer.html`
- Feature-engine's `ReciprocalTransformer()`: `https://feature-engine.readthedocs.io/en/latest/vartransformers/ReciprocalTransformer.html`

Using square and cube root to transform variables

The square and cube root transformations are two specific forms of power transformations where the exponents are 1/2 and 1/3, respectively. In this recipe, we will implement square and cube root transformations using NumPy and scikit-learn.

 The square root transformation is not defined for negative values, so make sure you only transform those variables whose values are >=0; otherwise, you will introduce NaN or receive an error message.

How to do it...

Let's begin by importing the necessary libraries and getting the dataset ready:

1. Import the required Python libraries and classes:

```
import numpy as np
import pandas as pd
from sklearn.datasets import load_boston
from sklearn.preprocessing import FunctionTransformer
```

2. Let's load the Boston House Prices dataset into a pandas dataframe:

```
boston_dataset = load_boston()
data = pd.DataFrame(boston_dataset.data,
columns=boston_dataset.feature_names)
```

Now, let's make a square root transformation using NumPy.

3. First, let's make a copy of the original dataframe using pandas `copy()`:

```
data_tf = data.copy()
```

4. Let's apply the square root transformation with NumPy to a group of variables and capture it in the new dataframe:

```
data_tf[['LSTAT', 'NOX', 'DIS', 'RM']] = np.sqrt(data[['LSTAT',
'NOX', 'DIS', 'RM']])
```

5. If we want to apply the cube root transformation instead, we can do so with NumPy's `cbrt()`, like so :

```
data_tf[['LSTAT', 'NOX', 'DIS', 'RM']] = np.cbrt(data[['LSTAT',
'NOX', 'DIS', 'RM']])
```

We can check the effect of the variable transformation by using the diagnostic plot function that we described in *step 3* of the *Transforming variables with the logarithm* recipe in this chapter.

Now, let's apply the square root transformation with scikit-learn.

6. Let's create a transformer by passing NumPy's `sqrt()` as an argument:

```
transformer = FunctionTransformer(np.sqrt)
```

If we want to perform the cube root transformation, we need to set up the transformer using `transformer = FunctionTransformer(np.cbrt)`.

7. Now, let's transform a subset of variables from the dataset:

```
data_tf = transformer.transform(data[['LSTAT', 'NOX', 'DIS',
'RM']])
```

To transform the returned NumPy array into a pandas dataframe, we can use the `data_tf = pd.DataFrame(data_tf, columns=[LSTAT', 'NOX', 'DIS', 'RM'])` command.

8. If we want to capture the transformed variables within the original dataset, we can do so as follows:

```
data_tf = data.copy()
data_tf[['LSTAT', 'NOX', 'DIS', 'RM']] =
transformer.transform(data[['LSTAT', 'NOX', 'DIS', 'RM']])
```

The preceding code block returns a pandas dataframe with the original variables. However, the `LSTAT`, `NOX`, `DIS`, and `RM` variables are transformed with the square root.

How it works...

In this recipe, we applied the square and cube root transformations to variables in the Boston House Prices dataset using NumPy and scikit-learn.

To apply the square or cube root transformations with NumPy, we created a copy of the original dataframe with pandas `copy()` and then used `sqrt()` or `cbrt()` on a slice of the dataset with the variables to be transformed. This procedure returned a pandas dataframe with the original variables, while `LSTAT`, `NOX`, `DIS`, and `RM` were transformed with the square root.

To apply the square root transformation with scikit-learn, we used `FunctionTransformer()`, which applies a user-defined function – in this case, `np.sqrt` – to a dataset and returns the result in a NumPy array. The `transform()` method applied `np.sqrt()` to a slice of the dataset and returned the transformed variables in a NumPy array.

There's more...

To perform square root or cube root transformations with Feature-engine, we can follow the steps that were provided in the next, *Using power transformations on numerical variables* recipe, and define the exponents as 1/2 or 1/3, respectively. There is also an example of its application in the Jupyter Notebook for this recipe, in the accompanying GitHub repository: `https://github.com/PacktPublishing/Python-Feature-Engineering-Cookbook/blob/master/Chapter04/Recipe-3-square-cube-root.ipynb`.

Using power transformations on numerical variables

Exponential or power functions are mathematical transformations that follow $X_t = X^{lambda}$, where lambda can be any exponent. The square and cube root transformations are special cases of power transformations where lambda is 1/2 or 1/3, respectively. In practice, we try different lambdas to determine which one offers the best transformation. In this recipe, we will carry out power transformations using NumPy, scikit-learn, and Feature-engine.

How to do it...

Let's begin by importing the libraries and getting the dataset ready:

1. Import the required Python libraries and classes:

```
import numpy as np
import pandas as pd
from sklearn.datasets import load_boston
from sklearn.preprocessing import FunctionTransformer
from feature_engine.variable_transformers import PowerTransformer
```

2. Let's load the Boston House Prices dataset into a pandas dataframe:

```
boston_dataset = load_boston()
data = pd.DataFrame(boston_dataset.data,
columns=boston_dataset.feature_names)
```

Now, we need to perform power transformations using NumPy.

3. First, let's make a copy of the original dataframe using pandas `copy()` so that we can modify the values in the copy and not in the original dataframe, which we need for the rest of this recipe:

```
data_tf = data.copy()
```

Remember that executing `data_tf = data`, instead of using pandas `copy()`, creates an additional view of the same data. Therefore, changes that are made in `data_tf` will be reflected in the `data` as well.

4. Let's apply a power transformation with NumPy, where the exponent is 0.3:

```
data_tf[['LSTAT', 'NOX', 'DIS', 'RM']] = np.power(data[['LSTAT', 'NOX', 'DIS', 'RM']], 0.3)
```

With `np.power()`, we can apply any exponential transformation by changing the value of the exponent in the second position of the method.

Now, let's apply a power transformation with scikit-learn.

5. Let's call `FunctionTransformer()` while passing a power of 0.3 using `np.power` within a `lambda` function:

```
transformer = FunctionTransformer(lambda x: np.power(x, 0.3))
```

`FunctionTransformer()` from scikit-learn doesn't need to be fit to the data since there are no parameters that need to be learned.

6. Now, let's transform a group of variables:

```
data_tf = transformer.transform(data[['LSTAT', 'NOX', 'DIS', 'RM']])
```

`PowerTransformer()` returns an NumPy array with **only** the transformed variables.

Finally, let's perform an exponential transformation with Feature-engine.

7. Let's start `PowerTransformer()` with the exponent 0.3 and the variables to transform. Then, we'll fit it to the data:

```
et = PowerTransformer(variables = ['LSTAT', 'NOX', 'DIS', 'RM'], exp=0.3)
et.fit(data)
```

If we don't define the variables to transform, `PowerTransformer()` will select **all the numerical variables** in the dataframe.

8. Finally, let's transform the variables in our dataset:

```
data_tf = et.transform(data)
```

The transformer returns a dataframe with the original variables, and the four variables specified in *step 7* are transformed with the power function.

How it works...

In this recipe, we applied power transformations using NumPy, scikit-learn, and Feature-engine while using the Boston House Prices dataset from scikit-learn.

To apply exponential functions with NumPy, we created a copy of the original dataframe with pandas `copy()`. Next, we used the `power()` method on a slice of the dataset with the variables to transform and captured the transformed variables in the new dataframe. This procedure returned a pandas dataframe with the original variables, and `LSTAT`, `NOX`, `DIS`, and `RM` were transformed with a power of `0.3`.

To apply an exponential transformation with scikit-learn, we used `FunctionTransformer()`, which applies a user-defined function. We started the transformer with `np.power()` within a lambda function using `0.3` as the exponent. The `transform()` method applied the power transformation to a slice of the dataset and returned the transformed variables in a NumPy array.

Finally, we used Feature-engine's `PowerTransformer()`. We started the transformer with a list of the variables to be transformed and the exponent `0.3`. The `fit()` method checked that the indicated variables were numerical while the `transform()` method applied the transformation, returning a dataframe with the transformed variables among the original variables in the dataset.

There's more...

For an example of how to apply different power transformations to different group of variables using Feature-engine within a single pipeline, take a look at the Jupyter Notebook for this recipe in the accompanying GitHub repository: `https://github.com/PacktPublishing/Python-Feature-Engineering-Cookbook/blob/master/Chapter04/Recipe-4-power-transformation.ipynb`.

See also

For more details on the classes and methods that were used in this recipe, take a look at the following links:

- NumPy's `power()`: https://docs.scipy.org/doc/numpy/reference/generated/numpy.power.html
- Feature-engine's `PowerTransformer()`: https://feature-engine.readthedocs.io/en/latest/vartransformers/PowerTransformer.html

Performing Box-Cox transformation on numerical variables

The Box-Cox transformation belongs to the power family of functions and is defined by $\frac{X^\lambda - 1}{\lambda}$ if $X > 0$ or $log(X)$ if $X = 0$, where X is the variable and λ is the transformation parameter. In the Box-Cox transformation, several values of λ are considered and the λ that returns the best transformation is selected. In this recipe, we will perform Box-Cox transformation using SciPy, scikit-learn, and Feature-engine.

The Box-Cox transformation can only be used on positive variables. If your variables have negative values, try the Yeo-Johnson transformation, which is described in the next recipe, *Performing Yeo-Johnson transformation on numerical variables*.

How to do it...

Let's begin by importing the necessary libraries and getting the dataset ready:

1. Import the required Python libraries and classes:

```
import numpy as np
import pandas as pd
import scipy.stats as stats
from sklearn.datasets import load_boston
from sklearn.preprocessing import PowerTransformer
from feature_engine.variable_transformers import BoxCoxTransformer
```

2. Let's load the Boston House Prices dataset into a pandas dataframe:

```
boston_dataset = load_boston()
data = pd.DataFrame(boston_dataset.data,
columns=boston_dataset.feature_names)
```

Now, let's perform the Box-Cox transformation using `scipy.stats`.

3. First, let's make a copy of the original dataframe using pandas `copy()` so that we can modify the values in the copy and not in the original dataframe:

```
data_tf = data.copy()
```

4. Let's apply the Box-Cox transformation with SciPy to the `LSTAT` variable:

```
data_tf['LSTAT'], param = stats.boxcox(data['LSTAT'])
```

 `scipy.stats.boxcox()` can only be applied to one-dimensional data, and returns two parameters: the transformed variable and the optimal lambda for the transformation, which we capture in the `param` variable.

5. Let's print the optimal lambda that we identified for the Box-Cox transformation of `LSTAT`:

```
print('Optimal λ: ', param)
```

The following output shows the best lambda for this:

```
Optimal λ:   0.22776736744327938
```

 We can check the effect of the variable transformation by using the diagnostic plot function that we described in *step 3* of the *Transforming variables with the logarithm* recipe of this chapter.

Now, let's apply the Box-Cox transformation using scikit-learn.

6. Let's start `PowerTransformer()` by specifying Box-Cox as an argument:

```
transformer = PowerTransformer(method='box-cox', standardize=False)
```

7. Let's create a list with the variables we want to transform and then fit the transformer to the slice of the dataset that contains these variables:

```
cols = ['LSTAT', 'NOX', 'DIS', 'RM']
transformer.fit(data[cols])
```

 Remember that the parameters need to be learned from the train set and used to transform the train and test sets. Due to this, you should divide your data into train and test sets before fitting `PowerTransformer()`.

8. Now, let's transform the dataset:

```
data_tf = transformer.transform(data[cols])
```

Scikit-learn returns a NumPy array with the transformed variables, which we can convert into a pandas dataframe by executing `data_tf = pd.DataFrame(data_tf, columns=cols)`.

 Scikit-learn's `PowerTransformer()` stores the learned lambdas in its `lambdas_` attribute, which you can display by executing `transformer.lambdas_`.

Now, let's implement the Box-Cox transformation with Feature-engine.

9. Let's start `BoxCoxTransformer()` by specifying the variables to transform in a list and then fit it to the dataset:

```
bct = BoxCoxTransformer(variables = ['LSTAT', 'NOX', 'DIS', 'RM'])
bct.fit(data)
```

10. Now, we'll transform the indicated variables in our data:

```
data_tf = bct.transform(data)
```

 Note that, compared to `PowerTransformer()` from scikit-learn, `BoxCoxTransformer()` from Feature-engine can take the entire dataframe as input, but it will only transform the variables that are specified when we start the transformer.

Feature-engine's transformer returns a dataframe with the original variables where those indicated in *step 9* were transformed by Box-Cox.

11. The optimal lambdas for each variable are stored in the `lambda_dict_` attribute. Let's inspect them:

```
bct.lambda_dict_
```

The output of the precedent line of code is as follows:

```
{'LSTAT': 0.22776736744327938,
 'NOX': -0.9156121057973192,
 'DIS': -0.1556058423249141,
 'RM': 0.44895976107977725}
```

Now, you've learned how to implement the Box-Cox transformation with three different Python libraries.

How it works...

In this recipe, we applied the Box-Cox transformation using SciPy, scikit-learn, and Feature-engine to a subset of variables of the Boston House Prices dataset. To transform the variables with SciPy, we applied the `stats.boxcox()` method to the `LSTAT` variable and obtained the transformed variable and the optimal lambda for the transformation.

> The `stats.boxcox()` method operates on one-dimensional data, so we need to transform each variable individually.

To apply the Box-Cox transformation with scikit-learn, we used `PowerTransformer()`. Scikit-learn's `PowerTransformer()` can apply both Box-Cox and Yeo-Johnson transformations, so we needed to specify the method when we created the transformer. In this case, we passed the `box-cox` string. The `standardize` argument allowed us to determine whether we wanted to standardize (scale) the transformed values. Next, we fit the transformer to the slice of the dataframe that contained the variables to be transformed so that the transformer learned the optimal lambdas for each variable. `PowerTransformer()` stored the learned lambdas in its `lambdas_` attribute. Finally, we used the `transform()` method on the slice of the dataset to return the transformed variables in a NumPy array.

Finally, we applied the Box-Cox transformation using Feature-engine. We initialized `BoxCoxTransformer()` and specified the variables to be transformed into a list. We fit the transformer to the data so that it learned the optimal lambdas per variable, which were stored in the `lambda_dict_`, and transformed the desired variables using the `transform()` method. Feature-engine's `BoxCoxTransformer()` can take the entire dataframe as input, but it will only transform the indicated variables, returning the entire dataframe with the subset of the variables that were transformed.

See also

For more details on the classes and methods that were used in this recipe, take a look at the following links:

- `scipy.stats.boxcox()`: https://docs.scipy.org/doc/scipy/reference/generated/scipy.stats.boxcox.html
- Scikit-learn's `PowerTransformer()`: https://scikit-learn.org/stable/modules/generated/sklearn.preprocessing.PowerTransformer.html.
- Feature-engine's `BoxCoxTransformer()`: https://feature-engine.readthedocs.io/en/latest/vartransformers/BoxCoxTransformer.html

Performing Yeo-Johnson transformation on numerical variables

The Yeo-Johnson transformation is an extension of the Box-Cox transformation and can be used on variables with zero and negative values, as well as positive values. These transformations can be defined as follows:

- $\dfrac{(X+1)^{\lambda} - 1}{\lambda}$; if λ is not 0 and X >= zero
- $\ln(X+1)$; if λ is zero and X >= zero
- $\dfrac{(-X+1)^{2-\lambda} - 1}{2-\lambda}$; if λ is not 2 and X is negative
- $-\ln(-X+1)$; if λ is 2 and X is negative

In this recipe, we will perform the Yeo-Johnson transformation using SciPy, scikit-learn, and Feature-engine.

How to do it...

Let's begin by importing the necessary libraries and getting the dataset ready:

1. Import the required Python libraries and classes:

```
import numpy as np
import pandas as pd
import scipy.stats as stats
from sklearn.datasets import load_boston
from sklearn.preprocessing import PowerTransformer
from feature_engine.variable_transformers import
YeoJohnsonTransformer
```

2. Let's load the Boston House Prices dataset into a pandas dataframe:

```
boston_dataset = load_boston()
data = pd.DataFrame(boston_dataset.data,
columns=boston_dataset.feature_names)
```

Now, let's apply the Yeo-Johnson transformation using SciPy.

3. First, let's make a copy of the original dataframe with pandas `copy()` so that we can modify the values in the copy and not in the original dataframe:

```
data_tf = data.copy()
```

4. Let's apply the Yeo-Johnson transformation using SciPy to the LSTAT variable:

```
data_tf['LSTAT'], param = stats.yeojohnson(data['LSTAT'])
```

 `scipy.stats.yeojohnson()` can only be applied to one-dimensional data and returns two parameters: the transformed variable and the optimal lambda for the transformation, which we capture in the `param` variable.

5. Let's inspect the optimal lambda for the transformation:

```
print('Optimal λ: ', param)
```

The output of the preceding code is as follows:

```
Optimal λ:   0.15370552301825943
```

We can check the effect of the variable transformation wi
function that we described in *step 3* of the *Transforming va*
logarithm recipe.

Now, let's apply the Yeo-Johnson transformation with scikit-l

6. Let's initialize `PowerTransformer()` by passing the `yeo-jo`
   method:

   ```
   transformer = PowerTransformer(method='yeo-johnson')
   ```

7. Let's create a list with the variables we want to transform and then fit the
   transformer to the slice of the dataset that contains these variables:

   ```
   cols = ['LSTAT', 'NOX', 'DIS', 'RM']
   transformer.fit(data[cols])
   ```

Remember that the parameters for the Yeo-Johnson transformation should
only be learned using the train set, so you must divide your dataset into
train and test sets before fitting the transformer.

8. Now, let's transform the dataset to return a NumPy array with the transformed
   variables:

   ```
   data_tf = transformer.transform(data[cols])
   ```

`PowerTransformer()` stores the learned parameters in its attribute
lambda, which you can return by executing `transformer.lambda_`.

Finally, let's implement the Yeo-Johnson transformation with Feature-engine.

9. We'll initialize `YeoJohnsonTransformer()` by specifying which variables to transform and then fit it to the dataset:

```
yjt = YeoJohnsonTransformer(variables = ['LSTAT', 'NOX', 'DIS',
'RM'])
yjt.fit(data)
```

If the `variables` argument is left as `None`, the transformer selects and transforms **all the numerical variables** in the dataset.

Note that, compared to `PowerTransformer()` from scikit-learn, the Feature-engine's transformer can take the entire dataframe as an argument of the `fit()` method.

10. Let's transform the specified variables in our data:

```
data_tf = yjt.transform(data)
```

11. `YeoJohnsonTrasnformer()` stores the best parameters per variable in its `lambda_dict_` attribute, which we can print as follows:

```
yjt.lambda_dict_
```

The preceding code outputs the following dictionary:

```
{'LSTAT': 0.15370552301825943,
 'NOX': -3.9737110448770623,
 'DIS': -0.4488719212889845,
 'RM': 0.3329865194470187}
```

Now, you've learned how to implement the Yeo-Johnson transformation with three different libraries: SciPy, scikit-learn, and Feature-engine.

How it works...

In this recipe, we applied the Yeo-Johnson transformation using SciPy, scikit-learn, and Feature-engine to a subset of variables of the Boston House Prices dataset. To transform the variables with SciPy, we applied the `stats.yeojohnson()` method to the `LSTAT` variable and obtained both the transformed variable and the optimal lambda for the transformation.

The `statsyeojohnson()` method operates on one-dimensional data, so we need to transform each variable individually.

To apply the Yeo-Johsnon transformation with scikit-learn, we used `PowerTransformer()`. Scikit-learn's `PowerTransformer()` can apply both Box-Cox and Yeo-Johnson transformations, so we specified the transformation with the `yeo-johnson` string. The `standardize` argument allowed us to determine whether we wanted to standardize (scale) the transformed values. Next, we fit the transformer to the slice of the dataframe that contained the variables to be transformed so that the transformer learned the optimal lambdas for each variable. `PowerTransformer()` stored the learned lambdas in its `lambdas_` attribute. Finally, we used the `transform()` method on the slice of the dataset to return the transformed variables in a NumPy array.

Finally, we applied the Yeo-Johnson transformation using Feature-engine. We initialized `YeoJohnsonTransformer()` and specified the variables to be transformed into a list. We fit the transformer to the data so that it learned the optimal lambdas per variable, which were stored in `lambda_dict_`, and finally transformed the desired variables using the `transform()` method. Feature-engine's `YeoJohnnsonTransformer()` can take the entire dataframe as input, but it will only transform the specified variables, thus returning the entire dataframe with the variables transformed.

See also

For more details on the classes and methods that were used in this recipe, take a look at the following links:

- `scipy.stats.yeojohnson()`: https://docs.scipy.org/doc/scipy/reference/generated/scipy.stats.yeojohnson.html
- Scikit-learn's `PowerTransformer()`: https://scikit-learn.org/stable/modules/generated/sklearn.preprocessing.PowerTransformer.html.
- Feature-engine's `YeoJohnsonTransformer()`: https://feature-engine.readthedocs.io/en/latest/vartransformers/YeoJohnsonTransformer.html

5
Performing Variable Discretization

Discretization, or binning, is the process of transforming continuous variables into discrete variables by creating a set of contiguous intervals, also called bins, that span the range of the variable values. Discretization is used to change the distribution of skewed variables and to minimize the influence of outliers, and hence improve the performance of some machine learning models.

How does discretization minimize the effect of outliers? Discretization places outliers into the lower or higher intervals, together with the remaining *inlier* values of the distribution. Hence, these outlier observations no longer differ from the rest of the values at the tails of the distribution, as they are now all together in the same interval or bin. Also, if sorting observations across bins with equal frequency, discretization spreads the values of a skewed variable more homogeneously across the value range.

In this chapter, we will discuss supervised and unsupervised approaches to transform continuous variables into discrete ones. Unsupervised discretization methods do not use any information, other than the variable distribution, to create the contiguous bins. Supervised methods, on the other hand, use target information to create the intervals.

This chapter will cover the following recipes:

- Dividing the variable into intervals of equal width
- Sorting the variable values in intervals of equal frequency
- Performing discretization followed by categorical encoding
- Allocating the variable values in arbitrary intervals
- Performing discretization with k-means clustering
- Using decision trees for discretization

Technical requirements

We will use the following Python libraries: pandas, NumPy, Matplotlib, scikit-learn, and Feature-engine. In the *Technical requirements* section of `Chapter 1`, *Foreseeing Variable Problems in Building ML Models*, you will find instructions on how to install these libraries. To install Feature-engine, you can use `pip`: `pip install feature-engine`. Throughout the recipes, we will use the Boston House Prices dataset from scikit-learn, which contains no missing data.

 To perform discretization in your own datasets, make sure you impute missing data with any of the techniques covered in `Chapter 2`, *Imputing Missing Data*.

Dividing the variable into intervals of equal width

In equal-width discretization, the variable values are sorted into intervals of the same width. The number of intervals is decided arbitrarily and the width is determined by the range of values of the variable and the number of bins to create, so for the variable *X*, the interval width is given as follows:

$$Width = \frac{Max(X) - Min(X)}{Bins}$$

For example, if the values of the variable vary between 0 and 100, we can create five bins like this: *width = (100-0) / 5 = 20*; the bins will be 0-20, 20-40, 40-60, 80-100. The first and final bins (0-20 and 80-100) can be expanded to accommodate outliers, that is, values under 0 or greater than 100 would be placed in those bins as well, by extending the limits to minus and plus infinity.

In this recipe, we will carry out equal-width discretization using pandas, scikit-learn, and Feature-engine.

How to do it...

Let's first import the necessary Python libraries and get the dataset ready:

1. Import the required Python libraries and classes:

```
import numpy as np
import pandas as pd
import matplotlib.pyplot as plt
from sklearn.datasets import load_boston
from sklearn.model_selection import train_test_split
from sklearn.preprocessing import KBinsDiscretizer
from feature_engine.discretisers import EqualWidthDiscretiser
```

2. Let's load the predictor and target variables of the Boston House Prices dataset in a dataframe:

```
boston_dataset = load_boston()
data = pd.DataFrame(boston_dataset.data,
columns=boston_dataset.feature_names)
data['MEDV'] = boston_dataset.target
```

The boundaries for the intervals should be learned using variables in the train set only, and then used to discretize the variables in train and test sets.

3. Let's divide the data into train and test sets and their targets:

```
X_train, X_test, y_train, y_test = train_test_split(
    data.drop('MEDV', axis=1), data['MEDV'], test_size=0.3,
    random_state=0)
```

We will divide the LSTAT continuous variable into 10 intervals. The width of the intervals is given by the value range divided by the number of intervals.

4. Let's calculate the range of the LSTAT variable, that is, the difference between its maximum and minimum values:

```
lstat_range = X_train['LSTAT'].max() - X_train['LSTAT'].min()
lstat_range
```

The preceding code outputs the range of LSTAT:

```
35.25
```

5. Let's determine the interval width, which is the variable's value range divided by the number of bins:

```
inter_width = int(lstat_range / 10)
```

The value of `lstat_range` divided by ten is `3.525`. With `int()`, we capture the integer part of the number, which is `3`.

6. Let's capture in new variables, the rounded minimum and maximum values of `LSTAT`:

```
min_value = int(np.floor( X_train['LSTAT'].min()))
max_value = int(np.ceil( X_train['LSTAT'].max()))
```

7. Let's print the minimum and maximum values and the interval width captured in *step 5* and *step 6*:

```
print(min_value, max_value, inter_width)
```

The output of the preceding code block is as follows:

```
(1, 37, 3)
```

To divide a pandas Series into intervals, we will use pandas' `cut()` method, which takes as arguments the limits of the intervals.

8. Let's create a list with the interval limits using list comprehension and print out the limits:

```
intervals = [i for i in range(min_value, max_value + inter_width,
inter_width)]
intervals
```

The output of the preceding block provides the limits that we need to pass to pandas' `cut()` method:

```
[1, 4, 7, 10, 13, 16, 19, 22, 25, 28, 31, 34, 37]
```

9. Let's discretize `LSTAT` and capture the discretized variable in a new column in the dataframe:

```
X_train['lstat_disc'] = pd.cut(x=X_train['LSTAT'], bins=intervals,
include_lowest=True)
```

We set `include_lowest=True` to include the lowest value in the first interval.

10. Let's print the top 10 observations of the discretized and original variable, side by side:

```
print(X_train[['LSTAT', 'lstat_disc']].head(10))
```

We can see in the output that the `34.41` value was allocated to the interval 34-37, the `7.73` value was allocated to the interval 7-10, and so on:

```
        LSTAT    lstat_disc
141     34.41   (34.0, 37.0]
272      7.73    (7.0, 10.0]
135     16.96   (16.0, 19.0]
298      4.97     (4.0, 7.0]
122     17.93   (16.0, 19.0]
22      18.72   (16.0, 19.0]
68      13.09   (13.0, 16.0]
20      21.02   (19.0, 22.0]
437     26.45   (25.0, 28.0]
14      10.26   (10.0, 13.0]
```

In equal-width discretization, there is usually a different number of observations per interval.

11. Let's calculate the number of observations per interval:

```
X_train.groupby('lstat_disc')['LSTAT'].count()
```

In the output of the preceding code, we can see that different intervals have a different number of observations:

```
(4.0, 7.0]      67
(7.0, 10.0]     63
(10.0, 13.0]    49
(16.0, 19.0]    45
(13.0, 16.0]    44
(0.999, 4.0]    28
(19.0, 22.0]    21
(22.0, 25.0]    17
(28.0, 31.0]     9
(25.0, 28.0]     7
(34.0, 37.0]     4
(31.0, 34.0]     0
```

12. Now, let's discretize LSTAT in the test set using pandas' cut () method:

```
X_test['lstat_disc'] = pd.cut(x=X_test['LSTAT'], bins=intervals,
include_lowest=True)
```

If the variable distribution in the train and test sets are similar, we should expect a similar proportion of observations across the LSTAT intervals in the train and test sets.

13. Let's plot the proportion of observations across LSTAT intervals in the train and test sets:

```
t1 = X_train['lstat_disc'].value_counts() / len(X_train)
t2 = X_test['lstat_disc'].value_counts() / len(X_test)

tmp = pd.concat([t1, t2], axis=1)
tmp.columns = ['train', 'test']
tmp.plot.bar()
plt.xticks(rotation=45)
plt.ylabel('Number of observations per bin')
```

We can see in the output that the proportion of observations per interval is approximately the same in the train and test sets:

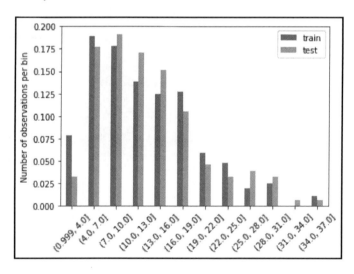

With Feature-engine, we can perform equal-width discretization in fewer lines of code and for many variables at a time. Let's first divide the data into train and test sets, as in *step 3*. Next, let's set up a discretizer.

14. Let's create an equal-width discretizer to sort 3 continuous variables into 10 intervals:

    ```
    disc = EqualWidthDiscretiser(bins=10, variables = ['LSTAT', 'DIS',
    'RM'])
    ```

15. Let's fit the discretizer to the train set so that the transformer learns the interval limits for each variable:

    ```
    disc.fit(X_train)
    ```

We can inspect the limits of the intervals in the `disc.binner_dict_` attribute.

16. Let's transform the variables in the train and test sets, that is, let's sort their values into bins:

    ```
    train_t = disc.transform(X_train)
    test_t = disc.transform(X_test)
    ```

    `EqualWidthDiscretiser()` returns a dataframe where the indicated variables are discretized.

`EqualWidthDiscretiser()` returns a digit indicating whether the value was sorted in the first, second, or tenth bin. If we want to return the bins as an object, we need to indicate `return_object=True` when we set up the discretizer in *step 14*.

Let's now do equal-width discretization with scikit-learn. First, let's divide the original data into train and test sets, as in *step 3*. Next, we set up a discretizer.

17. Let's create an equal-width discretizer with scikit-learn by setting its `strategy` to `uniform`:

    ```
    disc = KBinsDiscretizer(n_bins=10, encode='ordinal',
    strategy='uniform')
    ```

18. Let's fit the discretizer to the train set so that the transformer learns the interval limits for each variable:

```
disc.fit(X_train[['LSTAT', 'DIS', 'RM']])
```

 Scikit-learn's `KBinsDiscretiser()` will discretize all of the variables in the dataset, so we need to use the transformer only on the slice of the dataframe that contains the variables to discretize.

19. Finally, let's transform the train and test sets:

```
train_t = disc.transform(X_train[['LSTAT', 'DIS', 'RM']])
test_t = disc.transform(X_test[['LSTAT', 'DIS', 'RM']])
```

 We can inspect the bin boundaries learned by the transformer by executing `disc.bin_edges_`.

Remember that scikit-learn returns NumPy arrays. To convert the array into a pandas dataframe, we can execute `train_t = pd.DataFrame(train_t, columns = ['LSTAT', 'DIS', 'RM'])`.

How it works...

In this recipe, we performed equal-width discretization, that is, we sorted the variable values into equidistant intervals. We arbitrarily defined the number of bins as 10 and then calculated the difference between the maximum and minimum value of the `LSTAT` variable, using the pandas `max()` and `min()` methods. With NumPy's `floor()` and `ceil()` methods, we obtained the rounded-down or rounded-up minimum and maximum values, respectively. We then estimated the interval length by dividing the value range, that is, the maximum minus the minimum values, by the number of bins. Finally, we captured the interval limits in a list, utilizing the minimum and maximum values, and the interval width within a list comprehension.

To discretize the `LSTAT` variable, we used the pandas `cut()` method and the interval limits that we created with the list comprehension, to allocate the variable values into each interval. We then used pandas' `value_counts()` method to count the number of observations per interval.

To compare the distribution of observations in the equal-width intervals in train and test sets, we produced a bar plot with the percentage of observations per interval in each dataset. To create this plot, we used pandas' `value_counts()` method to count the number of observations per interval and divided these counts by the total number of observations in the train or test sets, which we calculated using Python's built-in `len()` method, to determine the percentage of observations per interval. To plot these proportions, we first concatenated the train and test series using pandas' `concat()` in a temporary dataframe, and then we assigned the column names of `train` and `test` to it. Finally, we used pandas' `plot.bar()` to display a bar plot. We rotated the labels with Matplotlib's `xticks()` method and added the *y* legend with `ylabel()`.

To perform equal-width discretization with Feature-engine, we used `EqualWidthDiscretiser()` and indicated the number of bins and the variables to discretize as arguments. Using the `fit()` method and passing the train set as an argument, the discretizer learned the interval limits for each variable. With the `transform()` method, the discretizer sorted the values to each bin. The discretized variable values were digits, representing the bins to which the original values were allocated.

Finally, we discretized three continuous variables into equal-width bins with `KBinsDiscretizer()` from scikit-learn, indicating the number of bins as an argument and setting `strategy` to `uniform`. With the `fit()` method and the train set as an argument, the transformer learned the limits of the intervals for each variable in the dataframe, and with the `transform()` method, the transformer sorted the values into each interval, returning a NumPy array with the discretized variables. The values of the discretized variables are also digits representing the intervals.

See also

You can learn more about discretization with scikit-learn on the following web pages:

- https://scikit-learn.org/stable/modules/generated/sklearn.preprocessing.KBinsDiscretizer.html
- http://scikit-learn.org/stable/auto_examples/preprocessing/plot_discretization.html

To learn more about Feature-engine's discretizer, visit https://feature-engine.readthedocs.io/en/latest/discretisers/EqualWidthDiscretiser.html.

Sorting the variable values in intervals of equal frequency

Equal-frequency discretization divides the values of the variable into intervals that carry the same proportion of observations. The interval width is determined by quantiles, and therefore different intervals may have different widths. In summary, equal-frequency discretization using quantiles consists of dividing the continuous variable into N quantiles, with N to be defined by the user. This discretization technique is particularly useful for skewed variables as it spreads the observations over the different bins equally. In this recipe, we will perform equal-frequency discretization using pandas, scikit-learn, and Feature-engine.

How to do it...

Let's first import the necessary Python libraries and get the dataset ready:

1. Import the required Python libraries and classes:

```
import pandas as pd
from sklearn.datasets import load_boston
from sklearn.model_selection import train_test_split
from sklearn.preprocessing import KBinsDiscretizer
from feature_engine.discretisers import EqualFrequencyDiscretiser
```

2. Let's load the predictor and target variables of the Boston House Prices dataset into a dataframe:

```
boston_dataset = load_boston()
data = pd.DataFrame(boston_dataset.data,
columns=boston_dataset.feature_names)
data['MEDV'] = boston_dataset.target
```

The boundaries for the intervals, that is, the quantiles, should be learned using variables in the train set, and then used to discretize the variables in train and test sets.

3. Let's divide the data into train and test sets:

```
X_train, X_test, y_train, y_test = train_test_split(
    data.drop('MEDV', axis=1), data['MEDV'], test_size=0.3,
    random_state=0)
```

4. To divide the `LSTAT` variable into 10 quantiles, we use pandas `qcut()`, which returns both the discretized variable and the quantile limits, which we capture as a column of the dataframe and an individual variable, respectively:

```
X_train['lstat_disc'], intervals = pd.qcut(X_train['LSTAT'], 10,
labels=None, retbins=True)
```

If we print the values of `intervals` with the `print(intervals)` command, we obtain the following output:

```
array([ 1.73 ,  4.623,  6.202,  7.528,  9.5  , 11.16 , 13.26 ,
15.565, 18.06 , 22.453, 36.98 ])
```

5. Let's print the top 10 observations of the discretized and original variable, side by side:

```
print(X_train[['LSTAT', 'lstat_disc']].head(10))
```

We can see in the output that the `34.41` value was allocated to the interval 22-36, the `7.73` value was allocated to the interval 7.5-9.5, and so on:

```
        LSTAT       lstat_disc
141     34.41   (22.453, 36.98]
272      7.73      (7.528, 9.5]
135     16.96   (15.565, 18.06]
298      4.97    (4.623, 6.202]
122     17.93   (15.565, 18.06]
22      18.72   (18.06, 22.453]
68      13.09    (11.16, 13.26]
20      21.02   (18.06, 22.453]
437     26.45   (22.453, 36.98]
14      10.26      (9.5, 11.16]
```

6. Let's determine the proportion of observations per bin:

```
X_train['lstat_disc'].value_counts() / len(X_train)
```

Note how different intervals have a similar proportion of observations in the output of the preceding code block:

```
(7.528, 9.5]        0.104520
(22.453, 36.98]     0.101695
(15.565, 18.06]     0.101695
(13.26, 15.565]     0.101695
(1.729, 4.623]      0.101695
(11.16, 13.26]      0.098870
(6.202, 7.528]      0.098870
```

```
(4.623, 6.202]        0.098870
(18.06, 22.453]       0.096045
(9.5, 11.16]          0.096045
```

7. Now, let's discretize `LSTAT` in the test set, using pandas' `cut()` method and the interval limits determined in *step 4*:

```
X_test['lstat_disc'] = pd.cut(x = X_test['LSTAT'], bins=intervals)
```

> We can compare the distribution of observations in the discretized variables of the train and test sets, as we did in *step 13* of the *Dividing the variable into intervals of equal width* recipe.

With Feature-engine, we can perform equal-frequency discretization in fewer steps and for many variables at the time. Let's first divide the data into train and test sets like in *step 3*. Next, let's set up a discretizer.

8. Let's create an equal-frequency discretizer to sort the values of three continuous variables into 10 quantiles:

```
disc = EqualFrequencyDiscretiser(q=10, variables = ['LSTAT', 'DIS',
'RM'])
```

9. Let's fit the discretizer to the train set so that it learns the quantile limits for each variable:

```
disc.fit(X_train)
```

> The transformer stores the limits of the intervals for each variable in a dictionary in its `disc.binner_dict_` attribute.

10. Let's transform the variables in the train and test sets:

```
train_t = disc.transform(X_train)
test_t = disc.transform(X_test)
```

> `EqualFrequencyDiscretiser()` returns a digit indicating whether the value was sorted in the first, second, or tenth bin. If we want to return the bins as an object, we should indicate `return_object=True` when we set up the discretizer in *step 8*.

Let's now do equal-frequency discretization with scikit-learn. First, let's divide the original data into train and test sets, as in *step 3*. Next, we set up a discretizer:

11. Let's create an equal-frequency discretizer by setting `strategy` to `quantile` and the number of bins to `10`:

```
disc = KBinsDiscretizer(n_bins=10, encode='ordinal',
strategy='quantile')
```

12. Let's fit the discretizer to the train set so that it learns the interval limits:

```
disc.fit(X_train[['LSTAT', 'DIS', 'RM']])
```

 Scikit-learn's `KBinsDiscretiser()` will discretize all of the variables in the dataset, so we need to use the transformer only in the slice of the dataframe that contains the variables of interest.

13. Finally, let's transform the train and test sets:

```
train_t = disc.transform(X_train[['LSTAT', 'DIS', 'RM']])
test_t = disc.transform(X_test[['LSTAT', 'DIS', 'RM']])
```

 We can inspect the bin edges with `disc.bin_edges_`.

Remember that scikit-learn returns a NumPy array, which we can convert in a pandas dataframe with this command: `train_t = pd.DataFrame(train_t, columns = ['LSTAT', 'DIS', 'RM'])`.

How it works...

With equal-frequency discretization, we sorted the variable values into intervals with a similar proportion of observations. The interval limits were determined by the quantiles. First, we arbitrarily defined the number of bins as 10. Next, we used pandas' `qcut()` method to determine the limits of the intervals and sort the `LSTAT` variable in the train set into those intervals. Next, using pandas' `cut()` method and the interval limits determined with pandas' `qcut()` method, we discretized `LSTAT` in the test set.

Finally, we used pandas `value_counts()` to count the number of observations per interval and divided it by the total number of observations, obtained with the built-in Python `len()` method, to determine the proportion of observations per interval.

To perform equal-frequency discretization with Feature-engine, we used `EqualFrequencyDiscretiser()` and indicated the number of quantiles and the variables to discretize as arguments. With the `fit()` method applied to the train set, the discretizer learned and stored the interval limits for each of the indicated variables in its `binner_dict_` attribute. With the `transform()` method, the variable values were allocated to the bins. The values of the discretized variables are digits, representing the 1st, 2nd, 3rd and so on bins.

Finally, we discretized variables with `KBinsDiscretizer()` from scikit-learn, indicating 10 as the number of bins and setting `strategy` to `quantile`. With the `fit()` method, the transformer learned and stored the limits of the intervals in its `bin_edges_` attribute, and with the `transform()` method, the discretizer sorted the values of the variables to each interval. Note that, differently from Feature-engine's `EqualFrequencyDiscteriser()`, `KBinsDiscretizer()` will transform all of the variables in the dataset.

Performing discretization followed by categorical encoding

After discretization, the intervals of the variable can be treated as a discrete numerical variable, or as categories in a categorical variable. If treated as categorical, we can follow up the discretization by reordering the intervals according to the target value, as we did in the *Encoding with integers in an ordered manner* recipe in Chapter 3, *Encoding Categorical Variables*, to create a monotonic relationship between the intervals and the target. In this recipe, we will combine these two feature engineering techniques using Feature-engine and the Boston House Prices dataset from scikit-learn.

How to do it...

To perform equal-frequency discretization followed by ordering the intervals according to the target mean, we need to import from Feature-engine the `EqualFrequencyDiscretiser()` and the `OrdinalCategoricalEncoder()`, among other Python libraries and classes:

1. Import the required Python libraries and classes:

    ```
    import pandas as pd
    import matplotlib.pyplot as plt
    from sklearn.datasets import load_boston
    from sklearn.model_selection import train_test_split
    ```

```
from feature_engine.discretisers import EqualFrequencyDiscretiser
from feature_engine.categorical_encoders import
OrdinalCategoricalEncoder
```

2. Let's load the predictor variables and target from the Boston House Prices dataset:

```
boston_dataset = load_boston()
data = pd.DataFrame(boston_dataset.data,
columns=boston_dataset.feature_names)
data['MEDV'] = boston_dataset.target
```

The interval limits and order should be learned from the train set, and then used to transform variables in both train and test sets.

3. Let's divide the data into train and test sets:

```
X_train, X_test, y_train, y_test = train_test_split(
    data.drop('MEDV', axis=1), data['MEDV'], test_size=0.3,
    random_state=0)
```

4. Let's create an equal-frequency discretizer using Feature-engine to divide three continuous variables into 10 quantiles:

```
disc = EqualFrequencyDiscretiser(q=10, variables = ['LSTAT', 'DIS',
'RM'], return_object=True)
```

With `return_object` set to `True`, the transformer will return the discretized variables cast as an object, which is needed to follow up with the ordinal encoder.

5. Let's fit the discretizer to the train set so that it learns the interval limits:

```
disc.fit(X_train)
```

6. Let's discretize the variables in the train and test sets:

```
train_t = disc.transform(X_train)
test_t = disc.transform(X_test)
```

Let's explore whether the discretized `LSTAT` variable shows a monotonic relationship with the target.

7. Let's concatenate the transformed train set with the target, and plot the target mean per interval of the variable DIS:

```
pd.concat([train_t, y_train],
axis=1).groupby('DIS')['MEDV'].mean().plot()
plt.ylabel('mean of survived')
plt.show()
```

In the output of the preceding code block, we can see that the relationship between DIS intervals and the target MEDV is not monotonic:

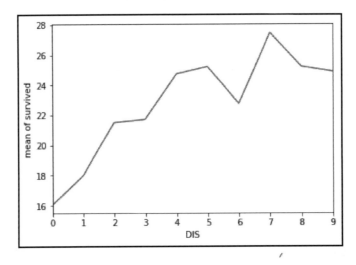

Let's now re-arrange the interval order following the target mean to create a monotonic relationship:

8. Let's create an ordinal encoder using Feature-engine:

```
enc = OrdinalCategoricalEncoder(encoding_method = 'ordered')
```

Feature-engine's `OrdinalCategoricalEncoder()` only works with variables cast as an object.

9. Let's fit the encoder to the train set with the **discretized** variables:

```
enc.fit(train_t, y_train)
```

With the `fit()` method, the encoder will order the intervals according to the mean target value per interval.

> `OrdinalCategoricalEncoder()` will automatically identify the discretized variables as categorical variables and encode them if we leave the `variables` argument set to `None` when initializing the transformer in *step 8*.

10. Let's encode the discretized variables:

```
train_t = enc.transform(train_t)
test_t = enc.transform(test_t)
```

We can execute the code in *step 7* to re-plot the discretized variable DIS versus the target and visualize the monotonic relationship, as shown in the following screenshot:

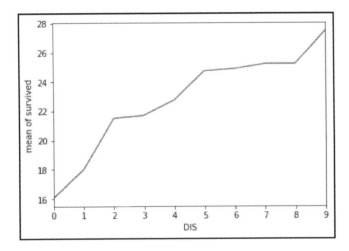

You have now learned how to combine two techniques to make variables more suitable for linear models.

How it works...

In this recipe, we first divided three variables into 10 equal-frequency intervals and then re-arranged the order of these intervals so that they displayed a monotonic relationship with the target.

To divide the variable into 10 equal-frequency intervals, we used `EqualFrequencyDiscretiser()` from Feature-engine. We passed a list of the variables to discretize, and set `return_object` to `True`, to return the discretized variables cast as an object. Then, we used `fit()` to let the transformer learn the interval boundaries and `transform()` to sort the variable values into the intervals.

To re-arrange the intervals so that they follow a monotonic relationship with the target, we used `OrdinalCategoricalEncoder()` from Feature-engine, which we described extensively in the *Encoding with integers in an ordered manner* recipe in Chapter 3, *Encoding Categorical Variables*. With the `fit()` method and passing the train set with the discrete variables and the target as arguments, the transformer learned the order of the intervals and stored it in a dictionary. With `transform()`, the transformer re-assigned the integer numbers to the intervals so that they showed a monotonic relationship with the target.

To visualize the monotonic relationship, after *step 6* and *step 10*, we calculated the mean of the target MEDV per interval of the discretized variable DIS and output a line plot utilizing pandas' `plot()` method.

See also

To learn more about Feature-engine's transformers, visit the following:

- `EqualFrequencyDiscretiser()`: https://feature-engine.readthedocs.io/en/latest/discretisers/EqualFrequencyDiscretiser.html
- `OrdinalCategoricalEncoder()`: https://feature-engine.readthedocs.io/en/latest/encoders/OrdinalCategoricalEncoder.html

Allocating the variable values in arbitrary intervals

In previous recipes, we have seen how to create intervals based on variable values and distribution. Sometimes, however, we want to divide the variables into intervals, the boundaries of which are arbitrarily determined by the user. In this recipe, we will learn how to discretize a variable into user pre-defined intervals using pandas and the Boston House Prices dataset from scikit-learn.

How to do it...

Let's first import the necessary Python libraries and get the dataset ready:

1. Import the required Python libraries and classes:

```
import numpy as np
import pandas as pd
import matplotlib.pyplot as plt
from sklearn.datasets import load_boston
from sklearn.model_selection import train_test_split
```

2. Let's load the predictor and target variables from the Boston House Prices dataset:

```
boston_dataset = load_boston()
data = pd.DataFrame(boston_dataset.data,
columns=boston_dataset.feature_names)
data['MEDV'] = boston_dataset.target
```

3. Let's divide the data into train and test sets:

```
X_train, X_test, y_train, y_test = train_test_split(
    data.drop('MEDV', axis=1), data['MEDV'], test_size=0.3,
random_state=0)
```

4. Let's plot a histogram of the LSTAT variable to find out its value range:

```
data['LSTAT'].hist(bins=30)
plt.show()
```

LSTAT values vary from 0 to approximately 40:

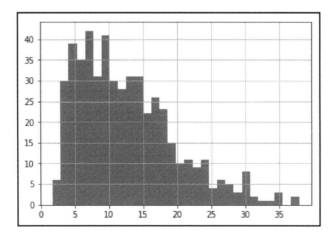

5. Let's create a list with the arbitrary interval limits, setting the upper limit to infinity to accommodate bigger values:

```
intervals = [0, 10, 20, 30, np.Inf]
```

6. Let's create a list with the interval limits as labels, that is, strings:

```
labels = ['0-10', '10-20', '20-30', '>30']
```

7. Let's discretize the LSTAT variable into the pre-defined limits we determined in *step 5*, and capture it in a new variable that takes **the label names** we created in *step 6* as values:

```
data['lstat_labels'] = pd.cut(data['LSTAT'], bins=intervals,
labels=labels, include_lowest=True)
```

8. Now, let's discretize the LSTAT variable into the pre-defined intervals and capture it in a new variable that takes the **interval limits** as values:

```
data['lstat_intervals'] = pd.cut(data['LSTAT'], bins=intervals,
labels=None, include_lowest=True)
```

The difference between *step 7* and *step 8* is that the discretized variable in *step 7* will take the label names as values, where the discretized variable in *step 8* will take the interval limits as values.

9. Let's inspect the first five rows of the original and discretized variables:

```
data[['LSTAT','lstat_labels', 'lstat_intervals']].head()
```

In the last two columns of the dataframe, we see the discretized variables; the first one with the strings we created in *step 6* as values, and the second one with the interval limits as returned by pandas' cut() method:

```
   LSTAT lstat_labels lstat_intervals
0   4.98         0-10  (-0.001, 10.0]
1   9.14         0-10  (-0.001, 10.0]
2   4.03         0-10  (-0.001, 10.0]
3   2.94         0-10  (-0.001, 10.0]
4   5.33         0-10  (-0.001, 10.0]
```

10. Finally, we can count the number of observations within each arbitrarily created interval:

```
data['lstat_intervals'].value_counts()
```

The number of observations per interval varies:

```
(-0.001, 10.0]     219
(10.0, 20.0]       213
(20.0, 30.0]        62
(30.0, inf]         12
Name: lstat_intervals, dtype: int64
```

You have now learned how to sort the values of a variable into user-defined intervals.

How it works...

We sorted the values of a variable into user-defined intervals using the Boston House Prices dataset. We first plotted a histogram of the LSTAT variable, to get an idea of the range of values of the variable. Next, we arbitrarily determined and captured the limits of the intervals in a list: we created intervals that vary from 0-10, 10-20, 20-30, and more than 30, by setting the upper limit to infinite with np.Inf. Next, we created a list with the interval names as strings.

Using pandas' cut() method and passing the list with the interval limits, we sorted the variable values into the pre-defined bins. We executed the command twice; in the first run, we set the labels argument to the list that contained the label names as strings, and in the second run, we set the labels argument to None. We captured the returned output in two variables, the first one displaying the interval limits as values and the second one with interval names as values. Finally, we counted the number of observations per variable using the pandas value_counts() method.

Performing discretization with k-means clustering

In discretization using k-means clustering, the intervals are the clusters identified by the k-means algorithm. The number of clusters (k) is defined by the user. The k-means clustering algorithm has two main steps. In the initialization step, k observations are chosen randomly as the initial centers of the k clusters, and the remaining data points are assigned to the closest cluster. In the iteration step, the centers of the clusters are re-computed as the average points of all of the observations within the cluster, and the observations are reassigned to the newly created closest cluster. The iteration step continues until the optimal k centers are found. In this recipe, we will perform k-means discretization with scikit-learn, using the Boston House Prices dataset.

How to do it...

Let's first import the necessary Python libraries and get the dataset ready:

1. Import the required Python libraries and classes:

```
import pandas as pd
from sklearn.datasets import load_boston
from sklearn.model_selection import train_test_split
from sklearn.preprocessing import KBinsDiscretizer
```

2. Let's load the Boston House Prices dataset into a pandas dataframe:

```
boston_dataset = load_boston()
data = pd.DataFrame(boston_dataset.data,
columns=boston_dataset.feature_names)
data['MEDV'] = boston_dataset.target
```

3. The k-means optimal clusters should be determined using the train set, so let's divide the data into train and test sets:

```
X_train, X_test, y_train, y_test = train_test_split(
    data.drop('MEDV', axis=1), data['MEDV'], test_size=0.3,
random_state=0)
```

4. Let's create a discretizer that uses k-means clustering to create 10 intervals by setting strategy to kmeans:

```
disc = KBinsDiscretizer(n_bins=10, encode='ordinal',
strategy='kmeans')
```

5. Let's fit the discretizer to the slice of the dataframe that contains the variables to discretize, so that the transformer finds the optimal clusters for each variable:

```
disc.fit(X_train[['LSTAT', 'DIS', 'RM']])
```

6. Let's inspect the limits of each interval or cluster:

```
disc.bin_edges_
```

Each array contains the limits for the 10 clusters for each of the 3 variables, LSTAT, DIS, and RM:

```
array([array([ 1.73, 5.45330009,  8.65519753, 12.03266667,
        15.46755102, 18.89709647, 22.15778075, 25.54037815,
        28.75339286, 32.6525,36.98]),
        array([ 1.1742, 2.26301884, 3.30153104, 4.48057886,
        5.60712611, 6.6482802, 7.56131797, 8.45406587, 9.7820881,
        11.37686667, 12.1265]),
        array([3.561, 3.987125, 4.73948864, 5.32155682,
        5.77190824, 6.14016449, 6.50284566, 6.91447956,
        7.43717157, 8.1095049, 8.78])], dtype=object)
```

7. Let's discretize the variables in the train set and then capture the returned NumPy array in a dataframe:

```
train_t = disc.transform(X_train[['LSTAT', 'DIS', 'RM']])
train_t = pd.DataFrame(train_t, columns = ['LSTAT', 'DIS', 'RM'])
```

With `print(train_t.head())`, we can inspect the first five rows of the returned dataframe, where we can see the number assigned to the different intervals or clusters:

```
   LSTAT  DIS   RM
0    9.0  0.0  2.0
1    1.0  2.0  6.0
2    4.0  0.0  5.0
3    0.0  6.0  5.0
4    4.0  0.0  4.0
```

8. Let's discretize the variables in the test set and then capture the returned NumPy array in a dataframe:

```
test_t = disc.transform(X_test[['LSTAT', 'DIS', 'RM']])
test_t = pd.DataFrame(test_t, columns = ['LSTAT', 'DIS', 'RM'])
```

We can compare the distribution of observations in the discretized variables of the train and test sets as we did in *step 13* of the *Dividing the variable into intervals of equal width* recipe.

How it works...

To perform k-means discretization, we used `KBinsDiscretizer()` from scikit-learn, setting `strategy` to `kmeans` and the number of clusters to 10 in the `n_bins` argument. With the `fit()` method, the transformer learned the cluster boundaries using the k-means algorithm. With the `transform()` method, the discretizer sorted the values of the variable to their corresponding cluster, returning a NumPy array with the discretized variables, which we converted into a dataframe.

Using decision trees for discretization

Discretization with decision trees consists of using a decision tree to identify the optimal bins in which to sort the variable values. The decision tree is built using the variable to discretize, and the target. When a decision tree makes a prediction, it assigns an observation to one of N end leaves, therefore, any decision tree will generate a discrete output, the values of which are the predictions at each of its N leaves. Discretization with decision trees creates a monotonic relationship between the bins and the target. In this recipe, we will perform decision tree-based discretization using scikit-learn and then automate the procedure with Feature-engine.

Getting ready

Discretization using decision trees was introduced by the winners of the KDD 2009 data science competition. You can find more details about this procedure in the *Winning the KDD Cup Orange Challenge with Ensemble Selection* article, on page 27 of the article series, *The 2009 Knowledge Discovery in Data Competition*, available at `http://www.mtome.com/Publications/CiML/CiML-v3-book.pdf`.

How to do it...

We will use the Boston House Prices dataset from scikit-learn. The target in this dataset is continuous, therefore, we will train a decision tree for regression with `DecisionTreeRegressor()` from scikit-learn:

1. Let's import the required Python libraries, classes and dataset:

```
import pandas as pd
import matplotlib.pyplot as plt
from sklearn.datasets import load_boston
```

```
from sklearn.model_selection import train_test_split
from sklearn.tree import DecisionTreeRegressor
from feature_engine.discretisers import DecisionTreeDiscretiser
```

2. Let's load the Boston House Prices dataset into a pandas dataframe:

```
boston_dataset = load_boston()
data = pd.DataFrame(boston_dataset.data,
columns=boston_dataset.feature_names)
data['MEDV'] = boston_dataset.target
```

3. Let's divide the data into train and test sets:

```
X_train, X_test, y_train, y_test = train_test_split(
    data.drop('MEDV', axis=1), data['MEDV'], test_size=0.3,
random_state=0)
```

4. Let's assemble a decision tree to predict the MEDV target, setting the maximum depth to 3 and random_state for reproducibility:

```
tree_model = DecisionTreeRegressor(max_depth=3, random_state=0)
```

For binary classification, we would use DecisionTreeClassifier() instead.

5. Let's fit the decision tree using the LSTAT variable to predict the MEDV target:

```
tree_model.fit(X_train['LSTAT'].to_frame(), y_train)
```

Scikit-learn predictors take dataframes as inputs. A single variable is a pandas Series, so we need to use the to_frame() method to transform it into a dataframe and make it compatible with scikit-learn.

6. Let's now predict `MEDV` from `LSTAT` and capture the output in a new variable in the train set:

```
X_train['lstat_tree'] =
tree_model.predict(X_train['LSTAT'].to_frame())
```

If we created a classification tree, we would use `predict_proba()` and retain the second column of the array, which is the probability of the target being 1; hence, we would execute `tree_model.predict_proba(X_train['LSTAT'].to_frame())[:,1]`.

7. Let's explore the end leaves, that is, bins, the tree created:

```
X_train['lstat_tree'].unique()
```

The decision tree produced eight different distinct predictions for all of the observations of the `LSTAT` variable:

```
array([12.91724138, 27.15384615, 16.36181818, 32.04285714, 20.555,
34.88333333, 23.71388889, 41.80740741])
```

8. Let's now discretize the `LSTAT` variable in the test set:

```
X_test['lstat_tree'] =
tree_model.predict(X_test['LSTAT'].to_frame())
```

9. Let's concatenate the test set with the target to plot the predictions versus the mean of the `MEDV` target per bin:

```
pd.concat([X_test, y_test],
axis=1).groupby(['lstat_tree'])['MEDV'].mean().plot()
plt.title('Monotonic relationship between discretised LSTAT and
target')
plt.ylabel('MEDV')
plt.show()
```

We can observe the monotonic relationship between the tree-derived intervals and the MEDV target in the output of the preceding code block:

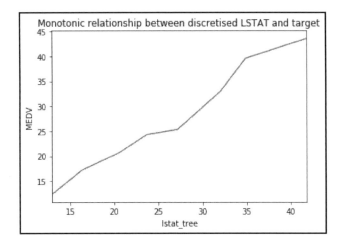

We can compare the distribution of observations in the discretized variables of train and test sets as we did in *step 13* of the *Dividing the variable into intervals of equal width* recipe.

Now let's implement decision tree discretization with Feature-engine. With Feature-engine, we can discretize multiple variables in just a few lines of code. First, we need to divide the dataset into train and test sets as we did in *step 3*.

10. Now, let's create a decision tree discretizer, which will optimize the maximum depth of the tree based on the negative mean square error metric using 10-fold cross-validation, for the LSTAT, RM, and DIS variables:

```
treeDisc = DecisionTreeDiscretiser(cv=10,
scoring='neg_mean_squared_error',variables=['LSTAT', 'RM', 'DIS'],
regression=True, param_grid={'max_depth': [1,2,3,4]})
```

If we were setting up a classification tree, we would use DecisionTreeClassifier() instead and set regression to False. We would also have to use metrics for classification such as roc_auc_score.

11. Let's `fit()` the discretizer using the train set and the target so that the discretizer finds the best decision trees, utilizing the provided grid of parameters for each of the variables indicated in the list:

```
treeDisc.fit(X_train, y_train)
```

12. Let's inspect the best parameters for the tree trained for the `LSTAT` variable:

```
treeDisc.binner_dict['LSTAT'].best_params_
```

The output of the preceding code shows that the optimal depth for the decision tree is 3:

```
{'max_depth': 3}
```

13. Let's transform the variables in the train and test sets:

```
train_t = treeDisc.transform(X_train)
test_t = treeDisc.transform(X_test)
```

 We can compare the distribution of observations in the discretized variables of the train and test sets as we did in *step 13* of the *Dividing the variable into intervals of equal width* recipe.

How it works...

To perform discretization with decision trees, we first loaded the dataset and divided it into train and test sets using the scikit-learn `train_test_split()` function. Next, we chose a variable, `LSTAT`, and fit a decision tree for regression using `DecisionTreeRegressor()` from scikit-learn. We used `to_frame()` to transform the pandas Series with the variable into a dataframe and make the data compatible with scikit-learn predictors. We used the `fit()` method to make the tree learn how to predict the `MEDV` target from `LSTAT`. With the `predict()` method, the tree estimated the target from `LSTAT` in the train and test sets. The decision tree returned eight distinct values, which were its predictions. These outputs represented the bins of the discretized variable.

To visualize the monotonic relationship between tree outputs and target, we created a plot of the bins predicted by the tree versus the mean target value for each of these bins. We first concatenated the test set and the target using pandas' `concat()` method. Next, we used pandas' `groupby()` method to group the observations per bin and then calculated the mean of `MEDV` in each bin. With pandas' `plot()` method, we plotted the relationship between the bins and `MEDV`.

To perform decision tree discretization using Feature-engine, we used
`DecisionTreeDiscretiser()`; indicated the cross-validation fold to use for the
optimization, the metric to evaluate the decision tree performance; set `regression` to `True`
to indicate that our target was continuous; and passed a dictionary with the parameters to
optimize in each tree. Next, we used the `fit()` method so that the discretizer fit the best
tree for each of the variables. And with the `transform()` method, we obtained the
discretized variables in the train and test sets.

There's more...

We can perform decision tree discretization with scikit-learn within a grid search to find the
optimal parameters to determine the most predictive decision tree. To do so, we first do the
imports, as in *step 1* of the main recipe, and we add one additional import:

1. Let's import the grid search from scikit-learn:

    ```
    from sklearn.model_selection import GridSearchCV
    ```

   Next, let's load the dataset and divide it into train and test sets, as in *step 2* and
   step 3 of the main recipe, and now let's set up a parameter search grid.

2. Let's set up a dictionary with the parameters we would like to test, in this case,
   four different tree depths:

    ```
    param_grid = {'max_depth': [1,2,3,4]}
    ```

3. Let's now set up the decision tree inside a grid search with 5-fold cross-validation
   and the negative mean squared error as a metric to optimize:

    ```
    tree_model = GridSearchCV(DecisionTreeRegressor(random_state=0),
                              cv = 5,
                              scoring = 'neg_mean_squared_error',
                              param_grid = param_grid)
    ```

4. Let's fit the tree to the `LSTAT` variable and the target:

    ```
    tree_model.fit(X_train['LSTAT'].to_frame(), y_train)
    ```

5. Finally, let's transform the variables with the best decision tree:

    ```
    X_train['lstat_tree'] =
    tree_model.predict(X_train['LSTAT'].to_frame())
    X_test['lstat_tree'] =
    tree_model.predict(X_test['LSTAT'].to_frame())
    ```

See also

For more details on how to perform a grid search with cross-validation with scikit-learn, follow `https://scikit-learn.org/stable/modules/generated/sklearn.model_selection.GridSearchCV.html`.

For more details about the parameters of a decision tree, visit the related documentation:

- `DecisionTreeRegressor()`: `http://scikit-learn.org/stable/modules/generated/sklearn.tree.DecisionTreeRegressor.html`
- `DecisionTreeClassifier()`: `http://scikit-learn.org/stable/modules/generated/sklearn.tree.DecisionTreeClassifier.html`

For details of the metrics, you can use to optimize the trees, visit scikit-learn's metrics web page at `https://scikit-learn.org/stable/modules/model_evaluation.html#the-scoring-parameter-defining-model-evaluation-rules`.

To visualize the structure of the tree we fit in the recipe with its various intermediate and Terminal leaves, visit the Jupyter Notebook in the accompanying GitHub repository, at `https://github.com/PacktPublishing/Python-Feature-Engineering-Cookbook/blob/master/Chapter05/Recipe-6-Discretisation-with-decision-trees.ipynb`.

6
Working with Outliers

An outlier is a data point that is significantly different from the remaining data. Statistical parameters such as the mean and variance are sensitive to outliers. Outliers may also affect the performance of some machine learning models, such as linear regression or AdaBoost. Therefore, we may want to remove or engineer the outliers in the variables of our dataset.

How can we engineer outliers? One way to handle outliers is to perform variable discretization with any of the techniques we covered in Chapter 5, *Performing Variable Discretization*. With discretization, the outliers will fall in the lower or upper intervals and, therefore, will be treated as the remaining lower or higher values of the variable. An alternative way to handle outliers is to assume that the information is missing, treat the outliers together with the remaining missing data, and carry out any of the missing imputation techniques described in Chapter 2, *Imputing Missing Data*. We can also remove observations with outliers from the dataset, or cap the maximum and minimum values of the variables, as we will discuss throughout this chapter.

In this chapter, we will discuss how to identify and remove outliers from a dataset, a process called trimming, and how to replace outliers by maximum or minimum values. We will also discuss how to use the mean and standard deviation for normally distributed variables or the inter-quartile range for skewed features or using percentiles, in a process commonly known as **winsorization**.

This chapter will cover the following recipes:

- Trimming outliers from the dataset
- Performing winsorization
- Capping the variable at arbitrary maximum and minimum values
- Performing zero-coding – capping the variable values at zero

Technical requirements

In this chapter, we will use the following Python libraries: pandas, NumPy, SciPy, and scikit-learn. I recommend installing the free Anaconda Python distribution (`https://www.anaconda.com/distribution/`), which contains all of these packages. For details on how to install the Python Anaconda distribution, visit the *Technical requirements* section in `Chapter 1`, *Foreseeing Variable Problems in Building ML Models*.

In this chapter, we will also use the open source Python library, Feature-engine, which I created and can be installed using `pip`:

```
pip install feature-engine
```

To find out more about Feature-engine, visit its documentation at `https://feature-engine.readthedocs.io`.

Trimming outliers from the dataset

Trimming, or truncating, is the process of removing observations that show outliers in one or more variables in the dataset. There are three commonly used methods to set the boundaries beyond which a value can be considered an outlier. If the variable is normally distributed, the boundaries are given by the mean plus or minus three times the standard deviation, as approximately 99% of the data will be distributed between those limits. For normally, as well as not normally, distributed variables, we can determine the limits using the inter-quartile range proximity rules or by directly setting the limits to the 5th and 95th quantiles. We covered the formula for the inter-quartile range proximity rule in the *Getting ready* section of the *Highlighting outliers* recipe in `Chapter 1`, *Foreseeing Variable Problems in Building ML Models*. In this recipe, we are going to use all three measures to identify and then remove outliers in the Boston House Prices dataset from scikit-learn, using pandas and NumPy.

How to do it...

Let's first import the necessary Python libraries:

1. Import the required Python libraries:

```
import pandas as pd
import numpy as np
import matplotlib.pyplot as plt
```

```
import seaborn as sns
from sklearn.datasets import load_boston
```

2. Let's load the Boston House Prices dataset from scikit-learn:

```
boston_dataset = load_boston()
```

3. Let's capture three of the variables, RM, LSTAT, and CRIM, in a pandas dataframe:

```
boston = pd.DataFrame(boston_dataset.data,
columns=boston_dataset.feature_names)[['RM', 'LSTAT', 'CRIM']]
```

You can visualize the loaded data using boston.head().

4. Let's make a boxplot of the RM variable to visualize outliers:

```
sns.distplot(boston['RM'], bins=30)
```

The outliers are the asterisks sitting outside the whiskers, which delimit the inter-quartile range proximity rule boundaries:

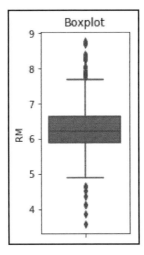

5. Let's create a function to find the boundaries of a variable distribution, using the inter-quartile range proximity rule:

```
def find_boundaries(df, variable, distance):
    IQR = df[variable].quantile(0.75) - df[variable].quantile(0.25)
    lower_boundary = df[variable].quantile(0.25) - (IQR * distance)
    upper_boundary = df[variable].quantile(0.75) + (IQR * distance)
    return upper_boundary, lower_boundary
```

 We can replace the code in the preceding function to instead find the boundaries using the mean and the standard deviation or the quantiles. For code on how to do this, visit the *There's more...* section at the end of this recipe.

6. Let's use the function from *step 5* to determine the limits of the RM variable:

```
RM_upper_limit, RM_lower_limit = find_boundaries(boston, 'RM', 1.5)
```

7. Let's print those limits beyond which we will consider a value an outlier:

```
RM_upper_limit, RM_lower_limit
```

The output of the preceding code is as follows:

```
(7.730499999999999, 4.778500000000001)
```

8. Let's create a Boolean vector to flag the outliers in RM:

```
outliers_RM = np.where(boston['RM'] > RM_upper_limit, True,
                       np.where(boston['RM'] < RM_lower_limit, True,
                       False)
```

9. Finally, let's remove the outliers from the dataset:

```
boston_trimmed = boston.loc[~(outliers_RM]
```

 With the code in *step 4*, you can visualize the distribution of the trimmed variable and see whether there are outliers remaining. If there are, you can adjust the boundaries and trim the data again, or try a different way of finding the boundaries, as shown in the *There's more...* section of this recipe.

How it works...

In this recipe, we removed the outliers of a variable of the Boston House Prices dataset from scikit-learn. To remove the outliers, we first identified those values visually through a boxplot. Next, we created a function to find the limits within which we found the majority of the values of the variable. Next, we created a Boolean vector to flag the values of the variable that sit beyond those boundaries, and, finally, we removed those observations from the dataset.

To load the data, we first imported the dataset from `sklearn.datasets` and then used `load_boston()`. Next, we captured the data in a dataframe using pandas' `DataFrame()`, indicating that the data is stored in `boston_dataset.data` and the variable names in `boston_dataset.feature_names`. To retain only the `RM`, `LSTAT`, and `CRIM` variables, we passed the column names in double square brackets (`[['RM', 'LSTAT', 'CRIM']]`) at the back of pandas' `DataFrame()`.

To identify outliers in our dataframe, we created a function to find the inter-quartile range proximity rule boundaries. The function takes the dataframe and the variable as arguments and calculates the inter-quartile range and the boundaries using the formula described in the *Getting ready* section of the *Highlighting outliers* recipe in `Chapter 1`, *Foreseeing Variable Problems in Building ML Models*. With the pandas' `quantile()` method, we can calculate the values for the 25th (`0.25`) and 75th quantiles (`0.75`). We then used this function to return the upper and lower boundaries for the `RM` variable.

To find the outliers of `RM`, we used `np.where()`, which produced a Boolean vector with `True` if the value was an outlier, that is, if the value was bigger or smaller than the upper or lower boundaries determined for `RM`.

Briefly, `np.where()` scanned the rows of the `RM` variable, and if the value was bigger than the upper boundary, it assigned `True`; whereas if the value was smaller, the second NumPy's `where()` method, nested in the first one, checked whether the value was smaller than the lower boundary, in which case, it also assigned `True`; otherwise, it assigned `False`.

Finally, we used the `loc[]` method from pandas to remove the observations that contained outliers for `RM`. The ~ symbol used with the pandas' `loc[]` method removes from the dataframe the outliers captured in the Boolean vector, `outliers_RM`.

There's more...

If instead of using the inter-quartile range proximity rule, we want to use the mean and standard deviation to find the limits, we need to replace the code in the function in *step 5*:

1. Find the outlier boundaries using the mean and standard deviation:

```
def find_boundaries(df, variable, distance):
    lower_boundary = df[variable].mean() - (df[variable].std() *
distance)
    upper_boundary = df[variable].mean() + (df[variable].std() *
distance)
    return upper_boundary, lower_boundary
```

To calculate the boundaries for the RM variable with the preceding function, we run the following code.

2. Calculate the boundaries for RM:

```
RM_upper_limit, RM_lower_limit = find_boundaries(boston, 'RM', 3)
```

Alternatively, if we want to use quantiles to calculate the limits, we should write the function like in the next step.

3. Find the outlier boundaries using quantiles:

```
def find_boundaries(df, variable):
    lower_boundary = df[variable].quantile(0.05)
    upper_boundary = df[variable].quantile(0.95)
    return upper_boundary, lower_boundary
```

And we calculate the boundaries for RM with the preceding function like in the next step.

4. Calculate the boundaries for RM:

```
RM_upper_limit, RM_lower_limit = find_boundaries(boston, 'RM')
```

The rest of the procedure is identical to the one described in *step 8* and *step 9*, in the *How to do it...* section of the recipe.

We can also remove outliers across multiple variables. To do this, we need to first run *step 1* to *step 5* described in the *How to do it...* section of the recipe, and then find the boundaries for multiple variables.

5. Let's calculate the boundaries for the RM, LSTAT, and CRIM variables:

```
RM_upper_limit, RM_lower_limit = find_boundaries(boston, 'RM', 1.5)
LSTAT_upper_limit, LSTAT_lower_limit = find_boundaries(boston,
'LSTAT', 1.5)
CRIM_upper_limit, CRIM_lower_limit = find_boundaries(boston,
'CRIM', 1.5)
```

6. Let's create Boolean vectors that flag the outliers for each one of RM, LSTAT, and CRIM:

```
outliers_RM = np.where(boston['RM'] > RM_upper_limit, True,
                np.where(boston['RM'] < RM_lower_limit, True, False))

outliers_LSTAT = np.where(boston['LSTAT'] > LSTAT_upper_limit,
                  True,
                  np.where(boston['LSTAT'] < LSTAT_lower_limit,
True,
                  False))

outliers_CRIM = np.where(boston['CRIM'] > CRIM_upper_limit, True,
                  np.where(boston['CRIM'] < CRIM_lower_limit, True,
                  False))
```

7. Finally, let's remove the observations with outliers in any of the variables:

```
boston_trimmed = boston.loc[~(outliers_RM + outliers_LSTAT +
outliers_CRIM)]
```

With the code in *step 4* in the *How to do it...* section, you can visualize the outliers in the trimmed dataset.

Performing winsorization

Winsorization, or winsorizing, is the process of transforming the data by limiting the extreme values, that is, the outliers, to a certain arbitrary value, closer to the mean of the distribution. Winsorizing is different from trimming because the extreme values are not removed, but are instead replaced by other values. A typical strategy involves setting outliers to a specified percentile.

For example, with 90% winsorization, we set all data below the 5th percentile to the value at the 5th percentile and all data above the 95th percentile to the value at the 95th percentile. Winsorization is symmetric; therefore, the winsorized mean of a symmetric distribution provides an unbiased representation of the distribution of the variable. In this recipe, we will perform winsorization using pandas, NumPy, and Feature-engine.

How to do it...

Let's first import the necessary Python libraries:

1. Import the required Python libraries:

```
import pandas as pd
import numpy as np
import matplotlib.pyplot as plt
import seaborn as sns
from sklearn.datasets import load_boston
```

2. Let's load the Boston House Prices dataset from scikit-learn:

```
boston_dataset = load_boston()
```

3. Let's capture three of the variables, RM, LSTAT, and CRIM, in a pandas dataframe:

```
boston = pd.DataFrame(boston_dataset.data,
columns=boston_dataset.feature_names)[['RM', 'LSTAT', 'CRIM']]
```

 You can visualize the loaded data using `boston.head()`.

4. Let's make a function to winsorize a variable to arbitrary upper and lower limits:

```
def winsorize(df, variable, upper_limit, lower_limit):
    return np.where(df[variable] > upper_limit, upper_limit,
            np.where(df[variable] < lower_limit, lower_limit,
df[variable]))
```

5. Let's winsorize the RM variable:

```
boston['RM']= winsorize(boston, 'RM', boston['RM'].quantile(0.95),
boston['RM'].quantile(0.05))
```

If you make a Q-Q plot and a boxplot of the RM variable before and after the winsorization, you can easily see how the extreme values get replaced by the percentiles. You can find the code to make these plots in the corresponding recipe in the accompanying GitHub repository.

How it works...

In this recipe, we replaced the outliers of one variable of the Boston House Prices dataset from scikit-learn, by the 5th and 95th percentiles. We first loaded the data as described in the *How it works* section of the *Trimming outliers from the dataset* recipe in this chapter. To replace the outliers, we created a function, that takes the dataframe, the variable name, and the 5th and 95th percentiles and uses Numpy's where() to replace the values bigger or smaller than those percentiles by the values of those percentiles.

NumPy's where() scans each observation and if the value is bigger than the 95th percentile, it replaces it with the 95th percentile; otherwise, it evaluates whether the value is smaller than the 5th percentile, in which case, it replaces it with the 5th percentile. If not, it keeps the original value. Finally, we used the function to replace the extreme values in the RM variable.

There's more...

We can winsorize many variables at the time by utilizing the open source package, Feature-engine. To do this, we need to load the libraries and the data as we did in *step 1* and *step 2* of the recipe in the *How to do it...* section. Next, we need to import Feature-engine:

1. Import Winsorizer from Feature-engine:

   ```
   from feature_engine.outlier_removers import Winsorizer
   ```

2. Set up a Feature-engine Winsorizer indicating which variables we want to winsorize:

   ```
   windsorizer = Winsorizer(distribution='quantiles', tail='both',
   variables=['RM', 'LSTAT', 'CRIM'])
   ```

With Winsorizer from Feature-engine, we can replace the values by the percentiles at the left and right tails or only at one of the tails by setting the argument tail to either both, left, or right.

3. Fit `windsorizer` to the data so that it learns the percentiles:

```
windsorizer.fit(boston)
```

4. Winsorize the `RM`, `LSTAT`, and `CRIM` variables:

```
boston_t = windsorizer.transform(boston)
```

 Remember that it is good practice to separate the data into training and testing sets and train `Winsorizer` on the train set. This way, the transformer will use the percentiles learned from the train set to cap the variables in train, test, and all future data.

We can inspect the 5th percentiles learned by `winsorizer` like in the next step.

5. Inspect the learned 5th percentiles:

```
windsorizer.left_tail_caps_
```

The output of the preceding code is as follows:

```
{'RM': 5.314, 'LSTAT': 3.7075000000000005, 'CRIM':
0.027909999999999997}
```

And we can inspect the 95th percentiles learned by `windsorizer` like in the next step.

6. Inspect the learned 95th percentiles:

```
windsorizer.right_tail_caps_
```

The output of the preceding code is as follows:

```
{'RM': 7.5875, 'LSTAT': 26.8075, 'CRIM': 15.78915}
```

In the dictionary, we can see the values that the transformer will use to replace the outliers in each variable.

See also

In the accompanying GitHub repository, `https://github.com/PacktPublishing/Python-Feature-Engineering-Cookbook`, you will find code to create histograms, Q-Q plots, and boxplots, and compare the effect of winsorization in normal and skewed variables.

You can also find out more about handling outliers with Feature-engine in its documentation at `https://feature-engine.readthedocs.io/en/latest/outliercappers/Winsorizer.html`.

To learn more about the pros and cons of winsorization, visit this blog: `https://blogs.sas.com/content/iml/2017/02/08/winsorization-good-bad-and-ugly.html`.

Capping the variable at arbitrary maximum and minimum values

Similarly to winsorization, we can replace the extreme values by values closer to other values in the variable, by determining the maximum and minimum boundaries with the mean plus or minus the standard deviation, or the inter-quartile range proximity rule. This procedure is also called bottom and top coding, censoring, or capping. We can cap both extremes of the distribution or just one of the tails, depending on where we find the outliers in the variable. In this recipe, we will replace extreme values by the mean and standard deviation or the inter-quartile range proximity rule, using pandas, NumPy, and Feature-engine, and using the Boston House Prices dataset from scikit-learn.

How to do it...

Let's first import the necessary Python libraries:

1. Import the required Python libraries:

```
import pandas as pd
import numpy as np
import matplotlib.pyplot as plt
import seaborn as sns
from sklearn.datasets import load_boston
```

2. Let's load the Boston House Prices dataset from scikit-learn:

```
boston_dataset = load_boston()
```

3. Let's capture three of the variables, RM, LSTAT, and CRIM, in a pandas dataframe:

```
boston = pd.DataFrame(boston_dataset.data,
columns=boston_dataset.feature_names)[['RM', 'LSTAT', 'CRIM']]
```

You can visualize the loaded data using `boston.head()`.

4. Let's make a function to find the limits using the inter-quartile range proximity rule:

```
def find_skewed_boundaries(df, variable, distance):
    IQR = df[variable].quantile(0.75) - df[variable].quantile(0.25)
    lower_boundary = df[variable].quantile(0.25) - (IQR * distance)
    upper_boundary = df[variable].quantile(0.75) + (IQR * distance)
    return upper_boundary, lower_boundary
```

If, instead, we wanted to find the boundaries with the mean and standard deviation, we can rewrite our function as follows.

5. Let's make a function to find the limits using the mean and the standard deviation:

```
def find_normal_boundaries(df, variable, distance):
    upper_boundary = df[variable].mean() + distance *
df[variable].std()
    lower_boundary = df[variable].mean() - distance *
df[variable].std()
    return upper_boundary, lower_boundary
```

Once we have created the functions, we can go ahead and find the limits using either the mean and standard deviation with the function from *step 5* or the inter-quartile range with the function in *step 4*. In this recipe, I will continue by finding the limits using the mean and standard deviation.

If the variable is not normally distributed, it may be more useful to use the inter-quartile range proximity rule to find the outliers.

6. Let's find the boundaries for the RM, LSTAT, and CRIM variables:

```
RM_upper_limit, RM_lower_limit = \
find_normal_boundaries(boston, 'RM', 3)
LSTAT_upper_limit, LSTAT_lower_limit = \
find_normal_boundaries(boston, 'LSTAT', 3)
CRIM_upper_limit, CRIM_lower_limit = \
find_normal_boundaries(boston, 'CRIM', 3)
```

Next, we can go ahead and replace extreme values by those boundaries.

7. Replace extreme values by the limits in RM:

```
boston['RM']= np.where(boston['RM'] > RM_upper_limit,
            RM_upper_limit,
        np.where(boston['RM'] < RM_lower_limit,
            RM_lower_limit, boston['RM']))
```

To replace the values in LSTAT and CRIM, you need to repeat *step 7*, changing the variable name in the dataframe and the upper and lower limits.

To cap values only at the higher or lower end of the distribution, we can change the code in *step 7* to boston['RM']= np.where(boston['RM'] > RM_upper_limit, boston['RM']) to cap the right tail or boston['RM']= np.where(boston['RM'] < RM_lower_limit, RM_lower_limit, boston['RM']) to cap the left tail.

How it works...

In this recipe, we replaced the outliers of three variables in the Boston House Prices dataset from scikit-learn. To replace the outliers, we first identified those values using the mean and standard deviation and then replaced values beyond these boundaries with the values at the boundaries.

We first loaded the data as described in the *How it works...* section of the *Trimming outliers from the dataset* recipe in this chapter. To identify those outliers in our dataframe, in *step 4* and *step 5*, we created a function to find boundaries using the inter-quartile range proximity rule or the mean and standard deviation, respectively. The function in *step 4* takes the dataframe and the variable as arguments and calculates the inter-quartile range and the boundaries using the formula described in the *Getting ready* section of the *Highlighting outliers* recipe in Chapter 1, *Foreseeing Variable Problems in Building ML Models*.

With the pandas' quantile() method, we can calculate the values for the 25th (0.25) and 75th quantiles (0.75). The function in *step 5* takes the dataframe and the variable as arguments and calculates the boundaries as the mean plus or minus a factor of the standard deviation. The mean of the variable is determined using pandas' mean() and the standard deviation using pandas' std(). The factor can be entered by the user utilizing the distance argument and is usually 3.

In the recipe, we continued using the function created in *step 5* to calculate the limits in the RM, LSTAT, and CRIM variables. Next, it replaced the outliers of RM with NumPy's where(). Briefly, NumPy's where() scanned each observation of the variable, and if the value was bigger than the upper limit, it replaced it with the upper limit; otherwise, it evaluated whether the value was smaller than the lower limit, in which case, it replaced it with the lower limit. If not, it kept the original value.

There's more...

We can cap many variables at a time, utilizing the open source package, Feature-engine. To do this, we need to load the libraries and the data as we did in *step 1* and *step 2* of the recipe in the *How to do it...* section. Next, we need to import Feature-engine:

1. Import `Winsorizer` from Feature-engine:

   ```
   from feature_engine.outlier_removers import Winsorizer
   ```

2. Set up a Feature-engine `Winsorizer` indicating which variables we want to winsorize and that we want to use the mean and standard deviation to find the limits:

   ```
   windsorizer = Winsorizer(distribution='gaussian', tail='both',
   fold=3, variables=['RM', 'LSTAT', 'CRIM'])
   ```

    With `Winsorizer` from Feature-engine, we can replace the values by the mean and standard deviation setting the argument distribution to `gaussian` or the inter-quartile range proximity rule by setting the distribution to `skewed`. We can also replace outliers at both ends of the distributions or just the left or right tails, by setting the `tail` to `both`, `left`, or `right`. The `fold` argument works as the `distance` argument in the functions we created in *step 4* and *step 5* of the recipe.

3. Fit `windsorizer` to the data so that it learns the limits:

   ```
   windsorizer.fit(boston)
   ```

4. Winsorize the RM, LSTAT, and CRIM variables:

   ```
   boston_t = windsorizer.transform(boston)
   ```

   We can inspect the lower boundaries learned by `winsorizer` like in the next step.

5. Inspect the learned lower boundaries:

```
windsorizer.left_tail_caps_
```

The preceding code block outputs this:

```
{'RM': 4.176782957105816, 'LSTAT': -8.77012129293899, 'CRIM':
-22.19111175868521}
```

And we can inspect the upper limits learned by `winsorizer` like in the next step.

6. Inspect the learned upper boundaries:

```
windsorizer.right_tail_caps_
```

The preceding code block outputs this:

```
{'RM': 8.392485817597757, 'LSTAT': 34.07624777515244, 'CRIM':
29.418158873309714}
```

The dictionary stores the values that the transformer will use to replace the outliers in each variable.

See also

To learn more about handling outliers with Feature-engine, refer to the documentation at `https://feature-engine.readthedocs.io/en/latest/outliercappers/Winsorizer.html`.

Performing zero-coding – capping the variable at zero

In econometrics and statistics, top-coding and bottom-coding refer to the act of censoring data points, the values of which are above or below a certain number or threshold, respectively. In essence, top and bottom coding is what we have covered in the previous recipe, where we capped the minimum or maximum values of variables at a certain value, which we determined with the mean and standard deviation, the inter-quartile range proximity rule, or the percentiles. Zero-coding is a variant of bottom-coding and refers to the process of capping, usually the lower value of the variable, at zero. It is commonly used for variables that cannot take negative values, such as age or income. In this recipe, we will learn how to implement zero-coding in a toy dataframe using pandas and Feature-engine.

How to do it...

Let's begin the recipe by importing the necessary libraries:

1. Import the required Python libraries:

   ```
   import pandas as pd
   import numpy as np
   import matplotlib.pyplot as plt
   ```

   To proceed with this recipe, let's create a toy dataframe with three variables called x, y, and z, that follow a normal distribution and show a few negative values. To create this toy dataframe, we need to follow these steps:

2. Create the x, y, and z variables with a normal distribution:

   ```
   np.random.seed(29)
   n = 200
   x = np.random.randn(n) + 2
   y = np.random.randn(n) * 2 + 4
   z = np.random.randn(n) * 5 + 10
   ```

   Setting the seed for reproducibility using np.random.seed() will help you to get the outputs shown in this recipe.

3. Let's capture these variables in a dataframe and add the variable names:

   ```
   data = pd.DataFrame([x, y, z]).T
   data.columns = ['x', 'y', 'z']
   ```

4. Let's find out whether the variables have negative numbers by examining the minimum values:

   ```
   data.min()
   ```

   All three variables contain negative values:

   ```
   x    -1.505401
   y    -0.901451
   z    -1.552986
   dtype: float64
   ```

5. Let's plot the histograms of the variables:

```
data.hist(bins=30)
plt.show()
```

We can see the negative values of the variables in the created histograms:

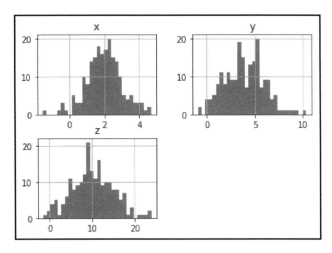

6. Let's cap the minimum values at zero:

```
data.loc[data['x'] < 0, 'x'] = 0
data.loc[data['y'] < 0, 'y'] = 0
data.loc[data['z'] < 0, 'z'] = 0
```

If you run `data.min()` after capping, the minimum values for all variables should be 0. You can also plot the histograms after capping, as we did in *step 5*, and compare the change in the distribution. You will see a small peak at 0, where the extreme values have been relocated with zero-coding.

How it works...

In this recipe, we replaced negative values with zero. To proceed with the recipe, we first created a toy dataframe with three independent variables that were normally distributed and showed a few negative values. Next, we examined the presence of negative values in the variables by looking at the minimum values and plotting the histograms. Finally, we replaced the negative values with 0.

To generate the toy dataframe, first, we created three independent variables, x, y, and z, which are normally distributed. We used NumPy's `random.randn()`, which extracts values at random from a normal distribution, and we multiplied the extracted values by a factor and added a constant value, to make the variables slightly different. Next, we captured the variables in a pandas dataframe using `pd.DataFrame()` and transposed it using the `T` method to return a 200-row by 3-column dataframe. We added the column names by passing them in a list to the pandas' `columns` attribute.

To examine whether the variables had negative numbers, we used pandas' `min()` to display the minimum values of the variables, and we saw that all of the minimum values were negative. Next, we used pandas' `hist()` to display the histograms of the three variables. To replace the negative values by zero, we used pandas' `loc[]`, which allowed us to select a slice of the dataframe based on a condition. The conditions we used was that the values of each variables were smaller than zero. With pandas' `loc[]` and the condition, we reset the negative values of the variables to zero.

There's more...

We can perform zero-coding in multiple variables at a time, utilizing the open source package, Feature-engine. To do this, we need to load the libraries and create the toy dataframe as we did in *step 1* to *step 3* of the recipe in the *How to do it...* section. Next, we need to import Feature-engine:

1. Import `ArbitraryOutlierCapper` from Feature-engine:

   ```
   from feature_engine.outlier_removers import ArbitraryOutlierCapper
   ```

2. Set up the `ArbitraryOutlierCapper` from Feature-engine indicating which variables we want to cap at zero:

   ```
   windsorizer = ArbitraryOutlierCapper(max_capping_dict=None,
   min_capping_dict={'x':0, 'y':0, 'z':0})
   ```

   With `Winsorizer` from Feature-engine, we can replace the values by any arbitrary value and at both ends of the distribution. We need only pass the dictionary with the capping values for the right tail at the `max_capping_dict` argument or with the capping values for the left tail at the `min_capping_dict` argument.

3. Fit `windsorizer` to the data:

```
windsorizer.fit(data)
```

4. Cap the variables at zero:

```
data_t = windsorizer.transform(data)
```

The transformed dataset, `data_t`, contains variables, the minimum values of which have been capped or censored at zero.

See also

To learn more about the arbitrary capper from Feature-engine, visit `https://feature-engine.readthedocs.io/en/latest/outliercappers/ArbitraryOutlierCapper.html`.

7

Deriving Features from Dates and Time Variables

Date and time variables are those that contain information about dates, times, or date and time. In programming, we refer to these variables as `datetime` variables. Examples of the `datetime` variables are date of birth, time of the accident, and date of last payment. The `datetime` variables usually contain a multitude of different labels corresponding to a specific combination of date and time. We do not utilize the `datetime` variables in their raw format when building machine learning models. Instead, we enrich the dataset dramatically by deriving multiple features from these variables. In this chapter, we will learn how to derive a variety of new features from date and time.

This chapter will cover the following recipes:

- Extracting date and time parts from a `datetime` variable
- Deriving representations of the year and month
- Creating representations of day and week
- Extracting time parts from a time variable
- Capturing the elapsed time between `datetime` variables
- Working with time in different time zones

Technical requirements

In this chapter, we will use the Python libraries, pandas and NumPy, and the built-in Python library, `datetime`. Visit the `requirements.txt` file in the accompanying Jupyter Notebook to check the library versions that we are using in the recipes.

Extracting date and time parts from a datetime variable

The datetime variables can take dates, time, or date and time as values. The datetime variables are not used in their raw format to build machine learning algorithms. Instead, we create additional features from them, and, in fact, we can enrich the dataset dramatically by extracting information from the date and time.

The pandas Python library contains a lot of capabilities for working with date and time. But to access this functionality, the variables should be cast in a data type that supports these operations, such as datetime or timedelta. Often, the datetime variables are cast as objects, particularly when the data is loaded from a CSV file. Pandas' dt, which is the accessor object to the datetime properties of a pandas Series, works only with datetime data types; therefore, to extract date and time parts, and, in fact, to derive any of the features we will discuss throughout this chapter, it is necessary to recast the variables as datetime.

In this recipe, we will learn how to separate the date and time parts of a datetime variable using pandas, and how to recast objects into datetime data types.

How to do it...

To proceed with the recipe, let's first import pandas and create a toy dataframe for the demonstration:

1. Import pandas:

   ```
   import pandas as pd
   ```

2. Let's create 20 datetime values, with values beginning from 2019-03-05 at midnight followed by increments of 1 minute. Then, let's capture the value range in a dataframe and display the top five rows:

   ```
   rng_ = pd.date_range('2019-03-05', periods=20, freq='T')
   df = pd.DataFrame({'date': rng_})
   df.head()
   ```

Our variable contains both date and time information, as we can see in the output of the preceding code block:

	date
0	2019-03-05 00:00:00
1	2019-03-05 00:01:00
2	2019-03-05 00:02:00
3	2019-03-05 00:03:00
4	2019-03-05 00:04:00

3. Let's display the data type of the variable we created:

```
df.dtypes
```

The variable is cast as `datetime`, the default output of pandas' `date_range()`, as we can see in the following output:

```
date        datetime64[ns]
dtype: object
```

4. Let's capture the **date** part of the `date` variable in a new feature using pandas' `dt` and then display the top five rows:

```
df['date_part'] = df['date'].dt.date
df['date_part'].head()
```

The newly created variable contains only the date part of the original values, as we can see in the following output:

```
0 2019-03-05
1 2019-03-05
2 2019-03-05
3 2019-03-05
4 2019-03-05
Name: date_part, dtype: object
```

5. Let's now capture the **time** part of the `datetime` variable created in *step 2* in a new feature and display the top rows:

```
df['time_part'] = df['date'].dt.time
df['time_part'].head()
```

The newly created variable contains only the time part of the original values, as we can see in the following output:

```
0      00:00:00
1      00:01:00
2      00:02:00
3      00:03:00
4      00:04:00
Name: time_part, dtype: object
```

In the second part of the recipe, let's learn how to change the data type of a variable into a datetime variable.

6. Let's first create a new dataframe where the datetime variable is cast as an object and display the output:

```
df = pd.DataFrame({'date_var':['Jan-2015', 'Apr-2013', 'Jun-2014', 'Jan-2015']})
df
```

We can see the five values of our new dataframe in the following output:

```
    date_var
0 Jan-2015
1 Apr-2013
2 Jun-2014
3 Jan-2015
```

If you now execute the df.dtypes command, you will see that the date_var variable is cast as an object.

7. Let's change the data type of the variable into datetime and display the dataframe:

```
df['datetime_var'] = pd.to_datetime(df['date_var'])
df
```

We can see in the following output that both the original and newly created variables are cast as object and datetime, respectively:

```
    date_var   datetime_var
0 Jan-2015   2015-01-01
1 Apr-2013   2013-04-01
2 Jun-2014   2014-06-01
3 Jan-2015   2015-01-01
```

Go ahead and execute df.dtypes to corroborate the data type of the variable we created in *step 7*.

8. Finally, let's extract the date and time part of the variable that was recast into datetime:

```
df['date'] = df['datetime_var'].dt.date
df['time'] = df['datetime_var'].dt.time
df
```

We can see the final dataframe with the date and time parts in the following output:

	date_var	datetime_var	date	time
0	Jan-2015	2015-01-01	2015-01-01	00:00:00
1	Apr-2013	2013-04-01	2013-04-01	00:00:00
2	Jun-2014	2014-06-01	2014-06-01	00:00:00
3	Jan-2015	2015-01-01	2015-01-01	00:00:00

Now that we know how to separate a datetime variable into date and time and how to cast variables into the datetime format, we are ready to proceed with the rest of the recipes in this chapter.

How it works...

In this recipe, we extracted the date and time parts of a datetime variable. We first created a toy dataframe with a variable that contained both the date and time in its values. To create the toy dataframe, we used the pandas date_range() method to create a range of values starting from an arbitrary date and increasing this by intervals of 1 minute. With the periods argument, we indicated the number of values to create in the range, that is, the number of dates; and with the freq argument, we indicated the size of the steps between the dates—we used T for minutes in our example. Finally, we transformed the date range into a dataframe with the pandas DataFrame() method.

With pandas' `head()`, we displayed the first five rows of our dataframe, and, with pandas' `dtypes`, we determined the data type of the variables. To extract the date part, we utilized pandas' `dt.date`, and, to extract the time part, we used pandas' `dt.time` on the `datetime` variable. These methods created two new `datetime` variables with the parts specified, which we captured as new columns of the dataframe.

Finally, we changed the data type of a variable into `datetime`. We created a toy dataframe where the variable was cast as an object. Pandas' `dt` only works with `datetime` values; hence, to extract the date and time parts, we first recast the variable into the `datetime` format using pandas' `to_datetime()`. Then, we used `dt.date` and `dt.time` as we did before, to extract the date and time parts, respectively.

See also

To learn how to create different `datetime` ranges with pandas `date_ranges()`, visit https://pandas.pydata.org/pandas-docs/stable/user_guide/timeseries.html#offset-aliases.

To learn more about pandas `dt`, visit https://pandas.pydata.org/pandas-docs/stable/reference/series.html#datetime-properties.

Deriving representations of the year and month

Some events occur more often at certain times of the year, for example, recruitment rates increase after Christmas and slow down toward the summer holidays in Europe. Businesses and organizations want to evaluate performance and objectives at regular intervals throughout the year, for example, at every quarter or every semester. Therefore, deriving these features from a date variable is very useful for both data analysis and machine learning. In this recipe, we will learn how to derive the year, month, quarter, and semester from a `datetime` variable using pandas and NumPy.

How to do it...

To proceed with the recipe, let's import the libraries and create a toy dataset:

1. Import pandas and NumPy:

   ```
   import numpy as np
   import pandas as pd
   ```

2. Let's create 20 `datetime` values, beginning from `2019-03-05` at midnight followed by increments of 1 month. Then, let's capture the value range in a dataframe and display the top five rows:

   ```
   rng_ = pd.date_range('2019-03-05', periods=20, freq='M')
   df = pd.DataFrame({'date': rng_})
   df.head()
   ```

   Note how the values increase by one month in the first five observations of the variable we created:

	date
0	2019-03-31
1	2019-04-30
2	2019-05-31
3	2019-06-30
4	2019-07-31

3. Let's extract the year part of the date in a new column and display the top five rows of the dataframe:

   ```
   df['year'] = df['date'].dt.year
   df.head()
   ```

We can see the year in the new variable in the following screenshot:

	date	year
0	2019-03-31	2019
1	2019-04-30	2019
2	2019-05-31	2019
3	2019-06-30	2019
4	2019-07-31	2019

Pandas' dt will raise a TypeError if the series does not contain datetime values. To convert variables from object into datetime, visit the *Extracting date and time parts from a datetime variable* recipe in this chapter.

4. Let's extract the month part of the date in a new column and display the top five rows of the dataframe:

```
df['month'] = df['date'].dt.month
df.head()
```

We can see the month in the newly created variable in the following screenshot:

	date	year	month
0	2019-03-31	2019	3
1	2019-04-30	2019	4
2	2019-05-31	2019	5
3	2019-06-30	2019	6
4	2019-07-31	2019	7

5. Let's capture the quarter in a new column and display the dataframe's top five rows:

```
df['quarter'] = df['date'].dt.quarter
df.head()
```

We can see the quarter in the following dataframe:

	date	year	month	quarter
0	2019-03-31	2019	3	1
1	2019-04-30	2019	4	2
2	2019-05-31	2019	5	2
3	2019-06-30	2019	6	2
4	2019-07-31	2019	7	3

To familiarize yourself with the distinct values of the new variables, you can use pandas' `unique()`, for example, `df['quarter'].unique()`.

6. Finally, let's capture the corresponding semester in a new column and display the dataframe's top rows:

```
df['semester'] = np.where(df['quarter'].isin([1,2]), 1, 2)
df.head()
```

We can see all of the derived features including the semester in the final view of the dataframe, as shown in the following screenshot:

	date	year	month	quarter	semester
0	2019-03-31	2019	3	1	1
1	2019-04-30	2019	4	2	1
2	2019-05-31	2019	5	2	1
3	2019-06-30	2019	6	2	1
4	2019-07-31	2019	7	3	2

You have now learned how to create features from a `datetime` variable that represent the most common and widely used year and month intervals. You can use those features in machine learning models or for data analysis and visualization.

How it works...

In this recipe, we created features that capture the year and month parts of a date variable. We first created a toy dataframe with a variable that contained dates. We used the pandas' date_range() method to create a range of 20 values starting from an arbitrary date and increasing this by intervals of 1 month. With the periods argument, we indicated the number of values we wanted to create, that is, the 20 dates and with the freq argument, we indicated the size of the steps between dates; we used M for months in our example. Finally, we transformed the date range into a dataframe with the pandas' DataFrame() method.

To extract the different parts of the date, we used pandas dt to access the datetime properties of a pandas Series, and then utilized the different properties required: year, month, and quarter to capture the year, month, and quarter in new columns of the dataframe, respectively. To find the semester, we used the where() method from NumPy in combination with the newly created variable quarter. NumPy's where() method scanned the values of the quarter variable. If they were 1 or 2, that is, for the first quarter, it assigned the value 1. Otherwise, it assigned the value 2, representing the first and second semester, respectively.

See also

To learn more about pandas dt and operations on time series, visit https://pandas.pydata.org/pandas-docs/stable/reference/series.html#time-series-related.

Creating representations of day and week

Some events occur more often on certain days of the week, for example, loan applications occur more likely during the week than over weekends, whereas others occur more often during certain weeks of the year. Businesses and organizations may also want to track some key performance metrics throughout the week. Therefore, deriving weeks and days from a date variable is very useful to support organizations in meeting their objectives, and they may also be predictive in machine learning. In this recipe, we will learn how to derive different representations of days and weeks from a datetime variable using pandas and NumPy.

How to do it...

To proceed with the recipe, let's import the required libraries and create a toy dataset:

1. Let's import pandas and NumPy:

```
import numpy as np
import pandas as pd
```

2. Let's create 20 `datetime` observations, beginning from `2019-03-05` at midnight followed by increments of 1 day. Then, let's capture the value range in a dataframe and display the top five rows:

```
rng_ = pd.date_range('2019-03-05', periods=20, freq='D')
df = pd.DataFrame({'date': rng_})
df.head()
```

Note how the values increase by 1 day in the first five observations of the variable we created:

	date
0	2019-03-05
1	2019-03-06
2	2019-03-07
3	2019-03-08
4	2019-03-09

3. Let's extract the day of the month, which can take values between 1 and 31, and capture it in a new column. Then, let's display the top rows of the dataframe:

```
df['day_mo'] = df['date'].dt.day
df.head()
```

We can see the day of the month in the new variable:

	date	day_mo
0	2019-03-05	5
1	2019-03-06	6
2	2019-03-07	7
3	2019-03-08	8
4	2019-03-09	9

Pandas' `dt` will raise a TypeError if the series does not contain `datetime` values. To convert variables from `object` into `datetime`, visit the *Extracting date and time parts from a datetime variable* recipe in this chapter.

4. Let's extract the day of the week, with values between 0 and 6, in a new column, and then let's display the top rows:

```
df['day_week'] = df['date'].dt.dayofweek
df.head()
```

We can see the day of the week in the new variable:

	date	day_mo	day_week
0	2019-03-05	5	1
1	2019-03-06	6	2
2	2019-03-07	7	3
3	2019-03-08	8	4
4	2019-03-09	9	5

You can check the unique values of the newly created variables using pandas `unique()`, for example, by executing `df['day_week'].unique()`.

5. Now, let's extract the name of the day of the week, that is, Monday, Tuesday, and so on, into a new column and output the top five rows of the dataframe:

```
df['day_week_name'] = df['date'].dt.weekday_name
df.head()
```

We can see the names of the days in the new variable:

	date	day_mo	day_week	day_week_name
0	2019-03-05	5	1	Tuesday
1	2019-03-06	6	2	Wednesday
2	2019-03-07	7	3	Thursday
3	2019-03-08	8	4	Friday
4	2019-03-09	9	5	Saturday

6. Next, let's create a binary variable that indicates whether the date was a weekend and then display the dataframe's top rows:

```
df['is_weekend'] = np.where(df['day_week_name'].isin(['Sunday',
'Saturday']), 1, 0)
df.head()
```

We can see the new `is_weekend` variable in the following screenshot:

	date	day_mo	day_week	day_week_name	is_weekend
0	2019-03-05	5	1	Tuesday	0
1	2019-03-06	6	2	Wednesday	0
2	2019-03-07	7	3	Thursday	0
3	2019-03-08	8	4	Friday	0
4	2019-03-09	9	5	Saturday	1

7. Finally, let's capture the corresponding week of the year, which can take values from 1 to 52, and display the dataframe's top rows:

```
df['week'] = df['date'].dt.week
df.head()
```

We can see the week of the year, corresponding to the date as shown in the following screenshot:

	date	day_mo	day_week	day_week_name	is_weekend	week
0	2019-03-05	5	1	Tuesday	0	10
1	2019-03-06	6	2	Wednesday	0	10
2	2019-03-07	7	3	Thursday	0	10
3	2019-03-08	8	4	Friday	0	10
4	2019-03-09	9	5	Saturday	1	10

You have now learned how to capture different representations of days and weeks, which can be quite handy for data analysis, visualization, and machine learning.

How it works...

In this recipe, we created features that capture representations of days and weeks from a date. We first created a toy dataframe with a `datetime` variable. We used the pandas `date_range()` method to create a range of 20 values starting from an arbitrary date and increasing this by intervals of 1 day. With the `periods` argument, we indicated the number of values to create, that is, 20 dates. And with the `freq` argument, we indicated the size of the steps between the dates—we used `D` for days in our example. Finally, we transformed the date range into a dataframe with the pandas `DataFrame()` method.

To extract the different representations of days and weeks, we used pandas `dt` to access the `datetime` properties of the pandas Series, and then we utilized the different properties as required: `week`, `day`, `dayofweek`, and `weekday_name`, capturing the features in new columns. To create a binary variable indicating whether the date was a weekend, we used the `where()` method from NumPy in combination with the newly created `day_week_name` variable, which contained the name of each day. NumPy's `where()` scanned the name of each day, and if they were Saturday or Sunday, it assigned the value 1, otherwise, it assigned the value 0. Like this, we created multiple features that we can use for data analysis and machine learning.

See also

To learn more about pandas `dt`, visit `https://pandas.pydata.org/pandas-docs/stable/reference/series.html#datetime-properties`.

Extracting time parts from a time variable

Some events occur more often at certain times of the day, for example, fraudulent activity occurs more likely during the night or early morning. Also, occasionally, organizations want to track whether an event occurred after another one, in a very short time window, for example, if sales increased on the back of displaying a TV or online advertisement. Therefore, deriving time features is extremely useful. In this recipe, we will extract different time parts of a `datetime` variable utilizing pandas and NumPy.

How to do it...

To proceed with the recipe, let's import the libraries and create a toy dataset:

1. Let's import pandas and NumPy:

   ```
   import numpy as np
   import pandas as pd
   ```

2. Let's create 20 datetime observations, beginning from 2019-03-05 at midnight followed by increments of 1 hour, 15 minutes, and 10 seconds. Then, let's capture the range in a dataframe and display the top five rows:

   ```
   rng_ = pd.date_range('2019-03-05', periods=20, freq='1h15min10s')
   df = pd.DataFrame({'date': rng_})
   df.head()
   ```

In the following screenshot, we can see the variable we just created, with a date and a time part, and the values increasing by intervals of 1 hour, 15 minutes, and 10 seconds:

	date
0	2019-03-05 00:00:00
1	2019-03-05 01:15:10
2	2019-03-05 02:30:20
3	2019-03-05 03:45:30
4	2019-03-05 05:00:40

3. Let's extract the hour, minute, and second parts of the time into three new columns, and then let's display the dataframe's top five rows:

```
df['hour'] = df['date'].dt.hour
df['min'] = df['date'].dt.minute
df['sec'] = df['date'].dt.second
df.head()
```

We can see the different time parts in the new columns of the dataframe:

	date	hour	min	sec
0	2019-03-05 00:00:00	0	0	0
1	2019-03-05 01:15:10	1	15	10
2	2019-03-05 02:30:20	2	30	20
3	2019-03-05 03:45:30	3	45	30
4	2019-03-05 05:00:40	5	0	40

Remember that pandas `dt` needs a `datetime` object to work. You can change the data type of an `object` variable into `datetime` using pandas' `to_datetime()`.

4. Let's perform the same operations that we did in *step 3* but now in one line of code:

```
df[['h','m','s']] = pd.DataFrame([(x.hour, x.minute, x.second) for
x in df['date']])
df.head()
```

We can see the newly created variables in the following screenshot:

	date	hour	min	sec	h	m	s
0	2019-03-05 00:00:00	0	0	0	0	0	0
1	2019-03-05 01:15:10	1	15	10	1	15	10
2	2019-03-05 02:30:20	2	30	20	2	30	20
3	2019-03-05 03:45:30	3	45	30	3	45	30
4	2019-03-05 05:00:40	5	0	40	5	0	40

Remember that you can display the unique values of a variable with pandas' `unique()`, for example, by executing `df['hour'].unique()`.

5. Finally, let's create a binary variable that flags whether the event occurred in the morning, between 6 AM. and 12 PM:

```
df['is_morning'] = np.where( (df['hour'] < 12) & (df['hour'] > 6),
1, 0 )
df.head()
```

We can see the `is_morning` variable in the following screenshot:

	date	hour	min	sec	h	m	s	is_morning
0	2019-03-05 00:00:00	0	0	0	0	0	0	0
1	2019-03-05 01:15:10	1	15	10	1	15	10	0
2	2019-03-05 02:30:20	2	30	20	2	30	20	0
3	2019-03-05 03:45:30	3	45	30	3	45	30	0
4	2019-03-05 05:00:40	5	0	40	5	0	40	0

You have now learned how to extract different time parts from a datetime variable. These features can be used for data analysis as well as to build machine learning models.

How it works...

In this recipe, we created features that capture representations of time. We first created a toy dataframe with a datetime variable. We used the pandas' date_range() method to create a range of 20 values starting from an arbitrary date and increasing this by intervals of 1 hour, 15 minutes, and 20 seconds. We used the '1h15min10s' string as the frequency term for the freq argument, to indicate the desired increments. Next, we transformed the date range into a dataframe with the pandas DataFrame() method.

To extract the different time parts, we used pandas' dt to access the properties required: hour, minute, and second, to extract the hour, minute, and second part of the time variable, respectively. To create a binary variable to indicate whether time was in the morning, we used the where() method from NumPy in combination with the hour variable. NumPy's where() scanned the hour variable and if its values were smaller than 12 and bigger than 6, it assigned the value 1; otherwise, it assigned the value 0. With these operations, we added several features to the dataframe that can be used for data analysis and to train machine learning models.

Capturing the elapsed time between datetime variables

The datetime variables offer value individually and they offer more value collectively when used together with other datetime variables to derive important insights. The most common example consists in deriving the age from the **date of birth** and **today** variable, or the day the customer had an accident or requested a loan. Like these examples, we can combine several datetime variables to derive the time that passed in between and create more meaningful features. In this recipe, we will learn how to capture the time between two datetime variables in different formats and the time between a datetime variable and the current day, utilizing pandas, NumPy, and the datetime library.

How to do it...

To proceed with the recipe, let's import the libraries and create a toy dataset:

1. Let's begin by importing `pandas`, `numpy`, and `datetime`:

```
import datetime
import numpy as np
import pandas as pd
```

2. Let's create 2 `datetime` variables with 20 values each, in which values start from `2019-05-03` and increase in intervals of 1 hour or 1 month, respectively. Then, let's capture the variables in a dataframe, add column names, and display the top rows:

```
rng_hr = pd.date_range('2019-03-05', periods=20, freq='H')
rng_month = pd.date_range('2019-03-05', periods=20, freq='M')
df = pd.DataFrame({'date1': rng_hr, 'date2': rng_month})
df.head()
```

We can see the first five rows of the created variables in the following output:

	date1	date2
0	2019-03-05 00:00:00	2019-03-31
1	2019-03-05 01:00:00	2019-04-30
2	2019-03-05 02:00:00	2019-05-31
3	2019-03-05 03:00:00	2019-06-30
4	2019-03-05 04:00:00	2019-07-31

3. Let's capture the difference in days between the two variables in a new feature, and then display the dataframe's top rows:

```
df['elapsed_days'] = (df['date2'] - df['date1']).dt.days
df.head()
```

We can see the difference in days in the following output:

	date1	date2	elapsed_days
0	2019-03-05 00:00:00	2019-03-31	26
1	2019-03-05 01:00:00	2019-04-30	55
2	2019-03-05 02:00:00	2019-05-31	86
3	2019-03-05 03:00:00	2019-06-30	116
4	2019-03-05 04:00:00	2019-07-31	147

Remember that pandas `dt` needs a `datetime` object to work successfully. For details on how to cast variables as `datetime`, visit the *Extracting date and time parts from a datetime variable* recipe at the beginning of this chapter.

4. Let's capture the difference in months between the two `datetime` variables in a new feature and then display the dataframe's top rows:

```
df['months_passed'] = ((df['date2'] - df['date1']) /
np.timedelta64(1, 'M'))
df['months_passed'] = np.round(df['months_passed'],0)
df.head()
```

We can see the difference in months between the variables in the following screenshot:

	date1	date2	elapsed_days	months_passed
0	2019-03-05 00:00:00	2019-03-31	26	1.0
1	2019-03-05 01:00:00	2019-04-30	55	2.0
2	2019-03-05 02:00:00	2019-05-31	86	3.0
3	2019-03-05 03:00:00	2019-06-30	116	4.0
4	2019-03-05 04:00:00	2019-07-31	147	5.0

5. Now, let's calculate the time in between the variables in minutes and seconds and then display the dataframe's top rows:

```
df['diff_seconds'] = (df['date2'] -
df['date1'])/np.timedelta64(1,'s')
df['diff_minutes'] = (df['date2'] -
df['date1'])/np.timedelta64(1,'m')
df.head()
```

We can see the new variables in the following output:

	date1	date2	elapsed_days	months_passed	diff_seconds	diff_minutes
0	2019-03-05 00:00:00	2019-03-31	26	1.0	2246400.0	37440.0
1	2019-03-05 01:00:00	2019-04-30	55	2.0	4834800.0	80580.0
2	2019-03-05 02:00:00	2019-05-31	86	3.0	7509600.0	125160.0
3	2019-03-05 03:00:00	2019-06-30	116	4.0	10098000.0	168300.0
4	2019-03-05 04:00:00	2019-07-31	147	5.0	12772800.0	212880.0

6. Finally, let's calculate the difference between one variable and the current day, and then display the first 5 rows of the dataframe:

```
df['to_today'] = (datetime.datetime.today() - df['date1'])
df.head()
```

We can see the new variable in the final column of the dataframe in the following screenshot:

	date1	date2	elapsed_days	months_passed	diff_seconds	diff_minutes	to_today
0	2019-03-05 00:00:00	2019-03-31	26	1.0	2246400.0	37440.0	234 days 16:46:28.095694
1	2019-03-05 01:00:00	2019-04-30	55	2.0	4834800.0	80580.0	234 days 15:46:28.095694
2	2019-03-05 02:00:00	2019-05-31	86	3.0	7509600.0	125160.0	234 days 14:46:28.095694
3	2019-03-05 03:00:00	2019-06-30	116	4.0	10098000.0	168300.0	234 days 13:46:28.095694
4	2019-03-05 04:00:00	2019-07-31	147	5.0	12772800.0	212880.0	234 days 12:46:28.095694

Note that the to_today variable on your computer will be different from the one in this book, due to the difference between the current date (at the time of writing) and when you execute the code.

How it works...

In this recipe, we captured different representations of the time in between two variables. To proceed with the recipe, we first created a toy dataframe with two variables, each one with 20 dates starting at an arbitrary date. The first variable increased its values in intervals of 1 hour and the second one in intervals of 1 month. We created the variables with pandas' `date_range()`, which we covered extensively in the previous recipes in this chapter.

To determine the difference between the variables, that is, to determine the time between them, we directly subtracted one variable from the other, that is, one pandas Series from the other. The difference of two pandas Series returns a new pandas Series. To capture the difference in days, we used pandas `dt` followed by `days`. To convert the difference in days into months, we used the `timedelta()` method from NumPy and indicated we wanted the difference in months, passing `M` in the second argument of the method. Instead, to capture the difference in seconds and minutes, we passed the `s` and `m` strings to `timedelta()`.

 NumPy's `timedelta()` method complements pandas `datetime`. The arguments for NumPy's `timedelta` method are a number, 1, in our examples, to represent the number of units, and a `datetime` unit, such as (D)ay, (M)onth, (Y)ear, (h)ours, (m)inutes, or (s)econds.

Finally, we captured the difference from one `datetime` variable to today's date. We obtained the date and time of today using the built-in Python library, `datetime`, with the `datetime.today()` method. We subtracted one of the `datetime` variables from our dataframe to today's date and captured the difference in days, hours, minutes, seconds, and nanoseconds, which is the default value of the operation.

See also

To learn more about NumPy's `timedelta`, visit `https://numpy.org/devdocs/reference/arrays.datetime.html#datetime-and-timedelta-arithmetic`.

Working with time in different time zones

Some organizations operate internationally; therefore, the information they collect about events may be recorded together with the time zone of the area where the event took place. To be able to compare events that occurred across different time zones, we first need to set all of the variables within the same zone. In this recipe, we will learn how to unify the time zones of a datetime variable and then learn how to reassign a variable to a different time zone using pandas.

How to do it...

To proceed with the recipe, let's import pandas and then create a toy dataframe with two variables, each one containing a date and time in different time zones:

1. Import pandas:

```
import pandas as pd
```

2. Let's create a toy dataframe with one variable with values in different time zones:

```
df = pd.DataFrame()

df['time1'] = pd.concat([
    pd.Series(
        pd.date_range(
            start='2015-06-10 09:00', freq='H', periods=3,
            tz='Europe/Berlin')),
    pd.Series(
        pd.date_range(
            start='2015-09-10 09:00', freq='H', periods=3,
            tz='US/Central'))
], axis=0)
```

3. Now, let's add another datetime variable to the dataframe, which also contains values in different time zones, and then display the resulting dataframe:

```
df['time2'] = pd.concat([
    pd.Series(
        pd.date_range(
            start='2015-07-01 09:00', freq='H', periods=3,
            tz='Europe/Berlin')),
    pd.Series(
        pd.date_range(
            start='2015-08-01 09:00', freq='H', periods=3,
            tz='US/Central'))
```

```
], axis=0)
```

```
df
```

We can see the toy dataframe with the variables in the different time zones in the following screenshot:

	time1	time2
0	2015-06-10 09:00:00+02:00	2015-07-01 09:00:00+02:00
1	2015-06-10 10:00:00+02:00	2015-07-01 10:00:00+02:00
2	2015-06-10 11:00:00+02:00	2015-07-01 11:00:00+02:00
0	2015-09-10 09:00:00-05:00	2015-08-01 09:00:00-05:00
1	2015-09-10 10:00:00-05:00	2015-08-01 10:00:00-05:00
2	2015-09-10 11:00:00-05:00	2015-08-01 11:00:00-05:00

The time zone is indicated with the **+02** and **-05** values, respectively.

4. To work with different time zones, first, we unify the time zone to the central zone setting, `utc = True`:

```
df['time1_utc'] = pd.to_datetime(df['time1'], utc=True)
df['time2_utc'] = pd.to_datetime(df['time2'], utc=True)
df
```

Note how, in the new variables, the UTC is zero, whereas, in the previous variables it varies:

	time1	time2	time1_utc	time2_utc
0	2015-06-10 09:00:00+02:00	2015-07-01 09:00:00+02:00	2015-06-10 07:00:00+00:00	2015-07-01 07:00:00+00:00
1	2015-06-10 10:00:00+02:00	2015-07-01 10:00:00+02:00	2015-06-10 08:00:00+00:00	2015-07-01 08:00:00+00:00
2	2015-06-10 11:00:00+02:00	2015-07-01 11:00:00+02:00	2015-06-10 09:00:00+00:00	2015-07-01 09:00:00+00:00
0	2015-09-10 09:00:00-05:00	2015-08-01 09:00:00-05:00	2015-09-10 14:00:00+00:00	2015-08-01 14:00:00+00:00
1	2015-09-10 10:00:00-05:00	2015-08-01 10:00:00-05:00	2015-09-10 15:00:00+00:00	2015-08-01 15:00:00+00:00
2	2015-09-10 11:00:00-05:00	2015-08-01 11:00:00-05:00	2015-09-10 16:00:00+00:00	2015-08-01 16:00:00+00:00

5. Now, let's calculate the difference in days between the variables and then display the dataframe:

```
df['elapsed_days'] = (df['time2_utc'] - df['time1_utc']).dt.days
df['elapsed_days'].head()
```

We can see the time between the values of the variables in the dataframe in the following output:

```
0    21
1    21
2    21
0   -40
1   -40
Name: elapsed_days, dtype: int64
```

6. Finally, let's change the time zone of the `datetime` variables to alternative ones and display the new variables:

```
df['time1_london'] = df['time1_utc'].dt.tz_convert('Europe/London')
df['time2_berlin'] = df['time1_utc'].dt.tz_convert('Europe/Berlin')

df[['time1_london', 'time2_berlin']]
```

We can see the variables in their respective time zones in the following screenshot:

	time1_london	time2_berlin
0	2015-06-10 08:00:00+01:00	2015-06-10 09:00:00+02:00
1	2015-06-10 09:00:00+01:00	2015-06-10 10:00:00+02:00
2	2015-06-10 10:00:00+01:00	2015-06-10 11:00:00+02:00
0	2015-09-10 15:00:00+01:00	2015-09-10 16:00:00+02:00
1	2015-09-10 16:00:00+01:00	2015-09-10 17:00:00+02:00
2	2015-09-10 17:00:00+01:00	2015-09-10 18:00:00+02:00

Note how, when changing time zones, not only the values of the zone changes—that is, the **+01** and **+02** values in the preceding screenshot, but the value of the hour changes as well.

How it works...

In this recipe, we changed the time zone of the variables and performed operations with variables in different time zones. To begin, we created a dataframe with two variables, the values of which started at an arbitrary date and increased hourly, and were set in different time zones. To combine the different time zone variables in one column within the dataframe, we concatenated the series returned by pandas' date_range(), utilizing the pandas' concat() method. We set the axis argument to 0, to indicate we wanted to concatenate the series vertically in one column. We covered the arguments of pandas' date_range() extensively in former recipes in this chapter; see, for example, the *Deriving representations of the year and month* recipe or *Creating representations of day and week* recipe for more details.

To reset the time zone of the variables to the central zone, we used the pandas' to_datetime() method and passed utc=True. To determine the time in between the variables, we subtracted the two pandas Series, as described in the *Capturing the elapsed time between datetime variables* recipe. To reassign a different time zone, we used the pandas' tz_convert() method, indicating the new time zone as argument.

See also

To learn more about the pandas' to_datetime() method, visit: https://pandas.pydata.org/pandas-docs/stable/reference/api/pandas.to_datetime.html.

To learn more about the pandas' tz_convert() method, visit https://pandas.pydata.org/pandas-docs/stable/reference/api/pandas.Series.dt.tz_convert.html.

8 Performing Feature Scaling

Many machine learning algorithms are sensitive to the scale and magnitude of the features. In particular, the coefficients of the linear models depend on the scale of the feature, that is, changing the feature scale will change the coefficients' value. In linear models, as well as algorithms that depend on distance calculations, such as clustering and principal component analysis, features with bigger value ranges tend to dominate over features with smaller ranges. Thus, having features within a similar scale allows us to compare feature importance, and also helps algorithms converge faster, thus improving performance and training times. We discussed the effect of feature magnitude on algorithm performance in more detail in the *Comparing feature magnitude* recipe of Chapter 1, *Foreseeing Variable Problems when Building ML Models*. In this chapter, we will implement multiple techniques in order to set numerical variables to similar value ranges.

This chapter will cover the following recipes:

- Standardizing the features
- Performing mean normalization
- Scaling to the maximum and minimum values
- Implementing maximum absolute scaling
- Scaling with the median and quantiles
- Scaling to vector unit length

Technical requirements

In this chapter, we will use the pandas, NumPy, and scikit-learn Python libraries. You can get all of these libraries from the Python Anaconda distribution, which you can install by following the steps described in the *Technical requirements* section of Chapter 1, *Foreseeing Variable Problems When Building ML Models*. For the recipes in this chapter, we will use the Boston House Prices dataset from scikit-learn. To abide by machine learning best practices, we will begin each recipe by separating the data into train and test sets.

For visualizations on how the scaling techniques described in this chapter affect variable distribution, visit the accompanying Jupyter Notebooks in the dedicated GitHub repository (`https://github.com/PacktPublishing/Python-Feature-Engineering-Cookbook`).

Standardizing the features

Standardization is the process of centering the variable at zero and standardizing the variance to 1. To standardize features, we subtract the mean from each observation and then divide the result by the standard deviation:

$$z = \frac{x - mean(x)}{std(x)}$$

The result of the preceding transformation is called the z-score and represents how many standard deviations a given observation *deviates* from the mean. In this recipe, we will implement standardization with scikit-learn.

How to do it...

To begin, we will import the required packages, load the dataset, and prepare the train and test sets:

1. Import the required Python packages, classes and functions:

```
import pandas as pd
from sklearn.datasets import load_boston
from sklearn.model_selection import train_test_split
from sklearn.preprocessing import StandardScaler
```

2. Let's load variables and target from the Boston House Prices dataset from scikit-learn into a dataframe:

```
boston_dataset = load_boston()
data = pd.DataFrame(boston_dataset.data,
columns=boston_dataset.feature_names)
data['MEDV'] = boston_dataset.target
```

3. Now, divide the data into train and test sets:

```
X_train, X_test, y_train, y_test = train_test_split(
    data.drop('MEDV', axis=1), data['MEDV'], test_size=0.3,
random_state=0)
```

4. Next, we'll set up a standard `scaler` transformer using `StandardScaler()` from scikit-learn and fit it to the train set so that it learns each variable's mean and standard deviation:

```
scaler = StandardScaler()
scaler.fit(X_train)
```

5. Now, let's standardize the train and test sets with the trained `scaler`; that is, we'll remove each variable's mean and divide the result by the standard deviation:

```
X_train_scaled = scaler.transform(X_train)
X_test_scaled = scaler.transform(X_test)
```

Scikit-learn scalers, just like any scikit-learn transformer, return NumPy arrays. To convert the array into a dataframe, you need to execute `X_train_scaled = pd.DataFrame(X_train_scaled, columns=X_train.columns)`.

`StandardScaler()` stores the mean and standard deviation that were learned from the train set variables in its `mean_` and `scale_` attributes. Let's visualize the learned parameters.

6. First, we'll print the mean values that were learned by the `scaler`:

```
scaler.mean_
```

The mean values per variable can be seen in the following output:

```
array([3.35828432e+00, 1.18093220e+01, 1.10787571e+01,
       6.49717514e-02, 5.56098305e-01, 6.30842655e+00,
       6.89940678e+01, 3.76245876e+00, 9.35310734e+00,
       4.01782486e+02, 1.84734463e+01, 3.60601186e+02,
       1.24406497e+01])
```

7. Now, let's print the standard deviation values that were learned by the `scaler`:

```
scaler.scale_
```

The standard deviation of each variable can be seen in the following output:

```
array([8.34141658e+00, 2.36196246e+01, 6.98393565e+00,
       2.46476009e-01, 1.15437239e-01, 7.01016354e-01,
       2.79987983e+01, 2.06473886e+00, 8.65974217e+00,
       1.70351284e+02, 2.22166426e+00, 8.55009244e+01,
       7.06848020e+00])
```

By doing this, you've learned how to standardize the variables in your datasets.

How it works...

In this recipe, we standardized the variables of the Boston House Prices dataset by utilizing scikit-learn. To standardize these features, we needed to learn and store the mean and standard deviation for each variable by utilizing the train set. Then, we used those parameters to standardize the variables in the train and test sets. To do this, we used `StandardScaler()` from scikit-learn, which can learn and store these parameters in its attributes.

First, we loaded the dataset and divided it into train and test sets using the `train_test_split()` function from scikit-learn. We passed the independent variables as arguments. To do this, we dropped the target from the dataset with pandas' `drop()`. Next, we passed the target as a pandas Series. Then, we specified the percentage of observations to be placed in the test set and set `random_state` to zero for reproducibility.

To standardize these features, we used `StandardScaler()` from scikit-learn with its default parameters. Using the `fit()` method and by taking the train set as an argument, the `scaler` learned each variable's mean and standard deviation and stored them in its `mean_` and `scale_` attributes. Using the `transform()` method, the `scaler` standardized the variables in the train and test sets, returning NumPy arrays.

See also

To learn more about `StandardScaler()` from scikit-learn, go to `http://scikit-learn.org/stable/modules/generated/sklearn.preprocessing.StandardScaler.html`.

Performing mean normalization

In mean normalization, we center the variable at zero and rescale the distribution to the value range. This procedure involves subtracting the mean from each observation and then dividing the result by the difference between the minimum and maximum values:

$$xscaled = \frac{x - mean(x)}{max(x) - min(x)}$$

This transformation results in a distribution centered at 0, with its minimum and maximum values within the range of -1 to 1. In this recipe, we will implement mean normalization with pandas and then with scikit-learn.

How to do it...

We'll begin by importing the required libraries, loading the dataset, and preparing the train and test sets:

1. Import pandas and the required scikit-learn class and function:

    ```
    import pandas as pd
    from sklearn.datasets import load_boston
    from sklearn.model_selection import train_test_split
    ```

2. Let's load the Boston House Prices dataset from scikit-learn into a pandas dataframe:

    ```
    boston_dataset = load_boston()
    data = pd.DataFrame(boston_dataset.data,
    columns=boston_dataset.feature_names)
    data['MEDV'] = boston_dataset.target
    ```

3. Let's divide the data into train and test sets:

    ```
    X_train, X_test, y_train, y_test = train_test_split(
        data.drop('MEDV', axis=1), data['MEDV'], test_size=0.3,
    random_state=0)
    ```

4. Let's learn the mean values from the variables in the train set using pandas and print the output:

    ```
    means = X_train.mean(axis=0)
    means
    ```

Performing Feature Scaling

 We set the `axis` to `0` to indicate we want the mean across all the rows, that is, across all the observations, which is the mean of each variable. If we set the `axis` to `1` instead, pandas will calculate the mean value per observation, across all the columns.

We can see the learned mean values per variable in the following output:

```
CRIM         3.358284
ZN          11.809322
INDUS       11.078757
CHAS         0.064972
NOX          0.556098
RM           6.308427
AGE         68.994068
DIS          3.762459
RAD          9.353107
TAX        401.782486
PTRATIO     18.473446
B          360.601186
LSTAT       12.440650
dtype: float64
```

5. Now, let's capture the difference between the maximum and minimum values per variable in the train set and then print them out:

```
ranges = X_train.max(axis=0)-X_train.min(axis=0)
ranges
```

We can see the value ranges per variable in the following output:

```
CRIM        88.96988
ZN         100.00000
INDUS       27.28000
CHAS         1.00000
NOX          0.48600
RM           5.21900
AGE         97.10000
DIS         10.95230
RAD         23.00000
TAX        524.00000
PTRATIO      9.40000
B          396.58000
LSTAT       35.25000
dtype: float64
```

The pandas `mean()`, `max()`, and `min()` methods return a pandas Series.

6. Now, we'll implement the mean normalization of the train and test sets by utilizing the learned parameters:

```
X_train_scaled = (X_train - means) / ranges
X_test_scaled = (X_test - means) / ranges
```

Note that this procedure returns pandas dataframes of the transformed train and test sets.

In order to score future data, you will need to store these parameters in a `.txt` or `.csv` file.

How it works...

In this recipe, we standardized the numerical variables of the Boston House Prices dataset from scikit-learn. To implement mean normalization, we learned and stored the mean, maximum, and minimum values from the variables in the train set, which we used to normalize the train and test sets.

We loaded the dataset and divided it into train and test sets using the `train_test_split()` function from scikit-learn. More details on this operation can be found in the *Standardizing the features* recipe of this chapter. To implement mean normalization, we captured the mean values of the numerical variables in the train set using the pandas `mean()` method. Next, we determined the difference between the maximum and minimum values of the numerical variables in the train set by utilizing the pandas `max()` and `min()` methods. Finally, we used the pandas Series with the mean values and the value ranges to implement normalization. We subtracted the mean from each observation in our train and test sets and divided the result by the value ranges. This returned the normalized variables in a pandas dataframe.

There's more...

There is no dedicated scikit-learn transformer to implement mean normalization, but we can implement mean normalization by combining the use of two transformers. To do this, we need to import pandas and load the data, just like we did in *step 1* to *step 3* in the *How it works...* section of this recipe:

1. Next, let's import the scikit-learn transformers:

   ```
   from sklearn.preprocessing import StandardScaler, RobustScaler
   ```

2. Let's set up the `StandardScaler()` from scikit-learn so that it learns and subtracts the mean but **does not** divide the result by the standard deviation:

   ```
   scaler_mean = StandardScaler(with_mean=True, with_std=False)
   ```

3. Now, let's set up the `RobustScaler()` from scikit-learn so that it **does not** remove the median from the values but divides them by the value range, that is, the difference between the maximum and minimum values:

   ```
   scaler_minmax = RobustScaler(with_centering=False,
   with_scaling=True, quantile_range=(0, 100))
   ```

    To divide by the difference between the minimum and maximum values, we need to specify `(0, 100)` in the `quantile_range` argument of `RobustScaler()`.

4. Let's fit the `scalers` to the train set so that they learn and store the mean, maximum, and minimum values:

   ```
   scaler_mean.fit(X_train)
   scaler_minmax.fit(X_train)
   ```

5. Finally, let's apply mean normalization to the train and test sets:

   ```
   X_train_scaled =
   scaler_minmax.transform(scaler_mean.transform(X_train))
   X_test_scaled =
   scaler_minmax.transform(scaler_mean.transform(X_test))
   ```

Note how we transform the data with `StandardScaler()` to remove the mean and then transform the resulting NumPy array with `RobustScaler()` to divide the result by the range between the minimum and maximum values. We described the functionality of `StandardScaler()` in the *Standardizing the features* recipe of this chapter and will cover `RobustScaler()` in the *Scaling with the median and quantiles* recipe of this chapter.

See also

To learn more about the scikit-learn scalers, take a look at the following links:

- `StandardScaler()`: http://scikit-learn.org/stable/modules/generated/ sklearn.preprocessing.StandardScaler.html
- `RobustScaler()`: http://scikit-learn.org/stable/modules/generated/ sklearn.preprocessing.RobustScaler.html

Scaling to the maximum and minimum values

Scaling to the minimum and maximum values squeezes the values of the variables between 0 and 1. To implement this scaling technique, we need to subtract the minimum value from all the observations and divide the result by the value range, that is, the difference between the maximum and minimum values:

$$xscaled = \frac{x - min(x)}{max(x) - min(x)}$$

In this recipe, we will implement scaling on the minimum and maximum values by utilizing scikit-learn.

How to do it...

To begin, we will import the required packages, load the dataset, and prepare the train and test sets:

1. Import pandas and the required scikit-learn classes and function:

```
import pandas as pd
from sklearn.datasets import load_boston
from sklearn.model_selection import train_test_split
from sklearn.preprocessing import MinMaxScaler
```

2. Let's load the Boston House Prices dataset from scikit-learn into a pandas dataframe:

```
boston_dataset = load_boston()
data = pd.DataFrame(boston_dataset.data,
columns=boston_dataset.feature_names)
data['MEDV'] = boston_dataset.target
```

3. Let's divide the data into train and test sets:

```
X_train, X_test, y_train, y_test = train_test_split(
    data.drop('MEDV', axis=1), data['MEDV'], test_size=0.3,
random_state=0)
```

4. Let's set up a minimum and maximum value scaler utilizing scikit-learn and then fit it to the train set so that it learns each variable's minimum and maximum:

```
scaler = MinMaxScaler()
scaler.fit(X_train)
```

5. Finally, let's scale the variables in the train and test sets with the trained scaler; that is, we'll subtract the minimum and divide by the value range:

```
X_train_scaled = scaler.transform(X_train)
X_test_scaled = scaler.transform(X_test)
```

MinMaxScaler() stores the maximum and minimum values and the value ranges in its data_max_, min_, and data_range_ attributes, respectively.

How it works...

In this recipe, we scaled the numerical variables of the Boston House Prices dataset that comes with scikit-learn to their minimum and maximum values. In order to learn and perpetuate these parameters, we used `MinMaxScaler()` from scikit-learn.

First, we loaded the dataset and divided it into train and test sets using the `train_test_split()` function from scikit-learn. To scale these features, we created an instance of `MinMaxScaler()` with its default parameters. Using the `fit()` method and by taking the train set as an argument, `scaler` learned each variable's maximum and minimum values, along with their differences, and stored these parameters in its `data_max_`, `min_`, and `data_range` attributes. With the `transform()` method, `scaler` removed the minimum value from each variable in the train and test sets and divided the result by the value range. This returned NumPy arrays.

See also

To learn more about `MinMaxScaler()` from scikit-learn, go to `http://scikit-learn.org/stable/modules/generated/sklearn.preprocessing.MinMaxScaler.html`.

Implementing maximum absolute scaling

Maximum absolute scaling scales the data to its maximum value; that is, it divides every observation by the maximum value of the variable:

$$x scaled = \frac{x}{max(x)}$$

The result of the preceding transformation is a distribution in which the values vary approximately within the range of -1 to 1. In this recipe, we will implement maximum absolute scaling with scikit-learn.

 Scikit-learn recommends using this transformer on data that is centered at zero or on sparse data.

How to do it...

Let's begin by importing the required packages, loading the dataset, and preparing the train and test sets:

1. Import pandas and the required scikit-learn classes and function:

```
import pandas as pd
from sklearn.datasets import load_boston
from sklearn.model_selection import train_test_split
from sklearn.preprocessing import MaxAbsScaler
```

2. Let's load the Boston House Prices dataset from scikit-learn into a pandas dataframe:

```
boston_dataset = load_boston()
data = pd.DataFrame(boston_dataset.data,
columns=boston_dataset.feature_names)
data['MEDV'] = boston_dataset.target
```

3. Let's divide the data into train and test sets:

```
X_train, X_test, y_train, y_test = train_test_split(
    data.drop('MEDV', axis=1), data['MEDV'], test_size=0.3,
random_state=0)
```

4. Let's set up the maximum absolute `scaler` from scikit-learn and fit it to the train set so that it learns the variable's maximum values:

```
scaler = MaxAbsScaler()
scaler.fit(X_train)
```

5. Now, let's divide each variable in the train and test sets by their maximum values by utilizing the trained `scaler`:

```
X_train_scaled = scaler.transform(X_train)
X_test_scaled = scaler.transform(X_test)
```

`MaxScaler()` stores the maximum values in its `max_abs_` attribute.

How it works...

In this recipe, we scaled the numerical variables of the Boston House Prices dataset to their maximum values. To scale these features to their maximum value, we learned and stored this parameter by utilizing `MaxAbsScaler()` from scikit-learn. First, we loaded the dataset and divided it into train and test sets using the `train_test_split()` function from scikit-learn. To scale the features, we created an instance of a `scaler` calling `MaxAbsScaler()` with its default parameters. With the `fit()` method, and by taking the train set as an argument, the `scaler` learned the maximum values for each variable and stored them in its `max_abs_` attribute. With the `transform()` method, the `scaler` divided the variables in the train and test sets by their maximum values. This returned NumPy arrays.

There's more...

We can center the variable distributions at 0 and then scale them to their absolute maximum, as recommended by scikit-learn, by combining the use of two transformers. To do this, we need to import the required packages and load the data, just like we did in *step 1* to *step 3* of this recipe:

1. Next, let's import the additional scikit-learn transformer:

   ```
   from sklearn.preprocessing import StandardScaler
   ```

2. Let's set up `StandardScaler()` from scikit-learn so that it learns and subtracts the mean but **does not** divide the result by the standard deviation:

   ```
   scaler_mean = StandardScaler(with_mean=True, with_std=False)
   ```

3. Now, let's set up `MaxAbsScaler()` with its default parameters:

   ```
   scaler_maxabs = MaxAbsScaler()
   ```

4. Let's fit the `scalers` to the train set so that they learn the required parameters:

   ```
   scaler_mean.fit(X_train)
   scaler_maxabs.fit(X_train)
   ```

5. Finally, let's transform the train and test sets:

   ```
   X_train_scaled =
   scaler_maxabs.transform(scaler_mean.transform(X_train))
   X_test_scaled =
   scaler_maxabs.transform(scaler_mean.transform(X_test))
   ```

Note how we transform the datasets with `StandardScaler()` to remove the mean and then transform the returned NumPy arrays with `MaxAbsScaler()` to scale the variables to their maximum values.

See also

To learn more about scikit-learn `scalers`, take a look at the following links:

- `StandardScaler()`: http://scikit-learn.org/stable/modules/generated/sklearn.preprocessing.StandardScaler.html
- `MaxAbsScaler()`: http://scikit-learn.org/stable/modules/generated/sklearn.preprocessing.MaxAbsScaler.html

Scaling with the median and quantiles

When scaling variables to the median and quantiles, the median value is removed from the observations and the result is divided by the **inter-quartile range (IQR)**. The IQR is the range between the 1st quartile and the 3rd quartile, or, in other words, the range between the 25th quantile and the 75th quantile:

$$xscaled = \frac{x - median(x)}{75thQuantile(x) - 25thQuantile(x)}$$

This method is known as *robust scaling* because it produces more robust estimates for the center and value range of the variable, and is recommended if the data contains outliers. In this recipe, we will implement scaling with the median and IQR by utilizing scikit-learn.

How to do it...

To begin, we will import the required packages, load the dataset, and prepare the train and test sets:

1. Import pandas and the required scikit-learn classes and function:

```
import pandas as pd
from sklearn.datasets import load_boston
from sklearn.model_selection import train_test_split
from sklearn.preprocessing import RobustScaler
```

2. Let's load the Boston House Prices dataset from scikit-learn into a pandas dataframe:

```
boston_dataset = load_boston()
data = pd.DataFrame(boston_dataset.data,
columns=boston_dataset.feature_names)
data['MEDV'] = boston_dataset.target
```

3. Let's divide the data into train and test sets:

```
X_train, X_test, y_train, y_test = train_test_split(
    data.drop('MEDV', axis=1), data['MEDV'], test_size=0.3,
random_state=0)
```

4. To perform scaling to the median and quantiles, we need to set up `RobustScaler()` from scikit-learn and fit it to the train set so that it learns and stores the median and IQR:

```
scaler = RobustScaler()
scaler.fit(X_train)
```

5. Finally, let's scale the variables in the train and test sets with the trained `scaler`:

```
X_train_scaled = scaler.transform(X_train)
X_test_scaled = scaler.transform(X_test)
```

6. Now, we can output the median values per variable that were learned and stored by `RobustScaler()`:

```
scaler.center_
```

The medians that are stored in the `center_` attribute of `RobustScaler()` can be seen in the following output:

```
array([2.62660e-01, 0.00000e+00, 8.56000e+00, 0.00000e+00,
       5.38000e-01, 6.21550e+00, 7.94500e+01, 3.21570e+00,
       5.00000e+00, 3.11000e+02, 1.91000e+01, 3.91605e+02,
       1.11600e+01])
```

7. Now, let's output the IQR stored in `RobustScaler()`:

```
scaler.scale_
```

We can see the IQR for each variable in the following output:

```
array([3.030275e+00, 2.000000e+01, 1.315000e+01, 1.000000e+00,
       1.792500e-01, 7.520000e-01, 4.857500e+01, 2.971650e+00,
       2.000000e+01, 3.900000e+02, 2.800000e+00, 1.963250e+01,
       9.982500e+00])
```

Remember that scikit-learn transformers return NumPy arrays.

How it works...

In this recipe, we scaled the numerical variables of the Boston House Prices dataset from scikit-learn to the median and IQR. To learn and perpetuate the median and the IQR, we used `RobustScaler()` from scikit-learn.

First, we loaded the dataset and divided it into train and test sets using the `train_test_split()` function from scikit-learn. To scale the features, we created an instance of `RobustScaler()` with its default parameters. With the `fit()` method and by taking the train set as an argument, `scaler` learned the median and IQR for each variable. With the `transform()` method, `scaler` subtracted the median from each variable in the train and test sets and divided the result by the IQR. Doing this returned NumPy arrays with the scaled variables.

See also

To learn more about `RobustScaler()` from scikit-learn, go to http://scikit-learn.org/stable/modules/generated/sklearn.preprocessing.RobustScaler.html.

Scaling to vector unit length

When scaling to vector unit length, we transform the components of a *feature* vector so that the transformed vector has a length of 1, or in other words, a norm of 1. Note that this scaling technique scales the *feature* vector, as opposed to each individual variable, compared to what we did in the other recipes in this chapter. A feature vector contains the values of each variable for a single observation. When scaling to vector unit length, we divide each feature vector by its norm.

Scaling to the unit norm is achieved by dividing each observation vector by either the Manhattan distance (l1 norm) or the Euclidean distance (l2 norm) of the vector. The Manhattan distance is given by the sum of the absolute components of the vector:

$$l1(X) = |x1| + |x2| + ... + |xn|$$

On the other hand, the Euclidean distance is given by the square root of the square sum of the component of the vector:

$$l2(X) = \sqrt{x1^2 + x2^2 + ... + xn^2}$$

Here, x1, x2, and xn are the values of variables 1, 2, and n for each observation.

In this recipe, we will implement scaling to vector unit length using scikit-learn.

How to do it...

To begin, we'll import the required packages, load the dataset, and prepare the train and test sets:

1. Import the required Python packages, classes, and function:

```
import numpy as np
import pandas as pd
from sklearn.datasets import load_boston
from sklearn.model_selection import train_test_split
from sklearn.preprocessing import Normalizer
```

2. Let's load the Boston House Prices dataset from scikit-learn into a pandas dataframe:

```
boston_dataset = load_boston()
data = pd.DataFrame(boston_dataset.data,
columns=boston_dataset.feature_names)
data['MEDV'] = boston_dataset.target
```

3. Let's divide the data into train and test sets:

```
X_train, X_test, y_train, y_test = train_test_split(
    data.drop('MEDV', axis=1), data['MEDV'], test_size=0.3,
random_state=0)
```

4. Let's set up the `Normalizer()` from scikit-learn to scale each observation to the Manhattan distance or `l1`:

```
scaler = Normalizer(norm='l1')
```

To normalize utilizing the Euclidean distance, you need to set the `norm` to `l2` using `scaler = Normalizer(norm='l2')`.

5. Let's fit `scaler` to the train set:

```
scaler.fit(X_train)
```

The `fit()` method of `Normalizer()` does nothing, as this normalization procedure depends exclusively on the values of the features for each observation. No parameters need to be learned from the train set.

6. Let's transform the train and test sets; that is, we'll divide each observation vector by its norm:

```
X_train_scaled = scaler.transform(X_train)
X_test_scaled = scaler.transform(X_test)
```

7. We can calculate the length, that is, the Manhattan distance of each observation vector, using `linalg()` from NumPy:

```
np.round( np.linalg.norm(X_train_scaled, ord=1, axis=1), 1)
```

You need to set `ord=1` for the Manhattan distance or `ord=2` for the Euclidean distance as arguments of NumPy's `linalg()`, depending on whether you scaled the features to the `l1` or `l2` norm.

We can see the normalized observation vectors in the following output:

```
array([1., 1., 1., 1., 1., 1., 1., 1., 1., 1., 1., 1., 1., 1., 1., 1., 1.,
       1., 1., 1., 1., 1., 1., 1., 1., 1., 1., 1., 1., 1., 1., 1., 1.,
       1., 1., 1., 1., 1., 1., 1., 1., 1., 1., 1., 1., 1., 1., 1., 1.,
       1., 1., 1., 1., 1., 1., 1., 1., 1., 1., 1., 1., 1., 1., 1., 1.,
       1., 1., 1., 1., 1., 1., 1., 1., 1., 1., 1., 1., 1., 1., 1., 1.,
       1., 1., 1., 1., 1., 1., 1., 1., 1., 1., 1., 1., 1., 1., 1., 1.,
       1., 1., 1., 1., 1., 1., 1., 1., 1., 1., 1., 1., 1., 1., 1., 1.,
       1., 1., 1., 1., 1., 1., 1., 1., 1., 1., 1., 1., 1., 1., 1., 1.,
       1., 1., 1., 1., 1., 1., 1., 1., 1., 1., 1., 1., 1., 1., 1., 1.,
```

```
1., 1., 1., 1., 1., 1., 1., 1., 1., 1., 1., 1., 1., 1., 1., 1., 1.,
1., 1., 1., 1., 1., 1., 1., 1., 1., 1., 1., 1., 1., 1., 1., 1., 1.,
1., 1., 1., 1., 1., 1., 1., 1., 1., 1., 1., 1., 1., 1., 1., 1., 1.,
1., 1., 1., 1., 1., 1., 1., 1., 1., 1., 1., 1., 1., 1., 1., 1., 1.,
1., 1., 1., 1., 1., 1., 1., 1., 1., 1., 1., 1., 1., 1., 1., 1., 1.,
1., 1., 1., 1., 1., 1., 1., 1., 1., 1., 1., 1., 1., 1., 1., 1., 1.,
1., 1., 1., 1., 1., 1., 1., 1., 1., 1., 1., 1., 1., 1., 1., 1., 1.,
1., 1., 1., 1., 1., 1., 1., 1., 1., 1., 1., 1., 1., 1., 1., 1., 1.,
1., 1., 1., 1., 1., 1., 1., 1., 1., 1., 1., 1., 1., 1., 1., 1., 1.,
1., 1., 1., 1., 1., 1., 1., 1., 1., 1., 1., 1., 1., 1., 1., 1., 1.,
1., 1., 1., 1., 1., 1., 1., 1., 1., 1., 1., 1., 1., 1., 1., 1., 1.,
1., 1., 1., 1., 1., 1., 1., 1., 1., 1., 1., 1., 1.])
```

As expected, the feature length for each observation is 1.

> You can compare the output of *step 7* with the distance of the unscaled data by executing `np.round( np.linalg.norm(X_train, ord=1, axis=1), 1)`.

How it works...

In this recipe, we scaled the numerical variables of the Boston House Prices dataset from scikit-learn to the vector unit norm by utilizing the Manhattan or Euclidean distance. First, we loaded the dataset and divided it into train and test sets using the `train_test_split()` function from scikit-learn. To scale the features, we created an instance of the `Normalizer()` from scikit-learn and set the norm to `l1` for the Manhattan distance. For the Euclidean distance, we set the norm to `l2`. Then, we applied the `fit()` method, although there were no parameters to be learned. Finally, with the `transform()` method, `scaler` divided each observation by its norm. This returned a NumPy array with the scaled dataset.

See also

To learn more about `Normalizer()` from scikit-learn, go to `http://scikit-learn.org/stable/modules/generated/sklearn.preprocessing.Normalizer.html`.

9
Applying Mathematical Computations to Features

New features can be created by combining two or more variables. Variables can be combined automatically or by using domain knowledge of the data and the industry. For example, in finance, we combine information about the **income** and the **acquired debt** to determine the **disposable income**:

disposable income = income - total debt.

Similarly, if a client has debt across many financial products, for example, a car loan, a mortgage, and credit cards, we can determine the **total debt** by adding all of those variables up:

Total debt = car loan balance + credit card balance + mortgage balance

In the previous examples, the mathematical functions used to combine the existing variables are derived via domain knowledge of the industry. We can also combine variables automatically, by creating polynomial combinations of the existing variables in the dataset or by using off-the-shelf algorithms such as decision trees and **Principal Component Analysis (PCA)**. In this chapter, we will create new features using multiple mathematical functions and off-the-shelf algorithms with Python.

This chapter will cover the following recipes:

- Combining multiple features with statistical operations
- Combining pairs of features with mathematical functions
- Performing polynomial expansion
- Deriving new features with decision trees
- Carrying out PCA

Technical requirements

In this chapter, we will use the following Python libraries: pandas, NumPy, Matplotlib, seaborn, and scikit-learn. You can get all of these libraries with the Python Anaconda distribution, which you can install following the steps described in the *Technical requirements* section in `Chapter 1`, *Foreseeing Variable Problems in Building ML Models*.

Combining multiple features with statistical operations

New features can be created by performing mathematical and statistical operations over existing variables. We previously mentioned that we can calculate the total debt by summing up the debt across individual financial products:

$$Total\ debt = car\ loan\ debt + credit\ card\ debt + mortgage\ debt$$

We can also derive other insightful features using alternative statistical operations. For example, we can determine the maximum debt of a customer across financial products, the minimum time they spent surfing one page of our website, or the mean time they spent reading an article of our magazine:

$$maximum\ debt = max(car\ loan\ balance,\ credit\ card\ balance,\ mortgage\ balance)$$

$$minimum\ time\ on\ page = min(time\ on\ homepage,\ time\ on\ about\ page,\ time\ on\ the\ contact\ us\ page)$$

$$mean\ time\ reading\ article = (time\ on\ article\ 1 + time\ on\ article\ 2 + time\ on\ article\ 3)\ /\ count(articles)$$

We can, in principle, use any mathematical or statistical operation to create new features, such as product, mean, standard deviation, or maximum or minimum values, to name a few. In this recipe, we will implement these mathematical operations using pandas.

Getting ready

In this recipe, we will use the Breast Cancer dataset that comes with scikit-learn, which contains information about tumors and other medical abnormalities, and a target indicating whether they are cancerous. To become familiar with the dataset, run the following commands in a Jupyter Notebook or Python console:

```
from sklearn.datasets import load_breast_cancer
data = load_breast_cancer()
print(data.DESCR)
```

The preceding code block should print out the description of the dataset and an interpretation of its variables.

How to do it...

In this recipe, we will create new features by combining information, that is, variables about tumors, using multiple mathematical operations:

1. Let's begin by loading pandas and the dataset from scikit-learn:

    ```
    import pandas as pd
    from sklearn.datasets import load_breast_cancer
    ```

2. Let's load the Breast Cancer dataset into a pandas dataframe:

    ```
    data = load_breast_cancer()
    df = pd.DataFrame(data.data, columns=data.feature_names)
    df['target'] = data.target
    ```

 Scikit-learn stores the data, feature names, and target in the `data`, `feature_names`, and `target` attributes, respectively. So, we need to reconstitute the dataset bit by bit.

In the following code lines, we will create new features using multiple mathematical operations across a subset of the features in the dataset.

3. Let's begin by creating a list with the subset of features to which we will apply the different mathematical operations:

```
features = ['mean smoothness', 'mean compactness',
            'mean concavity', 'mean concave points',
            'mean symmetry']
```

4. Create a new feature with the sum of the selected variables:

```
df['added_features'] = df[features].sum(axis=1)
```

5. Derive a new feature using the product of the selected features:

```
df['prod_features'] = df[features].prod(axis=1)
```

6. Obtain a new feature corresponding to the mean value of the variables selected in *step 3*:

```
df['mean_features'] = df[features].mean(axis=1)
```

7. Capture the standard deviation of the features in a new variable:

```
df['std_features'] = df[features].std(axis=1)
```

8. Find the maximum value across the selected variables:

```
df['max_features'] = df[features].max(axis=1)
```

9. Find the minimum value across the selected features:

```
df['min_features'] = df[features].min(axis=1)
```

We can perform *step 4* to *step 9* in one line of code using the pandas' `agg()` method: `df_t = df[features].agg(['sum', 'prod','mean','std', 'max', 'min'], axis='columns')`.

To find out more about the mathematical operations supported by pandas, follow this link: `https://pandas.pydata.org/pandas-docs/stable/reference/frame.html#computations-descriptive-stats`.

How it works...

The pandas library has plenty of built-in operations to return the desired mathematical and statistical computations over the indicated axis, that is, across the rows or the columns of a dataframe. In this recipe, we leveraged the power of pandas to create new features from existing ones. We loaded the Breast Cancer dataset from scikit-learn. Then, we made a list of the features to combine with the multiple mathematical operations. We used the pandas `sum()`, `prod()`, `mean()`, `std()`, `max()`, and `min()` methods to determine the sum, product, mean, standard deviation, and maximum and minimum values of those features.

To perform these operations across the columns, that is, across the variables, we added the `axis=1` argument within the methods, and we captured the new features as new columns of the dataframe. Finally, with the pandas' `agg()` method, we carried out all of the mathematical combinations in one line of code. Pandas' `agg()` takes, as arguments, a list of strings corresponding to the methods to apply and the `axis` to which the operations should be applied, which can be either columns or rows. It returns a pandas dataframe with the feature combination as columns.

There's more...

With visualizations, we can easily understand whether new features provide valuable information. In this section, we will create violin plots to visualize the distribution of one of the newly created features. We will plot the distribution of the feature separately, for those tumors that were cancerous and those that were not. To create the plot, we first need to execute *step 1* to *step 4* from the *How to do it...* section of this recipe. Then, we can create a violin plot of the resulting feature as follows:

1. Let's first import the visualization libraries:

```
import matplotlib.pyplot as plt
import seaborn as sns
```

2. Create a violin plot of the newly created feature:

```
sns.violinplot(x="target", y="added_features", data=df)
plt.title('Added Features')
plt.show()
```

The preceding code block returns the following plot, where we can see that the distribution of the newly created feature is different between cancerous and normal tumors:

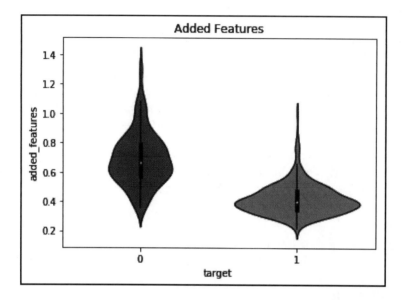

You can check this and more plots, including those from the original variables, in the Jupyter Notebook in the accompanying GitHub repository: `https://github.com/PacktPublishing/Python-Feature-Engineering-Cookbook`.

See also

To find out more about the mathematical operations supported by pandas, visit this link: `https://pandas.pydata.org/pandas-docs/stable/reference/frame.html#computations-descriptive-stats`.

To learn more about pandas aggregate, follow this link: `https://pandas.pydata.org/pandas-docs/stable/reference/api/pandas.DataFrame.aggregate.html`.

Combining pairs of features with mathematical functions

In the previous recipe, *Combining multiple features with statistical operations*, we created new features by performing statistical operations across several variables. Some mathematical operations, however, such as subtraction or division, make more sense when performed between two features, or when considering multiple features against one reference variable. These operations are very useful to derive ratios, such as the **debt-to-income ratio**:

debt-to-income ratio = total debt / total income

Or we can use them for differences, for example, the **disposable income**:

disposable income = income - total debt

In this recipe, we will learn how to derive new features by subtraction or division utilizing pandas, and more generally, we will learn how to perform operations against one reference variable.

Getting ready

We will use the Breast Cancer dataset that comes with scikit-learn. To learn more about this dataset, follow the steps indicated in the *Getting ready* section of the *Combining multiple features with statistical operations* recipe in this chapter.

How to do it...

Let's begin by loading the Python libraries and the Breast Cancer dataset from scikit-learn:

1. Load pandas and the dataset from scikit-learn:

```
import pandas as pd
from sklearn.datasets import load_breast_cancer
```

2. Let's load the Breast Cancer dataset into a pandas dataframe:

```
data = load_breast_cancer()
df = pd.DataFrame(data.data, columns=data.feature_names)
df['target'] = data.target
```

3. Let's now capture the difference between two features in a new variable:

```
df['difference'] = df['worst compactness'].sub(df['mean
compactness'])
```

We can perform the same calculation with this command:
`df['difference'] = df['worst compactness'] - (df['mean compactness'])`.

4. Let's now create a new feature with the ratio between two variables:

```
df['quotient'] = df['worst radius'].div(df['mean radius'])
```

We can calculate the ratio with the alternative command:
`df['quotient'] = df['worst radius'] / (df['mean radius'])`.

Next, we will compare a group of features to the aggregated view of another subset of features. Let's begin by capturing these subsets of variables into lists.

5. Make a list of the features we want to compare:

```
features = ['mean smoothness', 'mean compactness', 'mean
concavity', 'mean concave points', 'mean symmetry']
```

6. Make a list of the features we want to aggregate:

```
worst_f = ['worst smoothness', 'worst compactness',
           'worst concavity', 'worst concave points',
           'worst symmetry']
```

7. Create a new feature with the sum of the features in *step 6*:

```
df['worst'] = df[worst_f].sum(axis=1)
```

We discussed the code in *step 7* in the previous recipe, *Combining multiple features with statistical operations*.

8. Let's obtain the ratio between each one of the features in *step 5* and the feature created in *step 7*:

```
df[features] = df[features].div(df['worst'], axis=0)
```

The preceding code block divides each of the features in the list we created in *step 5* by the `worst` feature, which we created in *step 7*. You can output the first five rows of the engineered features using `df[features].head()` to corroborate the result.

How it works...

The pandas library has plenty of built-in operations to compare one feature or a subset of features to a single reference variable. In this recipe, we used the pandas `sub()` and `div()` methods to determine the difference or the ratio between two variables or a subset of variables and one reference feature.

First, we loaded the Breast Cancer dataset from scikit-learn. Next, we subtracted one variable from another. To do this, we applied the `sub()` method to a pandas Series with the first variable, passing the second pandas Series with the second variable within the method, which returned a third pandas Series with the second variable subtracted from the first one. To divide one variable from another, we used the `div()` method, which works identically, that is, it divides the variable on the left by the variable passed as an argument of `div()`.

Next, we divided several variables by a reference one. To do this, we first created a feature corresponding to the sum of a group of features in the dataset, as explained in the *Combining multiple features with statistical operations* recipe. Next, we called the `div()` method over a dataframe with multiple variables, passing the reference variable, that is, a pandas Series, as an argument. The `div()` method divided each variable in the dataframe by the variable indicated within the method. The resulting variables were captured as columns in the same dataframe.

There's more...

Plots and visualizations are useful to understand the distribution of the newly created features and their relationship to the target. To learn how to do violin plots and have a look at the distribution of the features we created in this recipe, visit the Jupyter Notebook in the accompanying GitHub repository.

See also

To learn more about the binary operations supported by pandas, follow this link: `https://pandas.pydata.org/pandas-docs/stable/reference/frame.html#binary-operator-functions`.

Performing polynomial expansion

Existing variables can be combined to create new insightful features. We discussed how to combine variables using common mathematical and statistical operations in the previous two recipes, *Combining multiple features with statistical operations* and *Combining pairs of features with mathematical functions*. A combination of one feature with itself, that is, a polynomial combination of the same feature, can also be quite informative or increase the predictive power of our algorithms. For example, in cases where the target follows a quadratic relationship with a variable, creating a second degree polynomial of the feature allows us to use it in a linear model, as shown in the following screenshot:

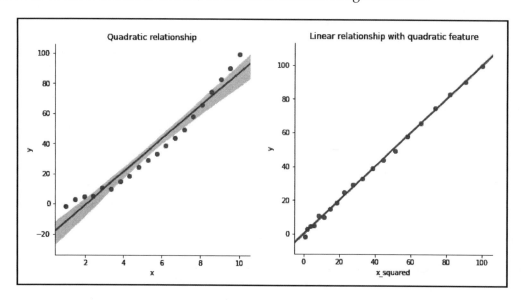

In the plot on the left, due to the quadratic relationship between the target, **y**, and the variable, **x**, there is a poor linear fit. Yet, in the plot on the right, we appreciate how the **x_squared** variable, which is a quadratic combination of **x**, shows a linear relationship with the target, **y**, and therefore improves the performance of the linear model, which predicts **y** from **x_squared**.

With similar logic, polynomial combinations of the same or different variables can return new variables that convey additional information and capture feature interaction and can, therefore, be better inputs for our machine learning algorithms, particularly for linear models. We can create polynomial variables automatically using scikit-learn, and, in this recipe, we will learn how to do so.

Getting ready

Polynomial expansion serves to automate the creation of new features, to capture feature interaction, and to capture potential non-linear relationships between the original variables and the target. The user determines which features to combine and which polynomial degree to use.

Keep in mind that high polynomial degrees or a large number of features to combine will return an enormous number of new features.

The `PolynomialFeatures()` transformer from scikit-learn creates all polynomial combinations of the features with a degree less than or equal to the specified degree, automatically. To follow up easily with the recipe, let's first understand the output of the `PolynomialFeatures()` transformer from scikit-learn, when used with second and third degree in a dataset with three variables.

Second degree polynomial combinations of three variables—a, b, and c—return the following new features:

$$[a, b, c]^2 = 1, a, b, c, ab, ac, bc, a^2, b^2, c^2, abc$$

Note how we have all possible interactions of degree, 1 and 2. The `PolynomialFeatures()` transformer also returns the bias term *1*.

Third degree polynomial combinations of the three variables—a, b, and c—return the following new features:

$$[a, b, c]^3 = 1, a, b, c, ab, ac, bc, abc, a^2b, a^2c, b^2a, b^2c, c^2a, c^2b, a^3, b^3, c^3$$

Note how we have all possible interactions of degree 1, 2, and 3 and the bias term 1.

Now that we understand the output of the polynomial expansion, let's jump into the recipe.

How to do it...

Let's begin by importing the required libraries and preparing the Boston House Prices dataset from scikit-learn:

1. Import pandas and the required functions, classes, and datasets from scikit-learn:

```
import pandas as pd
from sklearn.datasets import load_boston
from sklearn.model_selection import train_test_split
from sklearn.preprocessing import PolynomialFeatures
```

2. Load the Boston House Prices dataset into a pandas dataframe:

```
boston_dataset = load_boston()
data = pd.DataFrame(boston_dataset.data,
columns=boston_dataset.feature_names)
data['MEDV'] = boston_dataset.target
```

3. Separate the dataset into training and testing sets:

```
X_train, X_test, y_train, y_test = train_test_split(
    data.drop('MEDV', axis=1), data['MEDV'], test_size=0.3,
random_state=0)
```

Let's begin with the feature creation by polynomial expansion.

4. Let's set up the polynomial expansion transformer from scikit-learn, to create features by polynomial combination of a degree less than or equal to 3:

```
poly = PolynomialFeatures(degree=3, interaction_only=False,
include_bias=False)
```

5. Let's fit the transformer to the train set so that it learns all of the possible polynomial combinations of three of the variables:

```
poly.fit(X_train[['LSTAT', 'RM', 'NOX']])
```

6. Let's now create the new polynomial features in a new dataset:

```
train_t = poly.transform(X_train[['LSTAT', 'RM', 'NOX']])
test_t = poly.transform(X_test[['LSTAT', 'RM', 'NOX']])
```

Remember that scikit-learn returns NumPy arrays without the feature names, hence `train_t` and `test_t` are NumPy arrays.

7. Let's examine the names of the features created in *step 6*:

```
poly.get_feature_names(['LSTAT', 'RM', 'NOX'])
```

The preceding code returns a list with the names of each feature combination after the polynomial expansion:

```
['LSTAT',
 'RM',
 'NOX',
 'LSTAT^2',
 'LSTAT RM',
 'LSTAT NOX',
 'RM^2',
 'RM NOX',
 'NOX^2',
 'LSTAT^3',
 'LSTAT^2 RM',
 'LSTAT^2 NOX',
 'LSTAT RM^2',
 'LSTAT RM NOX',
 'LSTAT NOX^2',
 'RM^3',
 'RM^2 NOX',
 'RM NOX^2',
 'NOX^3']
```

Compare the returned feature with the explanation in the *Getting ready* section of this recipe to understand the output.

8. Finally, we can capture the arrays with the polynomial features in a dataframe as follows:

```
test_t = pd.DataFrame(test_t)
test_t.columns = poly.get_feature_names(['LSTAT', 'RM', 'NOX'])
```

Remember to pass the list with the features to `poly.get_feature_names()` in the same order as you did to `poly.fit()`; otherwise, the feature names will not coincide with the derived polynomial combinations.

How it works...

In this recipe, we derived new features automatically by creating polynomial combinations of three of the variables in our dataset. We first loaded the Boston House Prices dataset from scikit-learn and divided it into train and test sets.

To create the polynomial features, we used the `PolynomialFeatures()` transformer from scikit-learn, which generates a new feature matrix consisting of all polynomial combinations of the indicated features with a degree less than or equal to the specified degree. By setting `degree` to 3, we were able to create all possible polynomial combinations of degree 3 or smaller. To retain all of the terms of the expansion, we set `interaction_only` to `False`. And to avoid returning the bias term, we set the `include_bias` parameter to `False`.

Setting the `interaction_only` term to `True` returns only the terms, that is, the variables that contain combinations of two or more variables.

The `fit()` method learned all of the possible feature combinations based on the parameters specified. At this stage, the transformer did not perform actual mathematical computations. The `transform()` method performed the mathematical computations with the features to create the new variables. With the `get_feature_names()` method, we could identify the terms of the expansion, that is, how each new feature was calculated.

There's more...

Let's visualize the relationship of the polynomial variables with the target. First, let's run the main recipe as indicated in *step 1* to *step 8*. Then, let's import the Python visualization library and make the plots:

1. Import Matplotlib:

```
import matplotlib.pyplot as plt
```

2. Let's create a function to make multiple subplots, each displaying one of the new polynomial features in a scatter plot versus the target:

```
def plot_features(df, target):
    nb_rows = 5
    nb_cols = 4
    fig, axs = plt.subplots(nb_rows, nb_cols, figsize=(12, 12))
    plt.subplots_adjust(wspace=None, hspace=0.4)
```

```
n = 0
for i in range(0, nb_rows):
    for j in range(0, nb_cols):
        if n!=19:
            axs[i, j].scatter(df[df.columns[n]], target)
            axs[i, j].set_title(df.columns[n])
            n += 1
plt.show()
```

The function takes as argument the dataframe with the polynomial features and returns a multiple subplot visualization, where each subplot displays a scatter plot of a single polynomial feature against the target variable.

3. Run the function using the polynomial features derived from the test set:

```
plot_features(test_t, y_test)
```

We can see the output of the preceding code block in the following screenshot:

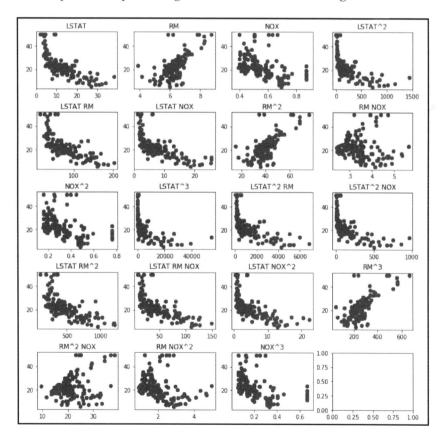

The function we created in *step 2* is tailored to our dataframe. If your dataframe contains more or less polynomial features, you need to adjust the number of rows and columns within the Matplotlib subplot: `plt.subplots(nb_rows, nb_cols, figsize=(12, 12))`.

See also

To learn more about `PolynomialFeatures()` from scikit-learn, follow this link: `https://scikit-learn.org/stable/modules/generated/sklearn.preprocessing.PolynomialFeatures.html`.

See also the Python `gplearn` package to automatically map out other relationships between the variables and the target: `https://gplearn.readthedocs.io/en/stable/intro.html`.

Deriving new features with decision trees

In the winning solution of the KDD competition in 2009, the authors created new features by combining two or more variables using decision trees and then used those variables to train the winning predictive model. This technique is particularly useful to derive features that are monotonic with the target, which is convenient for linear models. The procedure consists of building a decision tree using a subset of the features, typically two or three at a time, and then using the prediction of the tree as a new feature.

Creating new features with decision trees not only creates monotonic relationships between features and target, but it also captures feature interactions, which is useful when building models that do not do so automatically, such as linear models.

In this recipe, we will learn how to create new features with decision trees using pandas and scikit-learn.

Getting ready

To learn more about the procedure implemented by the winners of the 2009 KDD data competition, read the article that begins on page 21 of the following book: `http://www.mtome.com/Publications/CiML/CiML-v3-book.pdf`.

In this recipe, we will work with the Boston House Prices dataset that comes within scikit-learn.

How to do it...

Let's begin by importing the required libraries and getting the dataset ready:

1. Import pandas and the required functions, classes, and datasets from scikit-learn:

```
import pandas as pd
from sklearn.datasets import load_boston
from sklearn.model_selection import train_test_split
from sklearn.tree import DecisionTreeRegressor
from sklearn.model_selection import GridSearchCV
```

2. Load the Boston House Prices dataset into a pandas dataframe:

```
boston_dataset = load_boston()
data = pd.DataFrame(boston_dataset.data,
columns=boston_dataset.feature_names)
data['MEDV'] = boston_dataset.target
```

3. Let's separate the dataset into train and test sets to conform to machine learning best practices:

```
X_train, X_test, y_train, y_test = train_test_split(
    data.drop('MEDV', axis=1), data['MEDV'], test_size=0.3,
random_state=0)
```

Remember to set `random_state`, as indicated in *step 3*, for reproducibility.

In the following lines, we are going to create a new feature from three existing variables in the dataset using a decision tree. We are going to build this decision tree within `GridSearch()` so that we can optimize one of its parameters.

4. Let's create a dictionary with the parameter to optimize:

```
param_grid = {'max_depth': [3, 4, None]}
```

 You can optimize as many parameters of the tree as you wish. To find out which parameters you can optimize, follow this link: `https://scikit-learn.org/stable/modules/generated/sklearn.tree.DecisionTreeClassifier.html`.

5. Let's set up the decision tree within a scikit-learn `GridSearch()` with 5-fold cross-validation, adding the dictionary with the parameters to optimize created in *step 4*, and indicating the metric we would like to optimize:

```
tree_model = GridSearchCV(DecisionTreeRegressor(random_state=0),
                          cv = 5,
                          scoring = 'neg_mean_squared_error',
                          param_grid = param_grid)
```

 We use `DecisionTreeRegressor()` from scikit-learn because the target in this dataset, MEDV, is continuous. If you have a binary target or are performing classification, use `DecisionTreeClassifier()`, also from scikit-learn. Note that you will have to change the scoring metric to those permitted for classification.

6. Train the decision tree using three selected features from the dataset:

```
tree_model.fit(X_train[['LSTAT', 'RM', 'NOX']], y_train)
```

7. Derive the new feature using the decision tree in the train and test sets:

```
X_train['new_feat'] = tree_model.predict(X_train[['LSTAT', 'RM',
'NOX']])
X_test['new_feat'] = tree_model.predict(X_test[['LSTAT', 'RM',
'NOX']])
```

We have now created a new feature by combining the information of three existing features using a decision tree.

How it works...

In this recipe, we combined the information of three variables from the Boston House Prices dataset into a new variable utilizing a decision tree. We loaded the dataset from scikit-learn and then separated the data into train and test sets using the `train_test_split()` function. Next, we created a dictionary with the decision tree parameter to optimize as keys, and a list of the values to examine as values.

Next, we created an instance of a decision tree for regression using `DecisionTreeRegressor()` from scikit-learn inside `GridSearch()`, indicating the fold cross-validation, the metric to optimize, and the dictionary with the parameters and values to examine. Next, we fit the decision tree to the three variables of interest, and, finally, with the `predict()` method, we obtained the predictions derived by the tree from those three features, which we captured as a new feature in the dataframe.

There's more...

We can create visualizations to understand whether the derived feature shows the desired monotonic relationship as well as its distribution. After we run all of the steps in the *How to do it...* section of this recipe, we can create a simple scatter plot as follows:

1. Import the visualization library:

```
import matplotlib.pyplot as plt
```

2. Create a scatter plot with the derived decision tree feature and the target:

```
plt.scatter(X_test['new_feat'], y_test)
plt.ylabel('MEDV')
plt.xlabel('new_feat')
plt.title('Tree derived feature vs House Price')
```

The preceding code block outputs the following plot, where you can see the monotonic relationship between the newly created feature and the target:

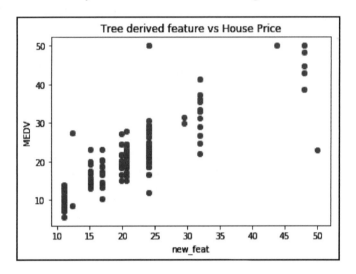

In the scatter plot, we can see a fairly decent monotonic relationship between the new feature and the target.

Carrying out PCA

PCA is a dimensionality reduction technique used to reduce a high dimensional dataset into a smaller subset of **Principal Components** (**PC**), which explain most of the variability observed in the original data. The first PC of the data is a vector along which the observations vary the most, or in other words, a linear combination of the variables in the dataset that maximizes the variance. Mathematically, the first PC minimizes the sum of the squared distances between each observation and the PC. The second PC is again a linear combination of the original variables, which captures the largest remaining variance and is subject to the constraint that is perpendicular to the first PC.

In general, we can build as many PCs as variables in the dataset. Each PC is a linear combination of the variables, orthogonal to the other components, and maximizes the remaining variance, which is left unexplained by previous PCs. The way these PCs are built means that it is often possible for a few of the first PCs to capture most of the information of the original data, as well as most of its relationships to the target.

In this recipe, we will implement PCA to reduce the dimensions of our data and create new features, the principal components, using scikit-learn.

Getting ready

If you are not familiar with PCA or want to know more about the mathematics underlying the functionality of this algorithm and how the components are built, these books are a good resource:

- *An Introduction to Statistical Learning*, by James G, Wittens D, Hastie T, and Tibshirani R, Springer Ed
- *Elements of Statistical Learning*, by Hastie T, Tibshirani R and J. Friedman, Springer Ed

The first book is better to get some intuition about the functionality of PCA, and the second book is better for mathematics. Both books are freely available online.

In this recipe, we are going to perform PCA using scikit-learn, that is, we are going to find the PCs of the Boston House Prices dataset that comes with scikit-learn and then identify the minimum number of components that capture most of the variance of the data.

How to do it...

Let's begin by importing the required libraries and preparing the Boston House Prices dataset from scikit-learn:

1. Import pandas and the required functions, classes, and data from scikit-learn:

```
import pandas as pd
import matplotlib.pyplot as plt
from sklearn.datasets import load_boston
from sklearn.model_selection import train_test_split
from sklearn.decomposition import PCA
```

2. Load the Boston House Prices dataset into a pandas dataframe:

```
boston_dataset = load_boston()
data = pd.DataFrame(boston_dataset.data,
columns=boston_dataset.feature_names)
data['MEDV'] = boston_dataset.target
```

3. Separate the dataset into train and test sets:

```
X_train, X_test, y_train, y_test = train_test_split(
    data.drop('MEDV', axis=1), data['MEDV'], test_size=0.3,
random_state=0)
```

We are now going to obtain the principal components:

4. Let's set up the PCA transformer from scikit-learn to return all possible components:

```
pca = PCA(n_components=None)
```

5. Let's find the principal components in the train set:

```
pca.fit(X_train)
```

6. Let's obtain the components for both train and test sets:

```
train_t = pca.transform(X_train)
test_t = pca.transform(X_test)
```

Remember that scikit-learn returns NumPy arrays, hence train_t and test_t are NumPy arrays.

When creating principal components, a few of the components will capture most of the variability of the original data. To identify how many components capture most of the variability in the Boston House Prices dataset, we can plot the percentage of variance explained (by each component) versus the component number.

7. Plot the percentage of the total variance explained by each component:

```
plt.plot(pca.explained_variance_ratio_)
plt.title('Percentage of Variance Explained')
plt.xlabel('Number of Components')
plt.ylabel('Percentage of Variance Explained')
```

Fortunately, the percentage of variance explained is captured and stored within scikit-learn's PCA object, so that we can easily retrieve it to identify the number of components that capture most of the variance.

The preceding code returns the following plot, where we can see that the first two components capture most of the variability of the data:

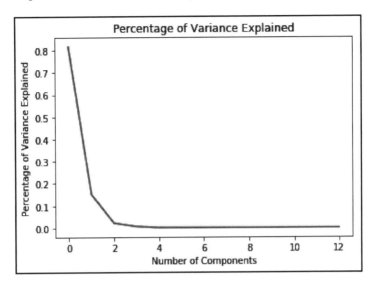

The preceding plot indicates that we can use the first two components to train our machine learning models using a linear model.

 PCA is sensitive to the scale of the features; therefore, it is advisable, if not compulsory to have features within a similar scale before fitting the PCA object from scikit-learn. You can rescale your features with the methods covered in Chapter 8, *Performing Feature Scaling*, of this book.

How it works...

In this recipe, we derived the principal components of the Boston House Prices dataset and then identified the minimum number of components that explain most of the variability observed in the data, using scikit-learn. We loaded the dataset from scikit-learn and then separated the data into train and test sets using the train_test_split() function. Next, we created an instance of a PCA transformer from scikit-learn, to derive all possible principal components, which equal the number of original features in the dataset.

By setting n_components to None, the transformer will return all of the derived principal components, which are the same number as the number of the original features in the dataset.

The fit() method from the PCA() transformer found the principal components in the train set, that is, the linear combinations of the variables that maximize the variance explained. The transform() method calculated the principal components for each observation. Finally, we plotted the percentage of variance explained by each component versus the component number to identify the minimum number of components that capture most of the variability.

See also

To learn more about the PCA transformer from scikit-learn, you can refer to https:// scikit-learn.org/stable/modules/generated/sklearn.decomposition.PCA.html.

To get an intuition into how PCA works, visit this thread on Stack Exchange: https:// stats.stackexchange.com/questions/2691/making-sense-of-principal-component-analysis-eigenvectors-eigenvalues.

10

Creating Features with Transactional and Time Series Data

Throughout this book, we've discussed multiple feature engineering techniques that we can use to engineer variables in tabular data, where each observation is independent and shows only 1 value for each available variable. However, data can also contain multiple values that are not independent for each entity. For example, there can be multiple records for each customer with the details of the customer's transactions within our organization, such as purchases, payments, claims, deposits, and withdrawals. In other cases, the values of the variables may change daily, such as stock prices or energy consumption per household. The first data sources are referred to as transactional data, whereas the second data sources are time series. Time series and transactional data contain time-stamped observations, which means they share a **time dimension**.

We often create features that aggregate or summarize the information from the historical data points of time series or transactions. For example, we can create features that capture the maximum amount that was spent by the customer in the last week, the number of transactions they made, or the time between transactions. The number of features we can create and the ways in which we can aggregate this information is enormous. In this chapter, we will discuss the most common ways of creating aggregated views of historical data by using pandas. Then, we will make a shallow dive into Featuretools, a library designed to automate feature creation from transactional data. Finally, we will point you to other Python libraries that have been devised specifically for analyzing signal complexity.

In this chapter, we will cover the following recipes:

- Aggregating transactions with mathematical operations
- Aggregating transactions in a time window
- Determining the number of local maxima and minima
- Deriving time elapsed between time-stamped events
- Creating features from transactions with Featuretools

Technical requirements

In this chapter, we will use the pandas, NumPy, SciPy, and Matplotlib Python libraries, all of which can be installed using the free Anaconda Python distribution. To do this, follow the instructions in the *Technical requirements* section of `Chapter 1`, *Foreseeing Variable Problems when Building ML Models*.

We will also use the open source Python library Featuretools, which can be installed using `pip` or `conda`. Follow the instructions in the following documentation: `https://docs.featuretools.com/en/stable/getting_started/install.html`.

Throughout the recipes in this chapter, we will work with a mock customer transaction dataset that comes with Featuretools and the **Appliances energy prediction** dataset, available in the UCI Machine Learning Repository: `http://archive.ics.uci.edu/ml/datasets/Appliances+energy+prediction`.

Dua, D. and Graff, C. (2019). *UCI Machine Learning Repository* [`http://archive.ics.uci.edu/ml`]. Irvine, CA: University of California, School of Information and Computer Science.

To download the Appliances energy prediction dataset, follow these steps:

1. Go to `http://archive.ics.uci.edu/ml/machine-learning-databases/00374/`.
2. Click on `energydata_complete.csv` to download the data:

3. Save `energydata_complete.csv` to the folder where you will run all the commands in this chapter.

Make sure you install Featuretools and download the dataset from the UCI Machine Learning repository before proceeding with this chapter, since we will be using both throughout.

Aggregating transactions with mathematical operations

Previously, we mentioned that we can aggregate information from historical data points into single observations like the maximum amount spent on a transaction, the total number of transactions, or the mean value of all transactions, to name a few examples. These aggregations are made with basic mathematical operations, such as the maximum, mean, and count. As you can see, mathematical operations are a simple yet powerful way to obtain a summarized view of historical data.

In this recipe, we will create a flattened dataset by aggregating multiple transactions using common mathematical operations. We will use pandas to do this.

In a flattened dataset, we remove the time-dimension from the transaction data or time series to obtain a single observation per entity.

Getting ready

In this recipe, we will use the mock customer transaction dataset that comes with Featuretools. This toy dataset contains information about transactions for five different customers. This data contains a unique identifier to distinguish between the customers, a unique identifier for each transaction, the transaction time, and the transaction amount, that is, the purchase amount. We will derive features from the purchase amount variable by performing mathematical operations with pandas.

How to do it...

Let's begin by importing the libraries and getting the dataset ready:

1. Let's import the required Python libraries:

```
import pandas as pd
import featuretools as ft
```

2. Let's load the dataset from Featuretools:

```
data_dict = ft.demo.load_mock_customer()
```

3. Let's merge the three different tables from Featuretools' mock dataset into a pandas dataframe:

```
data = data_dict["transactions"].merge(
        data_dict["sessions"]).merge(data_dict["customers"])
```

4. Now, we'll select the columns that identify each unique customer, each unique transaction, the time of the transaction, and the amount spent per transaction:

```
data = data[['customer_id', 'transaction_id', 'transaction_time',
'amount']]
```

For the purpose of this demo, we'll ignore the **sessions** table. To take a look at the data that's loaded after *step 4*, visit the accompanying Jupyter Notebook in this book's GitHub repository, or execute `data.head()`.

Now, we need to create a single view per customer that summarizes their purchase activity. To do this, we will remove the time dimension of the transactions to capture the historical behavior in different variables, thus obtaining one feature vector per customer.

5. Let's begin by making a list of the functions we will use to summarize the data:

```
operations = ['sum', 'max', 'min', 'mean', 'median', 'std',
'count']
```

6. Now, let's create a list with meaningful names for the features we will create with the preceding operations:

```
feature_names = [ 'total_amount', 'max_amount', 'min_amount',
                  'mean_amount', 'median_amount', std_amount',
                  'number of transactions']
```

7. Finally, we'll create a new dataframe with the features that capture the aggregated view of the transactions for each customer and then display the dataframe:

```
df = pd.DataFrame()
df[feature_names] =
data.groupby('customer_id')['amount'].agg(operations)
df
```

We can see the new features for each customer in the following screenshot:

customer_id	total_amount	max_amount	min_amount	mean_amount	median_amount	std_amount	number of transactions
1	9025.62	139.43	5.81	71.631905	69.715	40.442059	126
2	7200.28	146.81	8.73	77.422366	75.960	37.705178	93
3	6236.62	149.15	5.89	67.060430	58.930	43.683296	93
4	8727.68	149.95	5.73	80.070459	81.410	45.068765	109
5	6349.66	149.02	7.55	80.375443	78.870	44.095630	79

Each feature captures a bit of the historical information.

How it works...

In this recipe, we summarized the information that's available for each customer in an aggregated view that captures the main statistical parameters of the multiple transactions by using an example dataset from Featuretools.

First, we loaded the mock dataset from Featuretools' `demo` module with the `load_mock_demo()` method, which returns a dictionary with three main tables: the customer information, the session information, and the transaction information. Each table is a pandas dataframe and can be accessed individually by calling the dictionary and the respective key. For example, `data_dict["transactions"]` returns a pandas dataframe with the transactions table. With pandas `merge()`, we merged the three tables into one dataframe.

Pandas merge() automatically identified the columns those tables have in common and merged them using these columns' values.

After loading the dataset, we retained four columns, which were the unique identifiers for the customers and the transactions, the transaction time, and the amount spent per transaction. With that, we had the dataframe ready to carry on with the recipe.

To create the new features from the transactions, we made a list with the names of the mathematical operations to use to summarize the historical information. Next, we made a list of names for the new features. Finally, we used pandas groupby() to create groups of dataframes for each customer, and with pandas agg() and the list of the mathematical operations, we applied each operation to the transaction amount variable for each customer. This code returned a flattened view of the dataset without the time dimension, where each row corresponds to one customer and each variable contains information that summarizes their purchase behavior.

In this recipe, we aggregated the information in the entire dataset. However, generally, it's more useful to aggregate information that occurs in a **temporal window** prior to the event we want to predict. For details on how to aggregate features in time windows, take a look at the *Aggregating transactions in a time window* recipe of this chapter.

There's more...

We can also aggregate transactional data using the Featuretools library. To do that, let's import the required libraries and load the dataset, just like we did in *step 1* to *step 4* of this recipe. To work with Featuretools, we need to transform the dataframe into an **entity set**. Let's get started:

1. Let's create an entity set and give it a representative name:

```
es = ft.EntitySet(id="customer_data")
```

For more details on entity sets, take a look at the *Creating features from transactions with Featuretools* recipe of this chapter.

2. Let's add the dataframe to the entity set by indicating that the `transaction_id` is the unique transaction identifier and setting the transaction time as the time index of the entity set:

```
es.entity_from_dataframe(entity_id='transactions',
 dataframe=data,
 index="transaction_id",
 time_index='transaction_time')
```

Featuretools needs to identify the time index and unique transaction index to perform its operations.

3. To indicate that each customer is linked to certain transactions within the entity set, we need to create a new entity using the `normalize_entity()` method, give the entity a name—in this case, `customers`—and specify the unique identifier for the customers:

```
es.normalize_entity(base_entity_id="transactions",
                    new_entity_id="customers",
                    index="customer_id")
```

Now, we have the entity set ready to perform the feature aggregations.

In this recipe, we create an entity set from a dataframe, since this is often the format in which we have our data. However, we can load the data from Featuretools directly as an entity. For more details, go to `https://docs.featuretools.com/en/stable/automated_feature_engineering/afe.html`.

4. To create these features, we'll use Featuretools' `dfs()` transformer and specify the entity over which the data should be aggregated, that is, the customers, and then pass the list of mathematical operations that should be used to create the new features (we created a list with mathematical operations in *step 5* of the *How to do it...* section of this recipe):

```
feature_matrix, features = ft.dfs(entityset=es,
                                  target_entity="customers",
                                  agg_primitives=operations,
                                  trans_primitives=[],
                                  verbose=True,
                                  )
```

For details on how `dfs()` works, take a look at the *Creating features from transactions with Featuretools* recipe of this chapter.

The `dfs()` method from Featuretools will aggregate the features and return them in a new dataframe, which we can display by executing `feature_matrix`. The following output shows the aggregated features in `feature_matrix` when it's run on a Jupyter Notebook:

customer_id	SUM(transactions.amount)	MAX(transactions.amount)	MIN(transactions.amount)	MEAN(transactions.amount)	MEDIAN(transactions.amount)	STD
2	7200.28	146.81	8.73	77.422366	75.960	
5	6349.66	149.02	7.55	80.375443	78.870	
4	8727.68	149.95	5.73	80.070459	81.410	
1	9025.62	139.43	5.81	71.631905	69.715	
3	6236.62	149.15	5.89	67.060430	58.930	

Note that the values of this table are identical to those of the table in *step 7* of the *How to do it...* section of this recipe.

See also

In this recipe, we used Featuretools' `dfs()` with a list of mathematical functions to aggregate the features. If we omit the mathematical functions, `dfs()` will automatically perform a set of default operations to aggregate them. To discover the default feature aggregations that are returned by Featuretools' `dfs()`, go to https://docs.featuretools. com/en/stable/generated/featuretools.dfs.html#featuretools.dfs.

To learn more about Featuretools, check out its official documentation: https://docs. featuretools.com/en/stable/index.html.

Aggregating transactions in a time window

When we want to predict an event at a certain point in time, often, transactions or values closer to the event tend to be more relevant. Then, if we want to predict whether a customer will churn next week, the information in the last weeks or months tends to be more informative than the transactions of the customer in the past 5 years.

We can use mathematical operations to summarize historical data, just like we did in the previous recipe, but only for a certain temporal window. This way, we can create features such as the maximum amount spent in the last week or the number of transactions in the last month, to name a few examples. In this recipe, we will summarize time series data over discrete time windows using pandas.

Getting ready

In this recipe, we will use the Appliances energy prediction dataset from the UCI Machine Learning Repository. We will work with the **Appliances** and **lights** variables, which contain records of the electricity that's consumed by appliances or lights in a single household at intervals of 10 minutes for a period of 5 months. To become familiar with the dataset, visit the Jupyter Notebook that accompanies this recipe in this book's GitHub repository (https://github.com/PacktPublishing/Python-Feature-Engineering-Cookbook), where you will find visualizations so that you can understand the values, seasonality, and trends of these time series.

How to do it...

Let's begin by importing the libraries and getting the dataset ready:

1. First, we'll import pandas:

```
import pandas as pd
```

2. Now, we'll load three variables from the Appliances energy prediction dataset: the date and time in which the energy consumption was recorded and the energy that's consumed by appliances and lights:

```
cols = ['date', 'Appliances', 'lights']
data = pd.read_csv('energydata_complete.csv', usecols=cols)
```

3. At the moment, the data type of the date variable is an object. Let's change it so that it's a datetime:

```
data['date'] = pd.to_datetime(data['date'])
```

4. Let's create some new features that capture the average energy consumption by appliances and lights in the last 60 minutes, where six observations cover the 60 minutes and the aggregation is done over the `date` variable. Next, let's display the top 10 rows of the result:

    ```
    data_rolled = data.rolling(window=6, on='date').mean()
    data_rolled.head(10)
    ```

    The output of the preceding code shows the new features capturing the average electricity consumption of the six rows:

	date	Appliances	lights
0	2016-01-11 17:00:00	NaN	NaN
1	2016-01-11 17:10:00	NaN	NaN
2	2016-01-11 17:20:00	NaN	NaN
3	2016-01-11 17:30:00	NaN	NaN
4	2016-01-11 17:40:00	NaN	NaN
5	2016-01-11 17:50:00	55.000000	35.000000
6	2016-01-11 18:00:00	55.000000	38.333333
7	2016-01-11 18:10:00	55.000000	41.666667
8	2016-01-11 18:20:00	56.666667	43.333333
9	2016-01-11 18:30:00	60.000000	43.333333

We can create the same features by specifying the time window as a string instead. We can do this using `data_rolled = data.rolling(window='`**60min**`', on='date', min_periods=6).mean()`.

We can speed up the feature creation process by aggregating multiple operations in each time window.

5. Let's begin by making a list of the functions we will use to summarize the data in each time window:

    ```
    operations = ['sum', 'max', 'min', 'mean', 'median', 'std']
    ```

6. Now, we'll create a dictionary specifying which operation to apply to each variable. In this case, we will apply all the operations to both variables and then display the dictionary:

```
op_dict = {key: operations for key in ['Appliances', 'lights']}
op_dict
```

The output of the preceding block is the following dictionary:

```
{'Appliances': ['sum', 'max', 'min', 'mean', 'median', 'std'],
 'lights': ['sum', 'max', 'min', 'mean', 'median', 'std']}
```

7. Finally, we'll create a new dataframe with the new features that capture the aggregated view of the energy consumption in the last hour. Then, we'll display the top 10 rows:

```
data_rolled = data.set_index('date').rolling(
                            window='60min').agg(op_dict)
data_rolled.head(10)
```

We can see the summarized energy consumption pattern in the past hour, for every 10 minutes, in the following screenshot:

	Appliances						lights					
	sum	max	min	mean	median	std	sum	max	min	mean	median	std
date												
2016-01-11 17:00:00	60.0	60.0	60.0	60.000000	60.0	NaN	30.0	30.0	30.0	30.000000	30.0	NaN
2016-01-11 17:10:00	120.0	60.0	60.0	60.000000	60.0	0.000000	60.0	30.0	30.0	30.000000	30.0	0.000000
2016-01-11 17:20:00	170.0	60.0	50.0	56.666667	60.0	5.773503	90.0	30.0	30.0	30.000000	30.0	0.000000
2016-01-11 17:30:00	220.0	60.0	50.0	55.000000	55.0	5.773503	130.0	40.0	30.0	32.500000	30.0	5.000000
2016-01-11 17:40:00	280.0	60.0	50.0	56.000000	60.0	5.477226	170.0	40.0	30.0	34.000000	30.0	5.477226
2016-01-11 17:50:00	330.0	60.0	50.0	55.000000	55.0	5.477226	210.0	40.0	30.0	35.000000	35.0	5.477226
2016-01-11 18:00:00	330.0	60.0	50.0	55.000000	55.0	5.477226	230.0	50.0	30.0	38.333333	40.0	7.527727
2016-01-11 18:10:00	330.0	60.0	50.0	55.000000	55.0	5.477226	250.0	50.0	30.0	41.666667	40.0	7.527727
2016-01-11 18:20:00	340.0	60.0	50.0	56.666667	60.0	5.163978	260.0	50.0	40.0	43.333333	40.0	5.163978
2016-01-11 18:30:00	360.0	70.0	50.0	60.000000	60.0	6.324555	260.0	50.0	40.0	43.333333	40.0	5.163978

Note that each observation in the new dataframe is the average of the six previous observations. This means they aren't independent and can be very similar. The larger the temporal windows, the more similar the resulting aggregations tend to be.

How it works...

In this recipe, we created new features that summarize the information that occurred in a certain temporal window by using the Appliances energy prediction time series dataset.

First, we loaded the columns with the date of the energy consumption record and the energy that's consumed by appliances and lights into a pandas dataframe. The dataset contained records of energy consumption at regular 10 minute intervals.

To determine the mean energy that was consumed in the previous hour, we used pandas rolling(), followed by pandas mean(). The energy consumption is recorded every 10 minutes; this means that six observations span one hour of energy consumption. Thus, we specified six to the window argument of pandas rolling(). The pandas rolling() method applied mean() to six consecutive observations and displayed it in the last of the six observations it averaged.

The first five rows of the returned dataframe contain NaN values because rolling() needed a minimum of six precedent values to return the average. We can change this behavior by changing the default value of the min_periods argument.

Alternatively, we set up pandas rolling() with the '60min' string and specified the datetime variable to the on parameter.

Setting pandas rolling() with window=6 makes the method operate over the six **last available** consecutive rows, whereas setting rolling() with window='60min' makes the method specifically identify the last available **60 minutes** of data, thereby getting the time information from the datetime variable.

The min_periods parameter from pandas rolling() specifies the minimum number of observations that are needed to return the indicated average. When we set windows=6, min_periods is automatically set to 6. This means that an average will only be displayed for those observations for which there are five precedent rows of data available. When we set window='60min', we need to specify min_periods=6; otherwise, the result will contain the average of the last six rows if they exist or the average of the available precedent rows.

Compare the result that's returned by data.rolling(window='60min', on='date').mean() with that of data.rolling(window=6, on='date').mean().

Finally, we automated the creation of features in a time window by calculating multiple mathematical operations simultaneously. First, we captured the name of the mathematical operations in a list. Next, we made a dictionary with the name of the variables as keys and the operations to apply to each variable as values. To create the features, we set the date columns as an index of the dataframe with pandas `set_index()` and used pandas `rolling()` with a 60-minute window, followed by pandas `agg()` with the dictionary as an argument. This operation returned a new dataframe with the date as an index and the features with the mathematical computations as columns.

There's more...

In this recipe, we created new features that aggregate energy consumption with commonly used mathematical computations, which are built into pandas. We can also apply **user-defined** computations. In this section, we will create two functions to detect the number of local maxima and minima in time series, and then calculate those values per day of energy consumption.

To do this, we'll import pandas, load the data, and parse the date variable into `datetime` format, just like we did in *step 1* to *step 3* of this recipe:

1. First, let's import a function to find the local maxima from SciPy's `signal` module:

   ```
   from scipy.signal import find_peaks
   ```

2. Let's create two functions to count the number of local maxima and minima in a time series:

   ```
   def find_no_peaks(x):
       peaks, _ = find_peaks(x)
       return len(peaks)

   def find_no_valleys(x):
       valleys, _ = find_peaks(1/x)
       return len(valleys)
   ```

> We'll discuss the preceding code in more detail in the *Determining the number of local maxima and minima* recipe of this chapter.

3. Now, we can apply the functions we created using pandas by rolling over a window of 1 day:

```
data_rolled = data.set_index('date').rolling(
                      window='1d').agg([find_no_peaks,
find_no_valleys])
```

4. To discover the number of peaks per day, execute the following command, which returns the value of the number of local minima and maxima every one day:

```
for row in range(144, 1440, 144):
    print(data_rolled.iloc[[row]])
```

You can view the output of this command in the accompanying Jupyter Notebook in this book's GitHub repository (`https://github.com/PacktPublishing/Python-Feature-Engineering-Cookbook`).

Energy consumption is recorded every 10 minutes. This means that 144 rows contain the energy that's consumed in 1 day.

See also

Featuretools offers awesome functionality that we can use to aggregate features within a temporal window prior to user-defined cut-off times. This is usually set up ahead of the event we want to predict. To learn more about this functionality, take a look at the following links:

- `https://docs.featuretools.com/en/stable/automated_feature_engineering/handling_time.html#what-is-the-cutoff-time`
- `https://docs.featuretools.com/en/stable/automated_feature_engineering/handling_time.html#creating-and-flattening-a-feature-tensor`

Another commonly used feature is the **percentage change** in value between the current and the precedent observation, which we can create automatically with pandas `pct_change()`. You can find an example of how to use this command with the Appliances energy prediction dataset in the accompanying Jupyter Notebook. For more information about this method, take a look at the official documentation: `https://pandas.pydata.org/pandas-docs/stable/reference/api/pandas.DataFrame.pct_change.html`.

Finally, you can find out more about pandas `rolling()` in its official documentation:
`https://pandas.pydata.org/pandas-docs/stable/reference/api/pandas.DataFrame.rolling.html`.

Determining the number of local maxima and minima

Time series can be regarded as a signal, such as sound or electrocardiograms, and thus we can extract features that capture some of the complexity of the signal. Examples of signal complexity include the maximum or mean values, as we discussed in the previous recipes. We can also extract more complex features such as the number of local maxima or minima, or even more complex ones, such as the coefficients of the courier transform.

In this recipe, we will determine the number of local maxima and minima manually using the signal module from SciPy in combination with pandas. Then, we will point you to a Python package that extracts these and other complex signal processing parameters automatically that you can explore and use to expand your toolset.

Getting ready

Local maxima or local minima, also known as extrema, are the largest or smallest values of a function either within a certain range or in the entire domain of the function. They signal a change in the trend of the function. Here, local maxima come after an increase and prior to a decrease in the values of the function, whereas local minima come after a decrease and prior to an increase in the values of the function.

To find local extrema, we will use the `find_peaks` function from the `signal` module from SciPy, which finds all the local maxima by performing a simple comparison of neighboring values.

How to do it...

Let's begin by importing the libraries and getting the data set ready:

1. Let's import the required libraries and function:

    ```
    import numpy as np
    import pandas as pd
    ```

```
import matplotlib.pyplot as plt
from scipy.signal import find_peaks
```

2. Let's load the Appliances energy prediction dataset:

```
data = pd.read_csv('energydata_complete.csv')
```

3. The data type of the `date` variable is `object`; let's change it to `datetime`:

```
data['date'] = pd.to_datetime(data['date'])
```

4. Now, we need to extract the day, month, and hour part from the `datetime` variable into new columns:

```
data[['day', 'month', 'hr']] = pd.DataFrame([(x.day, x.month,
x.hour) for x in data['date']])
```

 We discussed the code in the preceding step in the *Deriving representations of year and month* and *Extracting time parts from a time variable* recipes of `Chapter 7`, *Deriving Features from Date and Time Variables*.

5. Let's make a plot with the mean energy that's consumed by appliances per hour:

```
data.groupby('hr')['Appliances'].mean().plot()
plt.ylabel('Energy in Kh')
plt.title('Daily Cycle of Energy Consumption by Appliances')
```

The following plot shows the average energy that's consumed per hour throughout the day, where the baseline energy consumption throughout the night hours is below 60 Kh:

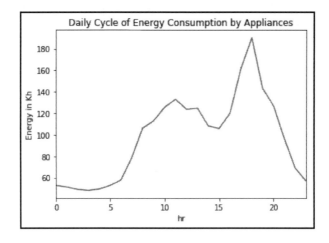

6. Let's make a plot of the mean energy that's consumed by appliances per day throughout the 5 months of data we have collected:

```
data.groupby(['month', 'day'])['Appliances'].mean().plot()
plt.ylabel('Energy in Kh')
plt.title('Mean daily Energy Consumption')
```

In the following plot, we can see that there are several local minima and maxima in the average energy that have been consumed per day in our 5 months of records:

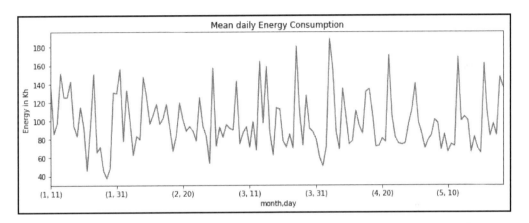

7. Let's create a pandas Series with the mean energy that's been consumed by appliances per day throughout the 5 months:

```
daily_ec = data.groupby(['month', 'day'])['Appliances'].mean()
```

8. Let's determine the local maxima in the preceding time series but with the constraint that the local maxima can't show values below the 60Kh baseline energy consumption:

```
peaks, _ = find_peaks(daily_ec, height=60)
```

9. Now, let's create a plot like the one in *step 6* and overlay red symbols on the local maxima that we identified with the function in *step 8,* and create a line at the baseline energy consumption level of 60 Kh:

```
plt.figure(figsize=(12, 4))
daily_ec.plot()
plt.plot(peaks, daily_ec.values[peaks], "o", color='red')
plt.plot(np.full_like(daily_ec, 60), "--", color="gray")
plt.show()
```

In the following output, we can see that the function in *step 8* correctly identified the days with maximum energy consumption throughout the 5 months of records we have:

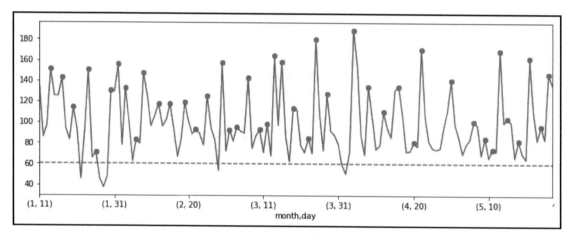

10. Now, let's find the local minima by using the same function from *step 8* and the **inverse** of the time series:

```
valleys, _ = find_peaks(1/daily_ec, height=(0, 1/60))
```

11. Now, let's create a plot like the one in *step 6* and overlay green symbols on the local minima that we identified with the function in *step 10*:

```
plt.figure(figsize=(12, 4))
daily_ec.plot()
plt.plot(valleys, daily_ec.values[valleys], "o", color='green')
plt.plot(np.full_like(daily_ec, 60), "--", color="gray")
plt.show()
```

In the following plot, we can see the days of minimum energy consumption throughout the 5 months of records we have:

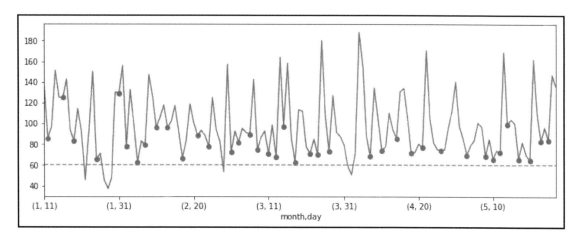

> Note how the minima under the baseline energy consumption of 60 Kh were omitted.

We can count the number of local maxima and minima in a temporal window of the time series to start getting insight into its complexity, just like we did in the *There's more* section in the previous recipe, *Aggregating transactions in a time window*.

How it works...

In this recipe, we identified the local maxima and minima in the daily energy consumed by house appliances. First, we loaded the Appliances energy prediction dataset from the UCI Machine Learning Repository and extracted different parts of time, that is, day, month, and hour, from the `datetime` variable, as we discussed in the *Deriving representations of year and month* and *Extracting time parts from a time variable* recipes of `Chapter 7`, *Deriving Features from Date and Time Variables*.

Next, we plotted the mean energy consumed per hour, or the mean energy consumed per day and month, using pandas `groupby()`, pandas `mean()`, and pandas `plot()`.

Next, we created a pandas time series with the mean energy consumed by appliances per day across the 5 months of data we have using pandas `groupby()`, followed by pandas `mean()`. To determine the local maxima in this pandas Series, we used the `find_peaks` function from the `signal` module from SciPy. The `find_peaks` function takes a time series and, optionally, a threshold with the minimum height the peaks should have (we specified 60 to the `height` argument in this recipe), and returns a Numpy array with the indices of the time series at which the local maxima were identified.

Next, we created a plot of the time series using pandas `plot()`. Then, using `plt.plot()`, we overlaid red dots at the location of the local maxima. With the NumPy `full_like()` method, we created an array with the length of the time series where all the values were the number 60, which we then overlaid on the plot to signal the baseline energy consumption of 60 Kh.

To determine the local minima, we used the `find_peaks` function over the **inverse** of the mean energy consumed per day. In other words, we turned the time series upside down to find the local maxima, which corresponds to the local minima of the original values. Then, we laid the local minima over the time series plot, as we explained in the preceding paragraph.

When we set up `find_peaks` with the inverse of the time series, we ignored the local minima where the values were below the 60 Kh baseline energy consumption by setting `height=(0, 1/60)`.

There's more...

In this recipe, we identified the local maxima and minima in a time series for a single household. But how could we determine the local maxima and minima for several houses? We can combine the use of pandas `groupby()`, pandas `agg()`, and user-defined functions to achieve this goal. To demonstrate how to do this, we will use the toy customer transactions dataset from Featuretools. Let's get started:

For more details about the customer transactions dataset from Featuretools, visit the *Getting ready* section of the *Aggregating transactions with mathematical operations* recipe in this chapter.

1. Let's import the required libraries and data:

```
import numpy as np
import pandas as pd
```

```
import matplotlib.pyplot as plt
from scipy.signal import find_peaks
import featuretools as ft
```

2. Let's load the mock customer transactions dataset while retaining four of the columns:

```
data_dict = ft.demo.load_mock_customer()
data = data_dict["transactions"].merge(
data_dict["sessions"]).merge(data_dict["customers"])
data = data[['customer_id', 'transaction_id', 'transaction_time',
             'amount']]
```

3. Let's create a new feature with the hour of transaction time:

```
data['hr'] = data['transaction_time'].dt.hour
```

4. Let's create a function that takes a time series and identifies and counts the number of local maxima:

```
def find_no_peaks(x):
    peaks, _ = find_peaks(x)
    return len(peaks)
```

5. Let's create a function that takes a time series and identifies and counts the number of local minima:

```
def find_no_valleys(x):
    valleys, _ = find_peaks(1/x)
    return len(valleys)
```

6. Finally, let's use the functions in *step 4* and *step 5* to count the local maxima and minima in the number of transactions per hour, per customer:

```
data.groupby(['customer_id', 'hr'])['amount'].mean().groupby(
    'customer_id').agg([find_no_peaks,find_no_valleys])
```

The preceding code returns the following dataframe, which shows the number of local maxima and minima in the mean transaction value per hour for each customer:

customer_id	find_no_peaks	find_no_valleys
1	2.0	2.0
2	1.0	0.0
3	1.0	2.0
4	1.0	2.0
5	1.0	1.0

You can find some plots where the local extrema were laid over the time series, and the code that was used to return them in the accompanying Jupyter Notebook of this book's GitHub repository (https://github.com/PacktPublishing/Python-Feature-Engineering-Cookbook).

See also

In the accompanying Jupyter Notebook, you will find more details about the output of each individual line of code and method that was used throughout this recipe.

For more details about find_peaks from SciPy signal, check out the following links:

- https://docs.scipy.org/doc/scipy/reference/generated/scipy.signal.find_peaks.html
- https://stackoverflow.com/questions/1713335/peak-finding-algorithm-for-python-scipy

For more information about the signal module from SciPy, go to https://docs.scipy.org/doc/scipy/reference/signal.html.

The Python library tsfresh contains multiple functionalities that we can use to automatically extract features that capture signal complexity. For more details, go to https://tsfresh.readthedocs.io/en/latest/.

Deriving time elapsed between time-stamped events

In the previous recipes, we performed mathematical operations over the **values** of the time series to obtain new features that summarize information about the variable, such as the mean and maximum values or the cumulative sum. It is also possible to perform these mathematical operations over the **time-stamp** and obtain information about the time between transactions or the time between specific events.

In this recipe, we will calculate the time between transactions, that is, the time between successive records of the variable values. Then, we will determine the time between specific events, such as the time between peaks of energy consumption, to demonstrate the power of pandas when it comes to aggregating time series data.

How to do it...

Let's begin by importing the necessary libraries and getting the dataset ready:

1. Let's import the required libraries and function:

```
import numpy as np
import pandas as pd
import matplotlib.pyplot as plt
from scipy.signal import find_peaks
```

2. Let's load the Appliances energy prediction dataset:

```
data = pd.read_csv('energydata_complete.csv')
```

3. The data type of the `date` variable is `object`; let's change it to `datetime`:

```
data['date'] = pd.to_datetime(data['date'])
```

4. First, let's calculate the time between transactions, that is, the time between each energy record, expressed in minutes:

```
data['time_since_previous'] = data['date'].diff()
data['time_since_previous'] =
data['time_since_previous']/np.timedelta64(1,'m')
```

We discussed the code in *step 4* in the *Combining pairs of features with mathematical functions* recipe of `Chapter 9`, *Applying Mathematical Computations to Features*, and the *Capturing elapsed time between datetime variables* recipe of `Chapter 7`, *Deriving features from Dates and Time Variables*.

Once we create the variable that captures **time since previous transactions**, we can use the mathematical operations that we used in the *Aggregating transactions with mathematical operations* recipe at the beginning of this chapter to create new features from it.

In the remaining part of this recipe, we will determine the time between specific events—in this case, the time between the local maxima in the daily mean energy consumed by appliances.

5. Let's extract the day and month from the `datetime` variable and put them into new variables:

```
data[['day', 'month']] = pd.DataFrame([(x.day, x.month) for x in
data['date']])
```

We discussed the code in the preceding step in the *Deriving representations of year and month* recipe of `Chapter 7`, *Deriving features from Date and Time Variables*.

6. Let's make the `datetime` variable the index of the series:

```
data.index = data['date']
```

7. Let's create a time series with the average electricity consumption by appliances per day:

```
elec_pday = data.groupby(['month', 'day'])['Appliances'].mean()
```

8. Let's find the indexes corresponding to the local maxima for the appliances' energy consumption time series and display the results:

```
peaks, _ = find_peaks(elec_pday.values, height=60)
peaks
```

The array contains the indices of the series with the local maxima:

```
array([  3,    6,    9,   13,   15,   19,   21,   23,   26,   28,   32,   35,
        39,   42,   45,   49,   51,   53,   56,   59,   61,   63,   65,   68,
        72,   74,   77,   84,   88,   92,   96,  100,  102,  110,  116,  119,
       121,  123,  125,  128,  131,  134,  136], dtype=int64)
```

9. Now, let's create a dataframe with **only** the local maxima of the appliance's mean energy consumption, reset its index to make month and day columns of the dataframe, and add a variable with the year, and display the top rows:

```
tmp = pd.DataFrame(elec_pday[peaks]).reset_index(drop=False)
tmp['year'] = 2016
tmp.head()
```

The resulting dataframe contains the peaks of daily energy that were consumed by appliances:

	month	day	Appliances	year
0	1	14	151.388889	2016
1	1	17	142.708333	2016
2	1	20	114.444444	2016
3	1	24	150.277778	2016
4	1	26	71.319444	2016

10. Now, let's reconstitute a datetime variable from the day, month, and year variables of the previous dataframe:

```
tmp['date'] = pd.to_datetime(tmp[['year', 'month', 'day']])
tmp.head()
```

We can see the additional `datetime` variable at the end of the dataframe:

	month	day	Appliances	year	date
0	1	14	151.388889	2016	2016-01-14
1	1	17	142.708333	2016	2016-01-17
2	1	20	114.444444	2016	2016-01-20
3	1	24	150.277778	2016	2016-01-24
4	1	26	71.319444	2016	2016-01-26

11. To determine the distance in days between the local maxima, we need to determine the distance between the rows, since each row in the previous dataframe contains a local maxima:

```
tmp['peak_distance'] = tmp['date'].diff()
tmp['peak_distance'] = tmp['peak_distance'].dt.days
tmp.head()
```

We can see the number of days between the maximum values of energy consumption in the last column of the dataframe:

	month	day	Appliances	year	date	peak_distance
0	1	14	151.388889	2016	2016-01-14	NaN
1	1	17	142.708333	2016	2016-01-17	3.0
2	1	20	114.444444	2016	2016-01-20	3.0
3	1	24	150.277778	2016	2016-01-24	4.0
4	1	26	71.319444	2016	2016-01-26	2.0

To find out how to capture *step 9* to *step 12* in a function that can be applied to any time series, or to determine the time that's elapsed between the maxima **and** minima of a time series, take a look at the accompanying Jupyter Notebook in this book's GitHub repository (`https://github.com/PacktPublishing/Python-Feature-Engineering-Cookbook`).

How it works...

In this recipe, we determined the time between energy records and then the time between specific events, such as the local maxima of a time series, using the Appliances energy prediction dataset.

We loaded the data and used pandas `to_datetime()` to change the format of the `date` variable so that it was a `datetime` variable. Next, we used pandas `diff()` to determine the difference in the `datetime` values between one row and its immediate precedent row, which returned the time between energy records.

Next, we extracted the day and month from the `datetime` variable. By using pandas `groupby()` over these features, followed by pandas `mean()`, we created a time series with the mean energy consumed daily by appliances. Next, we used `find_peaks()` from the `signal` module from SciPy to determine the local maxima in the time series. The output of `find_peaks()` is a NumPy array with the indexes of the time series where the maxima are located.

 We discussed `find_peaks()` extensively in the *Determining the number of local maxima and minima* recipe of this chapter.

Then, we used the indexes with the local maxima to slice the time series and obtain the values with the peaks of energy consumption. With pandas `DataFrame()`, we converted the series into a dataframe, retaining the day and month, which were in the index as columns of the dataframe. Next, we added a column for the year so that we could reconstitute the date from the day, month, and year variables using pandas `to_datetime()`. With pandas `diff()`, followed by `dt.days()` over the `datetime` variable, we determined the difference in days between one row and its previous row, that is, the difference in days between one local maxima and its previous one.

There's more...

We can determine the mean value of the time between the local maxima and minima for more than one entity. To demonstrate how to automate this procedure, we will use the mock customer transaction dataset from Featuretools. Let's get started:

1. Let's import the required libraries:

```
import numpy as np
import pandas as pd
from scipy.signal import find_peaks
import featuretools as ft
```

2. Let's load the customer transactions dataset into a pandas dataframe:

```
data_dict = ft.demo.load_mock_customer()
data = data_dict["transactions"].merge(
        data_dict["sessions"]).merge(data_dict["customers"])
data = data[['customer_id','transaction_id',
        'transaction_time','amount']]
```

3. Let's create a feature with the hour of the transaction:

```
data['hr'] = data['transaction_time'].dt.hour
```

4. Let's create a function to find the local maxima in a time series:

```
def find_no_peaks(x):
    peaks, _ = find_peaks(x)
    return peaks
```

5. Let's create a function to find the local minima in a time series:

```
def find_no_valleys(x):
    valleys, _ = find_peaks(1/x)
    return valleys
```

6. Let's create a function that concatenates and sorts the arrays by using the indices of the local maxima and minima:

```
def concatenate_pav(x):
    ids = np.concatenate([find_no_peaks(x), find_no_valleys(x)])
    ids.sort()
    return ids
```

7. Let's create a function that slices a time series into the values with the local maxima and minima and then determines the number of hours between them in order to return the mean number of hours between the extrema for the entire series:

```
def slice_and_measure(x):
    ids = concatenate_pav(x)
    tmp = pd.DataFrame(x.iloc[ids]).reset_index(drop=False)
    t = tmp['hr'].diff()
    return t.mean(skipna=True)
```

8. Finally, let's determine the mean time between the local maxima and minima of the mean purchase amount per hour, per customer:

```
data.groupby(['customer_id', 'hr'])['amount'].mean().groupby(
    'customer_id').apply(slice_and_measure)
```

We can see the returned Series in the following output:

```
customer_id
1    1.666667
2         NaN
3    1.000000
4    1.000000
5    3.000000
Name: amount, dtype: float64
```

The Series that was returned by *step 8* contains the mean time between the extrema in days. Customer 2 shows a NaN value, because there is only 1 maxima in its time series data, so it isn't possible to determine any distances.

See also

In the accompanying Jupyter Notebook, which can be found in this book's GitHub repository, you can find the output of the intermediate steps, along with some plots and visualizations that will help you understand the code that was presented in this recipe.

Creating features from transactions with Featuretools

Featuretools is an open source Python library that allows us to automatically create features from time series and transactional databases with multiple transaction records for each specific entity, such as customers. With Featuretools, we can automatically create features at the **transaction level**. Such features include the day, month, and year from a datetime variable, the time between transactions, or if the transaction occurred on a weekend, as well as the cumulative sum or the difference in value between transactions.

Featuretools also aggregates existing and new features at the **entity level**—in our example, at the customer level—using mathematical and statistical operations, such as the ones we used in the *Aggregating transactions with mathematical operations* recipe of this chapter or by using user-defined operations.

In this recipe, we will create features at the transaction level and then aggregate both new and existing features at the customer level by using Featuretool's automatic feature extraction functionality.

How to do it...

Let's begin by importing the necessary libraries and getting the dataset ready:

1. Let's import pandas and Featuretools:

```
import pandas as pd
import featuretools as ft
```

2. Let's load the mock customer transactions dataset from Featuretools into a dataframe:

```
data_dict = ft.demo.load_mock_customer()
data = data_dict["transactions"].merge(
        data_dict["sessions"]).merge(data_dict["customers"])
data = data[['customer_id', 'transaction_id',
        'transaction_time', 'amount']]
```

3. To work with Featuretools, we need to transform the dataframe into an entity set. To do this, we'll create an entity set and give it a representative name:

```
es = ft.EntitySet(id="customer_data")
```

4. We'll add the dataframe to the entity set by specifying that `transaction_id` is the unique transaction identifier, and by setting the transaction time as the time index of the entity set:

```
es.entity_from_dataframe(entity_id='transactions',
 dataframe=data,
 index="transaction_id",
 time_index='transaction_time')
```

Featuretools needs to identify the time index and unique transaction index to perform its operations.

5. Let's specify that, within the entity set, each customer is linked to certain transactions. To do this with Featuretools, we need to create a new entity using the `normalize_entity()` method, give the entity a name—in this case, `customers`—and specify the unique identifier for the customers:

```
es.normalize_entity(base_entity_id="transactions",
                    new_entity_id="customers",
                    index="customer_id")
```

Now that we have the entity set ready, we can start to build new features and perform feature aggregations. Let's begin by creating new features at a transaction level.

6. Let's make a list of the names of the operations we want to perform to create the new features:

```
transf_operations = ['is_weekend', 'cum_sum',
'cum_count','time_since_previous']
```

7. Now, let's set up `dfs()` from Featuretools so that we can return the previous features at the transaction level:

```
feature_matrix, features = ft.dfs(entityset=es,
                                  target_entity="transactions",
                                  agg_primitives=[],
                                  trans_primitives = transf_operations,
                                  verbose=True)
```

Note that we should leave `agg_primitives` as an empty list so that Featuretools doesn't aggregate the data at the customer level as well.

To visualize these new features, execute `feature_matrix.head()`.

In the rest of this recipe, we will aggregate new **and** existing features at the customer level.

8. Now, we will create a new feature at the transaction level that captures the time between transactions and then aggregates this feature and the transaction purchase amount at the customer level using the mean and maximum mathematical operations:

```
feature_matrix, features = ft.dfs(entityset=es,
                    target_entity="customers",
                    agg_primitives=["mean", 'max'],
                    trans_primitives=['time_since_previous'],
                    verbose=True)
```

Execute `feature_matrix` to return the five-row dataframe, along with the aggregated view of the features at the customer level.

How it works...

In this recipe, we automated the process of feature creation and aggregation using the open source Featuretools library. To proceed with this recipe, we loaded the mock customer transactions dataset as a pandas dataframe, which is the format we collect our data in the most.

To work with Featuretools, we needed to transform the dataset into an entity set, which is an object that specifies how the transactions are related to the different entities—in this case, customers. To transform the dataframe into an entity set, we used the Featuretools `entity_from_dataframe()` method and added the `transaction_id` as the unique transaction identifier and the transaction time as the time index of the entity set. Next, we created a new entity with the Featuretools `normalize_entity()` method and added `customer_id` as the unique customer identifier, so that Featuretools understands which transactions belong to which customer.

Feature creation with feature tools is done with the **deep feature synthesis** or `dfs` object. In the `dfs` object, we can specify whether we want to derive new features at the transaction level using the `trans_primitives` argument or aggregate features at the entity level using the `agg_primitives` argument. Then, we can specify which entity to aggregate these features over using the `target_entity` argument.

To create features at the transaction level, we set `target_entity` to `"transactions"` and passed a list with function names to the `trans_primitives` argument, leaving `agg_primitives` as an empty list so that Featuretools doesn't perform aggregations as well. The `dfs` object returned a pandas dataframe with the same number of rows as the original dataframe and the newly created features.

Featuretools includes a default set of built-in operations that can automatically create features at the transaction level. To find out about the operations that are supported by this feature, go to `https://docs.` `featuretools.com/en/stable/api_reference.html#transform-` `primitives`.

To create features at the customer level, we set `target_entity` to `"customers"` and passed a list with the `"time_since_previous"` string so that Featuretools creates a new feature with the time since the previous transaction, **before** making the aggregation. Then, we passed a list with the mathematical operations to use to the aggregate features at the customer level to the `agg_primitives` argument. The `dfs` object returned a pandas dataframe with five rows, with each one corresponding to one customer, and the features with the aggregated view of the transaction time and amount.

Featuretools includes a default set of built-in operations that can automatically aggregate features at a higher entity level. To find out about the operations that are supported by this feature, go to `https://docs.` `featuretools.com/en/stable/api_reference.html#aggregation-` `primitives`.

In our mock dataset, there was only one numerical variable, which was the transaction amount. If there were multiple numerical variables, Featuretools would apply the aggregation functions to all of them automatically.

Featuretools applies some aggregations such as the mean, maximum, and cumulative sum to **all the numerical** variables automatically. Other aggregations, such as the count, are applied to `integer` variables, that is, variables with unique identifiers. Finally, features that capture time between events are applied automatically to the `datetime` variable. Thus, when working with Featuretools, it is important to set the data types correctly before feature creation.

There's more...

With Featuretools, we can also create features at the transaction level or aggregate features at a higher entity level with user-defined operations. Here, we will determine the number of local maxima and minima per customer using Featuretools. Let's get started:

1. To implement user-defined aggregations with Featuretools, we need the `make_agg_primitive` function and the `Numeric` object to identify the data type of the variable that this function should be applied to. We also need the `find_peaks` function to find the local maxima:

```
from featuretools.primitives import make_agg_primitive
from featuretools.variable_types import Numeric
from scipy.signal import find_peaks
```

2. Let's create a function that determines the number of local maxima and another function that determines the number of local minima of a time series:

```
def find_no_peaks(column):
    peaks, _ = find_peaks(column)
    return len(peaks)

def find_no_valleys(column):
    valleys, _ = find_peaks(1 / column)
    return len(valleys)
```

> We discussed the preceding functions extensively in the *Determining the number of local maxima and minima* recipe of this chapter.

3. Now, we need to make the functions from *step 2* aggregate the primitives of Featuretools by specifying the data types over which they should automatically operate and the data type they should return:

```
FindNoPeaks = make_agg_primitive(function=find_no_peaks,
                                 input_types=[Numeric],
                                 return_type=Numeric)

FindNoValleys = make_agg_primitive(function=find_no_valleys,
                                   input_types=[Numeric],
                                   return_type=Numeric)
```

4. Finally, we can apply these functions to determine the mean and maximum number of local maxima and minima of the transaction amount time series, as well as the mean and maximum amount per transaction, per customer:

```
feature_matrix, features = ft.dfs(entityset=es,
                        target_entity="customers",
                        agg_primitives=[FindNoPeaks, FindNoValleys,
                                         'Mean', 'Max'],
                        trans_primitives=[],
                        verbose=True)
```

The returned `feature_matrix` dataframe contains five rows—one per customer—and the mean and maximum number of local extrema and transaction amount.

See also

In this recipe, we just scratched the surface of what is possible with Featuretools. To learn more about this amazing tool, take a look at the following links:

- Demonstration of how to use Featuretools in a Kaggle dataset: `https://www.kaggle.com/willkoehrsen/automated-feature-engineering-basics`
- Blog by a former Featuretools developer: `https://towardsdatascience.com/automated-feature-engineering-in-python-99baf11cc219`
- Demos of Featuretools on multiple datasets: `https://www.featuretools.com/demos/`
- Featuretools documentation: `https://docs.featuretools.com/en/stable/index.html`

To use Featuretools to create features in temporal windows, take a look at the following links:

- `https://docs.featuretools.com/en/stable/automated_feature_engineering/handling_time.html#what-is-the-cutoff-time`
- `https://docs.featuretools.com/en/stable/automated_feature_engineering/handling_time.html#creating-and-flattening-a-feature-tensor`

11
Extracting Features from Text Variables

Text can be part of the variables in our datasets. For example, in insurance, some variables that capture information about an incident may come from a free text field in a form. In data from a website that collects customer reviews or feedback, we may also encounter variables that contain short descriptions provided by text that has been entered manually by the users. Text is unstructured, that is, it does not follow a pattern, like the **tabular** pattern of the datasets we have worked with throughout this book. Text may also vary in length and content, and the writing style may be different. How can we extract information from text variables to inform our predictive models? This is the question we are going to address in this chapter.

The techniques we will cover in this chapter belong to the realm of **Natural Language Processing (NLP)**. NLP is a subfield of linguistics and computer science, concerned with the interactions between computer and human language, or, in other words, how to program computers to understand human language. NLP includes a multitude of techniques to understand the syntax, semantics, and discourse of text, and therefore to do this field justice would require a book in itself.

In this chapter, instead, we will discuss those techniques that will allow us to quickly extract features from short pieces of text, to complement our predictive models. Specifically, we will discuss how to capture text complexity by looking at some statistical parameters of the text such as the word length and count, the number of words and unique words used, the number of sentences, and so on. We will use the pandas and scikit-learn libraries, and we will make a shallow dive into a very useful Python NLP toolkit called **Natural Language Toolkit (NLTK)**.

This chapter will cover the following recipes:

- Counting characters, words, and vocabulary
- Estimating text complexity by counting sentences
- Creating features with bag-of-words and n-grams
- Implementing term frequency-inverse document frequency
- Cleaning and stemming text variables

Technical requirements

We will use the following Python libraries: pandas, Matplotlib, and scikit-learn, which you can get by installing the Python Anaconda distribution, following the steps described in the *Technical requirements* section in `Chapter 1`, *Foreseeing Variable Problems in Building ML Models*.

We will also use NLTK from Python, a comprehensive library for NLP and text analysis. You can find instructions to install NLTK here: `http://www.nltk.org/install.html`. If you are using the Python Anaconda distribution, follow these instructions to install NLTK: `https://anaconda.org/anaconda/nltk`.

After you install NLTK, open up a Python console and execute the following:

```
import nltk
nltk.download('punkt')
nltk.download('stopwords')
```

Those commands will download the necessary data to be able to run the recipes of this chapter successfully.

If you haven't downloaded these or other data sources necessary for NLTK functionality, NLTK will raise an error. Read the error message carefully because it will direct you to download the data required to run the command you are trying to execute.

Counting characters, words, and vocabulary

One of the salient characteristics of text is its complexity. Long descriptions are more likely to contain more information than short descriptions. Texts rich in different, unique words are more likely to be richer in detail than texts that repeat the same words over and over. In the same way, when we speak, we use many short words such as articles and prepositions to build the sentence structure, yet the main concept is often derived by the nouns and adjectives we use, which tend to be longer words. So, as you can see, even without reading the text, we can start inferring how much information the text provides by determining the number of words, the number of unique words, the lexical diversity, and the length of those words. In this recipe, we will learn how to extract these features from a text variable using pandas.

Getting ready

We are going to use the *20 Newsgroup dataset* that comes with scikit-learn, which comprises around 1,800 news posts on 20 different topics. More details about the dataset can be found in these links:

- Scikit-learn dataset website: `https://scikit-learn.org/stable/datasets/index.html#newsgroups-dataset`
- Home page for the 20 Newsgroup dataset: `http://qwone.com/~jason/20Newsgroups/`

Before jumping into the recipe, let's become familiar with the features we are going to derive from these text pieces. We mentioned that longer descriptions, more words in the article, a greater variety of unique words, and longer words, tend to correlate with the amount of information the article provides. Hence, we can capture text complexity by extracting the following information:

- The total number of characters in the text
- The total number of words
- The total number of unique words
- Lexical diversity = total number of words / number of unique words
- Word average length = number of characters / number of words

In this recipe, we will extract these numerical features using pandas, which is equipped with multiple string processing functionality that can be accessed via the `str` attribute.

How to do it...

Let's begin by loading pandas and getting the dataset ready to use:

1. Load pandas and the dataset from scikit-learn:

```
import pandas as pd
from sklearn.datasets import fetch_20newsgroups
```

2. Let's load the train set part of the 20 Newsgroup dataset into a pandas dataframe:

```
data = fetch_20newsgroups(subset='train')
df = pd.DataFrame(data.data, columns=['text'])
```

 You can print out an example of a text variable in the dataframe by executing `print(df['text'][1])`. Change the number between `[]` to navigate through different texts. Note how every text description is a single string composed of letters, numbers, punctuation, and spaces.

Now that we have the text in a pandas dataframe, we are ready to crack on with the feature extraction.

3. Let's capture the number of characters in each string in a new column:

```
df['num_char'] = df['text'].str.len()
```

 You can remove trailing whitespaces, including new lines, in a string before counting the number of characters by adding the `strip()` method before the `len()` method: `df['num_char'] = df['text'].str.strip().str.len()`.

4. Let's capture the number of words in each text in a new column:

```
df['num_words'] = df['text'].str.split().str.len()
```

5. Let's capture the number of **unique** words in each text in a new column:

```
df['num_vocab'] =
df['text'].str.lower().str.split().apply(set).str.len()
```

 Python will interpret the same word as two different words if one has a capital letter. To avoid this behavior, we introduce the `lower()` method before the `split()` method.

6. Let's create a feature that captures the lexical diversity, that is, the total number of words to the number of unique words:

```
df['lexical_div'] = df['num_words'] / df['num_vocab']
```

7. Let's calculate the average word length by dividing the number of characters by the number of words:

```
df['ave_word_length'] = df['num_char'] / df['num_words']
```

We have now extracted five different features that capture the text complexity, which we can use as inputs to our machine learning algorithms. With `df.head()`, you can peek at the values of the first five rows of the created features.

 In this recipe, we have created new features straight away from the raw data, without doing any data cleaning, removing punctuation, or even stemming words. Note that these are usual steps performed ahead of most NLP standard procedures. To learn more about this, visit the *Cleaning and stemming text variables* recipe at the end of this chapter.

How it works...

In this recipe, we created five new features that capture text complexity utilizing the pandas' `str` attribute to access built-in pandas functionality to work with strings. We worked with the text column of the train subset of the 20 Newsgroup dataset that comes with scikit-learn. Each row in this dataset is composed of a string with text.

We used pandas' `str` followed by `len()` to count the number of characters in each string, that is, the total number of letters, numbers, symbols, and spaces. We also combined `str.len()` with `str.strip()` to remove trailing whitespaces at the beginning and end of the string and in new lines, before counting the number of characters.

To count the number of words, we used pandas' `str` followed by `split()` to divide the string into a list of words. The `split()` method creates a list of words by breaking the string at the whitespaces between words. Next, we counted those words with pandas' `str.len()`, obtaining the number of words per string.

> **TIP**
> We can alter the behavior of `str.split()` by passing the string or character at which we would like to have the strings divided. For example, `df['text'].str.split(';')` divides a string at each occurrence of `;`.

To determine the number of unique words, we used pandas' `str.split()` to divide the string into a list of words. Next, we applied the built-in Python method `set()` within pandas' `apply()` to return a set of words; remember that a set contains **unique occurrences** of the elements in a list, that is unique words. Next, we counted those words with pandas' `str.len()` to return the vocabulary, or, in other words, the number of unique words in the string. Python interprets as different words those that are written in uppercase from those in lowercase; therefore, we introduced the pandas' `lower()` method to set all the characters in lowercase before splitting the string and counting the number of unique words.

To create the **lexical diversity** and **average word length** features, we simply performed a vectorized division of two pandas Series. And that is it: we created five new features with information about the complexity of the text.

There's more...

We can go ahead and have a glimpse of the distribution of the newly created features in each of the 20 different news topics present in the dataset, by introducing some simple visualizations. To make histogram plots of the newly created features, after you run all of the steps from the *How it works...* section of this recipe, follow these commands:

1. Import Matplotlib:

    ```
    import matplotlib.pyplot as plt
    ```

2. Add the target with the news topics to the 20 Newsgroup dataframe:

    ```
    df['target'] = data.target
    ```

3. Create a function to display a histogram of a feature of your choice for each one of the news topics:

    ```
    def plot_features(df, text_var):
        nb_rows = 5
        nb_cols = 4
        fig, axs = plt.subplots(nb_rows, nb_cols, figsize=(12, 12))
        plt.subplots_adjust(wspace=None, hspace=0.4)

        n = 0
    ```

```
for i in range(0, nb_rows):
    for j in range(0, nb_cols):
        axs[i, j].hist(df[df.target==n][text_var], bins=30)
        axs[i, j].set_title(text_var + ' | ' + str(n))
        n += 1
plt.show()
```

4. Run the function for the **number of words** feature:

```
plot_features(df, 'num_words')
```

The preceding code block returns a plot where you can see the distribution of the number of words in each one of the 20 news topics, numbered from 0 to 19 in the plot title:

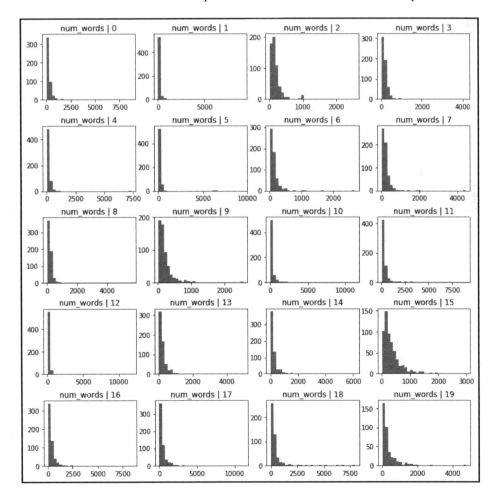

The number of words shows a different distribution depending on the news topics. Therefore, this feature is likely useful in a classification algorithm to predict the topic of the text.

See also

To learn more about the built-in string processing functionality from pandas' `str`, follow this link: `https://pandas.pydata.org/pandas-docs/stable/user_guide/text.html#method-summary`.

Estimating text complexity by counting sentences

One aspect of a text we can capture in features is its complexity. Usually, longer descriptions that contain multiple sentences spread over several paragraphs tend to provide more information than descriptions with very few sentences. Therefore, capturing the number of sentences may provide some insight into the amount of information provided by the text. This process is called sentence tokenization. Tokenization is the process of splitting a string into a list of pieces or tokens. In the previous *Counting characters, words, and vocabulary* recipe, we did word tokenization, that is, we divided the string into words. In this recipe, we will divide the string into sentences and then we will count them. We will use the NLTK Python library, which provides this functionality.

Getting ready

In this recipe, we will use the NLTK Python library. Make sure you have installed NLTK following the instructions for your operating system and then download the necessary data as described in the *Technical requirements* section of this chapter.

How to do it...

Let's begin with the recipe by importing the required libraries and dataset:

1. Load pandas, the sentence tokenizer from NLTK, and the dataset from scikit-learn:

   ```
   import pandas as pd
   from nltk.tokenize import sent_tokenize
   from sklearn.datasets import fetch_20newsgroups
   ```

2. To understand the functionality of the sentence tokenizer from NLTK, let's create a variable that contains a string with multiple sentences:

   ```
   text = """
   The alarm rang at 7 in the morning as it usually did on Tuesdays.
   She rolled over,
   stretched her arm, and stumbled to the button till she finally
   managed to switch it off.
   Reluctantly, she got up and went for a shower. The water was cold
   as the day before the engineers
   did not manage to get the boiler working. Good thing it was still
   summer.
   Upstairs, her cat waited eagerly for his morning snack. Miaow! he
   voiced with excitement
   as he saw her climb the stairs.
   """
   ```

3. Let's now separate the string we created in *step 2* into sentences using the NLTK sentence tokenizer:

   ```
   sent_tokenize(text)
   ```

   The sentence tokenizer returns the list of sentences shown in the following output:

   ```
   ['\nThe alarm rang at 7 in the morning as it usually did on
   Tuesdays.',
    'She rolled over,\nstretched her arm, and stumbled to the button
   till she finally managed to switch it off.',
    'Reluctantly, she got up and went for a shower.',
    'The water was cold as the day before the engineers\ndid not
   manage to get the boiler working.',
    'Good thing it was still summer.',
    'Upstairs, her cat waited eagerly for his morning snack.',
    'Miaow!',
    'he voiced with excitement\nas he saw her climb the stairs.']
   ```

The escape character followed by the letter \n, indicates a new line.

4. Let's count the number of sentences in the text variable:

```
len(sent_tokenize(text))
```

The code in the preceding line returns 7, which is the number of sentences in our text variable. Now, let's determine the number of sentences in an entire dataframe.

5. Let's load the train subset of the 20 Newsgroup dataset into a pandas dataframe:

```
data = fetch_20newsgroups(subset='train')
df = pd.DataFrame(data.data, columns=['text'])
```

6. To speed up the running of the following steps, let's work only with the first 10 rows of the dataframe:

```
df = df.loc[1:10]
```

7. Let's also remove the first part of the text, which contains information about the email sender, subject, and other details we are not interested in. Most of this information comes before the word Lines followed by :, so let's split the string at Lines: and capture the second part of the string:

```
df['text'] = df['text'].str.split('Lines:').apply(lambda x: x[1])
```

8. Finally, let's create a variable that captures the number of sentences per text variable:

```
df['num_sent'] = df['text'].apply(sent_tokenize).apply(len)
```

With the df command, you can display the entire dataframe with the text variable and the new feature containing the number of sentences per text. We can now use this new feature in machine learning algorithms.

How it works...

In this recipe, we separated a string with text into sentences using sent_tokenizer from the NLTK library. sent_tokenizer has been pre-trained to recognize capitalization and different types of punctuation that signal the beginning and the end of a sentence.

We first applied `sent_tokenizer` to a manually created string in order to become familiar with its functionality. The tokenizer divided the text into a list of seven sentences. We combined the tokenizer with the built-in Python method `len()` to count the number of sentences in the string.

Next, we loaded a dataset with text and, to speed up the computation, we retained only the first 10 rows of the dataframe using pandas' `loc[]`. Next, we removed the first part of the text with information about the email sender and subject. To do this, we split the string at `Line:` using pandas' `str.split()` returning a list with two elements, the strings before and after `Line:`. Utilizing a lambda function within pandas' `apply()`, we retained the second part of the text, that is, the second string in the list returned by pandas' `split()`.

Finally, we applied `sent_tokenizer` to each row in the dataframe with the pandas' `apply()` method, to separate the strings into sentences, and then subsequently applied the built-in Python method `len()` to the list of sentences to return the number of sentences per string. This way, we created a new feature that contains the number of sentences per text.

There's more...

NLTK has functionality for word tokenization among other useful features, which we can use instead of pandas to count and return the number of words. You can find more about NLTK's functionality here:

- *Python 3 Text Processing with NLTK 3 Cookbook* by Jacob Perkins, *Packt Publishing*
- NLTK documentation: `http://www.nltk.org/`

Creating features with bag-of-words and n-grams

A **bag-of-words (BoW)**, is a simplified representation of a text that captures the words that are present in the text and the number of times each word appears in the text. So, for the text string *Dogs like cats, but cats do not like dogs,* the derived BoW is as follows:

dogs	like	cats	but	do	not
2	2	2	1	1	1

Here, each word becomes a variable, and the value of the variable represents the number of times the word appears in the string. As you can see, BoW captures multiplicity but does not retain word order or grammar. That is why it is a simple, yet useful, way of extracting features and capturing some information about the texts we are working with.

To capture some syntax, BoW can be used together with n-grams. An n-gram is a contiguous sequence of *n* items in a given text. Continuing with the sentence *Dogs like cats, but cats do not like dogs*, the derived 2-grams are as follows:

- Dogs like
- like cats
- cats but
- but do
- do not
- like dogs

We can create, together with a BoW, a bag of n-grams, where the additional variables are given by the 2-grams and the values for each 2-grams are the number of times they appear in each string; for this particular example, the value is 1. So our final BoW with 2-grams would look like this:

dogs	like	cats	but	do	not	dogs like	like cats	cats but	but do	do not	like dogs
2	2	2	1	1	1	1	1	1	1	1	1

In this recipe, we will learn how to create BoWs with or without n-grams using scikit-learn.

Getting ready

Before jumping into the recipe, let's get familiar with some of the parameters of a BoW that we can adjust to make the BoW more or less comprehensive. When creating a BoW over several pieces of text, a new feature is created for each unique word that appears at least once in any of the text pieces we are analyzing. If the word appears only in one piece of text, it will show a value of 1 for that particular text and 0 for all of the others.

Therefore, BoWs tend to be sparse matrices, where most of the values are zeros. Also, the number of columns, that is, the number of words, can be quite large if we work with huge text corpora, and even bigger if we also include n-grams. To limit the number of columns created and the sparsity of the returned matrix, we can choose to retain words that appear across multiple texts; or, in other words, we can retain words that appear in, at least, a certain percentage of texts.

To reduce the number of columns and sparsity of the BoW, we should also work with words in the same case, for example, lowercase, as Python will identify words in a different case as different words. We can also reduce the number of columns and sparsity by removing **stop words**. Stop words are very frequently used words to make sentences flow, but that, per se, do not carry any useful information. Examples of stop words are pronouns such as **I**, **you**, and **he**, as well as prepositions and articles.

In this recipe, we will learn how to set words in lowercase, remove stop words, retain words with a minimum acceptable frequency, and capture n-grams all together with one single transformer from scikit-learn, CountVectorizer().

How to do it...

Let's begin by loading the libraries and getting the dataset ready:

1. Load pandas, CountVectorizer, and the dataset from scikit-learn:

```
import pandas as pd
from sklearn.datasets import fetch_20newsgroups
from sklearn.feature_extraction.text import CountVectorizer
```

2. Let's load the train set part of the 20 Newsgroup dataset into a pandas dataframe:

```
data = fetch_20newsgroups(subset='train')
df = pd.DataFrame(data.data, columns=['text'])
```

3. To make the interpretation of the results easier, let's remove punctuation and numbers from the text variable:

```
df['text'] = df['text'].str.replace(
        '[^\w\s]','').str.replace('\d+', '')
```

4. Let's now set up CountVectorizer() so that, before creating the BoW, it puts the text in lowercase, removes stop words, and retains words that appear at least in 5% of the text pieces:

```
vectorizer = CountVectorizer(lowercase=True,
                             stop_words='english',
                             ngram_range=(1, 1),
                             min_df=0.05)
```

To introduce n-grams as part of the returned columns, we can change the value of `ngrams_range` to, for example, `(1,2)`. The tuple provides the lower and upper boundaries of the range of n-values for different n-grams to be extracted. In the case of `(1,2)`, `CountVectorizer()` will return single words and arrays of two consecutive words.

5. Let's fit `CountVectorizer()` so that it learns which words should be used in the BoW:

```
vectorizer.fit(df['text'])
```

6. Let's now create the BoW:

```
X = vectorizer.transform(df['text'])
```

7. Finally, let's capture the BoW in a dataframe with the corresponding feature names:

```
bagofwords = pd.DataFrame(X.toarray(), columns =
vectorizer.get_feature_names())
```

We have now created a pandas dataframe that contains words as columns and the number of times they appeared in each text as values. You can inspect the result by executing `bagofwords.head()`. We can use the BoW as an input for a machine learning model.

How it works...

`CountVectorizer()` from scikit-learn converts a collection of text documents into a matrix of token counts. The tokens can be individual words or arrays of two or more consecutive words, that is, n-grams. In this recipe, we created a BoW from a text variable in a dataframe.

We loaded the 20 Newsgroup text dataset from scikit-learn and, first, we removed punctuation and numbers from the text rows using pandas' `replace()`, which can be accessed through pandas' `str`, to replace digits, `'\d+'`, or symbols, `'[^\w\s]'`, with empty strings, `''`. Then, we used `CountVectorizer()` to create the BoW. We set the `lowercase` parameter to `True`, to put the words in lowercase before extracting the BoW. We set the `stop_words` argument to `english` to ignore stop words, that is, to avoid stop words in the BoW. We set `ngram_range` to the `(1,1)` tuple to return only single words as columns. Finally, we set `min_df` to `0.05` to return words that appear in at least 5 % of the texts, or, in other words, in 5 % of the rows in the dataframe.

After setting up the transformer, we used the `fit()` method to allow the transformer to find the words that fulfill the preceding criteria. And with the `transform()` method, the transformer returned an object containing the BoW with its feature names, which we captured in a pandas dataframe.

See also

For more details about `CountVectorizer()`, visit the scikit-learn documentation at `https://scikit-learn.org/stable/modules/generated/sklearn.feature_extraction.text.CountVectorizer.html`.

Implementing term frequency-inverse document frequency

Term Frequency-Inverse Document Frequency (TF-IDF) is a numerical statistic that captures how relevant a word is in a document, with respect to the entire collection of documents. What does this mean? Some words will appear a lot within a text document as well as across documents, for example, the English words **the**, **a**, and **is**. These words generally convey little information about the actual content of the document and don't make it stand out of the crowd. TF-IDF provides a way to weigh the importance of a word, by contemplating how many times it appears in a document, with respect to how often it appears across documents. Hence, commonly occurring words such as **the**, **a**, and **is** will have a low weight, and words more specific to a topic, such as **leopard**, will have a higher weight.

TF-IDF is the product of two statistics, **term frequency** and **inverse document frequency**. Term frequency is, in its simplest form, the count of the word in an individual text. So, for term **t**, the term frequency is calculated as *tf(t) = count(t)* and is determined text by text. The inverse document frequency is a measure of how common the word is **across** all documents and is usually calculated on a logarithmic scale. A common implementation is given by the following:

$$idf(t) = log(\frac{n}{1 + df(t)})$$

Here, *n* is the total number of documents and *df(t)* the number of documents in which the term *t* appears. The bigger the value of *df(t)*, the lower the weighting for the term.

TF-IDF can be also used together with n-grams. Similarly, to weight an n-gram, we compound the n-gram frequency in a certain document by the times the n-gram appears across all documents.

In this recipe, we will learn how to extract features using TF-IDF with or without n-grams using scikit-learn.

Getting ready

The scikit-learn implementation of the TF-IDF uses a slightly different way to calculate the **IDF** statistic. For more details on the exact formula, visit the scikit-learn documentation: `https://scikit-learn.org/stable/modules/feature_extraction.html#tfidf-term-weighting`.

TF-IDF shares the characteristics of BoW when creating the term matrix, that is, high feature space and sparsity. To reduce the number of features and sparsity, we can remove stop words, set the characters to lowercase, and retain words that appear in a minimum percentage of observations. If you are unfamiliar with these terms, visit the *Creating features with bag-of-words and n-grams* recipe in this chapter for a recap.

In this recipe, we will learn how to set words in lowercase, remove stop words, retain words with a minimum acceptable frequency, capture n-grams, and then return the TF-IDF statistic of words, all using one single transformer from scikit-learn, `TfidfVectorizer()`.

How to do it...

Let's begin by loading the libraries and getting the dataset ready:

1. Load pandas, `TfidfVectorizer`, and the dataset from scikit-learn:

```
import pandas as pd
from sklearn.datasets import fetch_20newsgroups
from sklearn.feature_extraction.text import TfidfVectorizer
```

2. Let's load the train set part of the 20 Newsgroup dataset into a pandas dataframe:

```
data = fetch_20newsgroups(subset='train')
df = pd.DataFrame(data.data, columns=['text'])
```

3. To make the interpretation of the results easier, let's remove punctuation and numbers from the text variable:

```
df['text'] = df['text'].str.replace(
        '[^\w\s]','').str.replace('\d+', '')
```

4. Now, let's set up `TfidfVectorizer()` from scikit-learn so that, before creating the TF-IDF metrics, it puts all text in lowercase, removes stop words, and retains words that appear in at least 5% of the text pieces:

```
vectorizer = TfidfVectorizer(lowercase=True,
                             stop_words='english',
                             ngram_range=(1, 1),
                             min_df=0.05)
```

To introduce n-grams as part of the returned columns, we can change the value of `ngrams_range` to, for example, `(1,2)`. The tuple provides the lower and upper boundaries of the range of n-values for different n-grams to be extracted. In the case of `(1,2)`, `TfidfVectorizer()` will return single words and arrays of two consecutive words as columns.

5. Let's fit `TfidfVectorizer()` so that it learns which words should be introduced as columns of the TF-IDF matrix:

```
vectorizer.fit(df['text'])
```

6. Let's now create the TF-IDF matrix:

```
X = vectorizer.transform(df['text'])
```

7. Finally, let's capture the TF-IDF matrix in a dataframe with the corresponding feature names:

```
tfidf = pd.DataFrame(X.toarray(), columns =
vectorizer.get_feature_names())
```

We have now created a pandas dataframe that contains words as columns and the TF-IDF as values. You can inspect the result by executing `tfidf.head()`.

How it works...

In this recipe, we extracted the TF-IDF values of words present in at least 5% of the documents utilizing `TfidfVectorizer()` from scikit-learn.

We loaded the 20 Newsgroup text dataset from scikit-learn and then removed punctuation and numbers from the text rows using pandas' `replace()`, which can be accessed through pandas' `str`, to replace digits, `'\d+'`, or symbols, `'[^\w\s]'`, with empty strings, `''`. Then, we used `TfidfVectorizer()` to create TF-IDF statistics for words. We set the `lowercase` parameter to `True` to put words in lowercase before making the calculations. We set the `stop_words` argument to `english` to avoid stop words in the returned matrix. We set `ngram_range` to the `(1,1)` tuple to return single words as features. Finally, we set the `min_df` argument to `0.05` to return words that appear at least in 5 % of the texts or, in other words, in 5 % of the rows.

After setting up the transformer, we applied the `fit()` method to let the transformer find the words to retain in the final term matrix. With the `transform()` method, the transformer returned an object with the words and with the words and their TF-IDF values, which we then captured in a pandas dataframe with the appropriate feature names. We can now use these features in machine learning algorithms.

See also

For more details on `TfidfVectorizer()`, visit the scikit-learn documentation at `https://scikit-learn.org/stable/modules/generated/sklearn.feature_extraction.text.TfidfVectorizer.html`.

Cleaning and stemming text variables

We mentioned previously that some variables in our dataset can be created based on free text fields, which are manually completed by users. People have different writing styles, and we use a variety of punctuation marks, capitalization patterns, and verb conjugation to convey the content, as well as the emotion around it. We can extract information from text without taking the trouble to read it by creating statistical parameters that summarize the text complexity, keywords, and relevance of words in a document. We discussed these methods in the preceding recipes of this chapter. Yet, to derive these statistics and aggregated features, we should clean the text variables first.

Text cleaning or text preprocessing involves punctuation removal, the elimination of stop words, character case setting, and word stemming. Punctuation removal consists of deleting characters that are not letters, numbers, or spaces, and, in some cases, we also remove numbers. The elimination of stop words refers to removing common words that are used in our language to allow for the sentence structure and flow, but that individually convey little or no information. Examples of stop words are the articles, **the** and **a**, for the English language, as well as pronouns such as **I**, **you**, and **they**, and commonly used verbs in their various conjugations, such as the verbs **to be** and **to have** as well as the auxiliary verbs **would** and **do**.

To allow computers to identify words correctly, it is also necessary to set all words in the same case, as the word **Toy** and **toy** would be identified as different by a computer, due to the capital T in the first one. Finally, to focus on the **message** of the text and not to count them as different words that convey similar meaning if it weren't for their conjugation, we may also want to introduce word stemming as part of the preprocessing pipeline. Word stemming refers to reducing each word to its root or base so that the words **playing**, **plays**, and **played** become **play**, which, in essence, convey the same or very similar meaning.

In this recipe, we will learn how to remove punctuation and stop words, set words in lowercase, and perform word stemming with pandas and NLTK.

Getting ready

We are going to use the NLTK stem package to perform word stemming, which incorporates different algorithms to stem words from English and other languages. Each method differs in the algorithm it uses to find the root of the word; therefore, they may output slightly different results. I recommend you read more about it, try different methods, and choose the one that serves the project you are working on.

More information about NLTK stemmers can be found here: https://www.nltk.org/api/nltk.stem.html.

How to do it...

Let's begin by loading the libraries and getting the dataset ready:

1. Load `pandas`, `stopwords`, and `SnowballStemmer` from NLTK and the dataset from scikit-learn:

   ```
   import pandas as pd
   from nltk.corpus import stopwords
   ```

```
from nltk.stem.snowball import SnowballStemmer
from sklearn.datasets import fetch_20newsgroups
```

2. Let's load the train set part of the 20 Newsgroup dataset into a pandas dataframe:

```
data = fetch_20newsgroups(subset='train')
df = pd.DataFrame(data.data, columns=['text'])
```

Now, let's begin with the text cleaning.

Print an example text with this command, `print(df['text'][10])`, right after the execution of each line of code in this recipe, so you visualize straight away the changes introduced to the text.

3. First, let's remove the punctuation:

```
df["text"] = df['text'].str.replace('[^\w\s]','')
```

You can also remove the punctuation using the built-in `string` module from Python. First, import the module by executing `import string` and then execute `df['text'] = df['text'].str.replace('[{}]'.format(string.punctuation), '')`.

4. We can also remove characters that are numbers, leaving only letters, as follows:

```
df['text'] = df['text'].str.replace('\d+', '')
```

5. Let's now set all cases in lowercase:

```
df['text'] = df['text'].str.lower()
```

Now, let's remove stop words.

6. Let's create a function that splits a string into a list of words, then removes the stop words from the list if the words are within NLTK's English stop words list, and finally concatenates the remaining words back into a string:

```
def remove_stopwords(text):
    stop = set(stopwords.words('english'))
    text = [word for word in text.split() if word not in stop]
    text = ' '.join(x for x in text)
    return text
```

To be able to process the data with scikit-learn's `CountVectorizer()` or `TfidfVectorizer()`, we need the text to be in string format. Therefore, after removing the stop words, we need to return the words as a single string.

We transform NLTK's stop words list into a set because sets are faster to scan than lists. This improves the computation time.

7. Now, let's use the function we created in *step 6* to remove stop words from the `text` variable:

```
df['text'] = df['text'].apply(remove_stopwords)
```

Finally, let's stem the words in our data. We will use `SnowballStemmer` from NLTK.

8. Let's create an instance of `SnowballStemer` for the English language:

```
stemmer = SnowballStemmer("english")
```

Try the stemmer in a single word to see how it works, for example, run `stemmer.stem('running')`. You should see `run` as the result of that command. Try different words!

9. Let's create a function that splits a string into a list of words, then applies `stemmer` to each word, and finally concatenates the stemmed word list back into a string:

```
def stemm_words(text):
    text = [stemmer.stem(word) for word in text.split()]
    text = ' '.join(x for x in text)
    return text
```

10. Let's use the function we created in *step 9* to stem the words in our data:

```
df['text'] = df['text'].apply(stemm_words)
```

Now, our text is ready to create features based on character and word counts and to create BoWs or TF-IDF matrices, as we described in previous recipes of this chapter.

Note that the only feature that needs to be derived **before** removing punctuation is the count of the sentences, as punctuation and capitalization are needed to define the boundaries of each sentence.

How it works...

In this recipe, we removed punctuation, numbers, and stop words from a text variable, then we set the words in lowercase, and finally stemmed the words to their root. We removed punctuation and numbers from the text variable using pandas' `replace()`, which can be accessed through pandas' `str`, to replace digits, `'\d+'`, or symbols, `'[^\w\s]'`, with empty strings, `''`. Alternatively, we used the `punctuation` module from the built-in package `string`.

Run `string.punctuation` in your Python console after importing `string` to visualize the symbols that will be replaced by empty strings.

Next, utilizing pandas string processing functionality through `str`, we set all of the words to lowercase with the `lower()` method. To remove stop words from the text, we used the `stopwords` module from NLTK, which contains a list of words that are considered frequent, that is, the stop words. We created a function that takes a string and splits it into a list of words using pandas' `str.split()`, and then with a list comprehension, we looped over the words in the list and retained the non-stop words. Finally, with the `join()` method, we concatenated the retained words back into a string. We used the built-in Python `set()` method over the NLTK stop words list to improve computation efficiency, as it is faster to iterate over sets than over lists. Finally, with pandas' `apply()`, we applied the function to each row of our text data.

Run `stopwords.words('english')` in your Python console after importing `stopwords` from NLTK to visualize the list with the stop words that will be removed.

Finally, we stemmed the words using `SnowballStemmer` from NLTK. `stemmer` works one word at a time. Therefore, we created a function that takes a string and splits it into a list of words using pandas' `str.split()`. In a list comprehension, we applied `stemmer` word per word, and then concatenated the list of stemmed words back into a string, using the `join()` method. With pandas' `apply()`, we applied the function to stem words to each row of the dataframe.

The cleaning steps performed in this recipe resulted in strings containing the original text, without punctuation or numbers, in lowercase, without common words, and with the root of the word instead of its conjugated form. The data, as it is returned, can be used to derive features as described in the *Counting characters, words, and vocabulary* recipe or to create BoWs and TI-IDF matrices as described in the *Creating features with bag-of-words and n-grams* and *Implementing term frequency-inverse document frequency* recipes.

Other Books You May Enjoy

If you enjoyed this book, you may be interested in these other books by Packt:

Python Machine Learning Cookbook -Second Edition
Giuseppe Ciaburro, Prateek Joshi

ISBN: 978-1-78980-845-2

- Use predictive modeling and apply it to real-world problems
- Explore data visualization techniques to interact with your data
- Learn how to build a recommendation engine
- Understand how to interact with text data and build models to analyze it
- Work with speech data and recognize spoken words using Hidden Markov Models
- Get well versed with reinforcement learning, automated ML, and transfer learning
- Work with image data and build systems for image recognition and biometric face recognition
- Use deep neural networks to build an optical character recognition system

Python Machine Learning By Example - Second Edition
Yuxi (Hayden) Liu

ISBN: 978-1-78961-672-9

- Understand the important concepts in machine learning and data science
- Use Python to explore the world of data mining and analytics
- Scale up model training using varied data complexities with Apache Spark
- Delve deep into text and NLP using Python libraries such NLTK and gensim
- Select and build an ML model and evaluate and optimize its performance
- Implement ML algorithms from scratch in Python, TensorFlow, and scikit-learn

Leave a review - let other readers know what you think

Please share your thoughts on this book with others by leaving a review on the site that you bought it from. If you purchased the book from Amazon, please leave us an honest review on this book's Amazon page. This is vital so that other potential readers can see and use your unbiased opinion to make purchasing decisions, we can understand what our customers think about our products, and our authors can see your feedback on the title that they have worked with Packt to create. It will only take a few minutes of your time, but is valuable to other potential customers, our authors, and Packt. Thank you!

Index

L

lack human interpretability 134
linear relationship
  identifying 25, 26, 27, 28, 29, 30
lmplot()
  reference link 30
local maxima number
  determining 301, 302, 303, 304, 305, 306
local minima number
  determining 301, 302, 303, 304, 305, 306
logarithm
  variables, transforming with 142, 143, 144, 145, 146

M

mathematical functions
  pairs of features, combining with 269, 270, 271
mathematical operations
  used, for aggregating transactions 289, 290, 291, 292
maximum absolute scaling
  implementing 253, 254, 255
maximum and minimum values
  scaling 251, 252, 253
mean imputation
  performing 51, 52, 53, 54, 55
mean normalization
  performing 247, 248, 249, 250, 251
mean, of target
  encoding with 123, 124, 125, 126
median and quantiles
  scaling with 256
  working with 256, 257, 258
median imputation
  performing 51, 52, 53, 54, 55
metrics
  reference link 196
missing data
  qualifying 15, 16, 17, 18
  used, for removing observations 48, 49, 50
missing value indicator variable
  adding 75, 76, 77, 78, 79
  adding, with scikit-learn's SimpleImputer() 79
missing values

capturing, in bespoke category 65, 66, 67
replacing, with arbitrary number 61, 62, 64
replacing, with values 68, 69, 70, 71
mode imputation
  implementing 56, 57, 58, 59, 60
multivariate imputation by chained equations (MICE)
  performing 80, 81, 82
  references 80

N

n-grams
  used, for creating features 333, 334, 335, 336
Natural Language Processing (NLP) 323
Natural Language Toolkit (NLTK) 323
normal distribution
  identifying 31, 32, 33, 34
numerical variables
  Box-Cox transformation, performing on 158, 159, 160, 162
  identifying 11, 12, 13
  power transformations, using on 155, 157
  Yeo-Johnson transformation, performing on 162, 163, 164, 165, 166
NumPy's log()
  reference link 147
nunique() method
  using 21

O

observations
  removing, with missing data 48, 49, 50
one-hot encoding, of frequent categories
  performing 104, 105, 106, 107, 108
one-hot encoding
  binary variables, creating through 96, 97, 98, 99, 100, 101
  implementing, with Feature-engine 102, 103
ordinal encoding
  references 112
ordinal numbers
  categories, replacing with 108, 109, 110, 111
outliers, handling with Feature-engine
  reference link 207
outliers

time parts
extracting, from time variable 231, 232, 233, 234

time variable
time parts, extracting from 231, 232, 233, 234

time window
aggregating transactions 294, 295, 296, 297, 298, 299

time, in different time zone
working with 239, 240, 241, 242

transactional data
aggregating, with Featuretools library 292, 293, 294

transactions
aggregating, in time window 294, 295, 296, 297, 298, 299
aggregating, with mathematical operations 289, 290, 291, 292

U

user-defined computations
applying 299, 300

V

variable distribution
distinguishing 34, 36, 37

variable values
allocating, in arbitrary intervals 184, 186, 187
sorting, in intervals of equal-frequency discretization 176, 177, 179, 180

variables
capping, at arbitrary maximum values 207, 208, 209, 210
capping, at arbitrary minimum values 207, 208, 209, 210

dividing, into intervals of equal-width
discretization 168, 169, 171, 172, 173, 174, 175

histogram, creating 13, 14
transforming, with cube root 152, 153, 154
transforming, with logarithm 142, 143, 144, 145, 146
transforming, with reciprocal function 147, 148, 149, 150, 151
transforming, with square root 152, 153, 154

vector unit length
scaling to 258, 259, 260, 261

vocabulary
counting 325, 326, 327, 328

W

Weight of Evidence (WoE)
encoding with 126, 127, 128, 129
implementations, reference link 130

winsorization
about 197
performing 203, 204, 205, 206

words
counting 325, 326, 327, 328

Y

Yeo-Johnson transformation
performing, on numerical variables 162, 163, 164, 165, 166

Z

zero-coding
performing 211, 212, 213
performing, in multiple variables 214, 215

Made in the USA
Monee, IL
30 June 2020